CULTS AND NONCONVENTIONAL RELIGIOUS GROUPS

A Collection of Outstanding Dissertations and Monographs

Edited by
J. GORDON MELTON
Institute for the Study of American Religion

A GARLAND SERIES

SHAKUBUKU

A Study of the Nichiren Shoshu Buddhist Movement in America, 1960–1975

DAVID A. SNOW

GARLAND PUBLISHING, INC.
New York & London
1993

Library of Congress Cataloging-in-Publication Data

Snow, David Alan, 1943–
    Shakubuku : a study of the Nichiren Shoshu Buddhist movement in
America, 1960–1975 / by David A. Snow
        p.   cm. — (Cults and nonconventional religious groups)
    ISBN 0–8153–1137–0
    1. Nichiren Shōshū—Missions—United States. 2. Nichiren Shōshū of
America—History. I. Series.
BQ8443.6.U6S66 1993
294.3'928'097309046—dc20   92–39646
                                                             CIP

Printed on acid-free, 250-year-life paper

MANUFACTURED IN THE UNITED STATES OF AMERICA

To my parents, for reasons that require no explanation, and to my sister Deborah, whose involvement in a series of social movements in the late 1960s and early 1970s first stimulated my interest in the study of such activities.

CONTENTS

PREFACE

One of the more intriguing aspects of American culture in the kaleidoscopic decade between 1965 and 1975 was the flowering and diffusion of a veritable smorgasbord of alternative religious and psychotherapeutic philosophies and practices. Many of these philosophies were purely Eastern and exotic; others represented a blend of various imported practices, modern Western psychotherapy, and the teachings and advice of such "positive thinkers" as Dale Carnegie and Norman Vincent Peale; some were somatopsychic or based on a presumed correlation between the state of mind and the state of the body; some were based on a curious mixture of elements of the so-called hippie subculture with fundamentalist Christianity; and a few had been around for years but were repackaged and promoted with Madison Avenue gusto. However widely they varied in terms of their respective philosophical roots, the scope and content of their beliefs and goals, and the nature of their ritual practices and recruitment methods, all were directed in part or totally toward personal transformation or what is variously referred to, depending on the practice in question, as "nirvana," "human revolution," "enlightenment," "satori," "self-transcendence," "self-actualization," or just plain "it." Moreover, each maintained, some subtly and others quite blatantly, that theirs was the "one way" or "true path". They were known by, among other things, such names as Arica, the Divine Light Mission, EST, Functional Integration, Hare Krishna, Rolfing, Silva Mind Control, Transcendental Meditation, Yoga, Zen and so on.[1]

Reported in this volume is the study of one of these movements - Nichiren Shoshu of America. Probably best known for its chant of Nam-Myoho-Renge-Kyo, Nichiren Shoshu - which also goes by the name of Nichiren Shoshu Academy or by the acronym NSA - is a noncommunal, proselytizing Buddhist movement that has sought to change the world by changing individuals in accordance with its own version of Buddhism, regarded by core members as "orthodox" or "true Buddhism." Introduced into America around 1960, largely as a spiritual outpost for the Japanese brides and girlfriends of American G.I.s, it grew dramatically from a few hundred followers to a claimed membership of nearly a quarter of million adherents by the mid-1970s, and it continues to thrive today.

This book provides an analytic and historical description of the movement's development and flowering in America between 1960 and 1975, focusing in particular on its goals and ideology, its attendant ritual practices, its promotion and recruitment efforts, the characteristics of its membership, the factors that account for why some individuals rather than others became members, and the nature and consequences of the conversion process. In the course of addressing these concerns, sociological and social psychological assumptions and theories about social movement recruitment and participation are critically assessed and theoretically refined.

The research on which the book is based was conducted over a year-and-a-half period, between January of 1974 and July of 1975, while I was a doctoral candidate in Sociology at the University of California, Los Angeles. The final product was my dissertation, which was completed and approved in the late summer of 1976. This book constitutes the formal publication of that dissertation, with the exception of some editorial modifications, a few deletions and additions here and there, and the inclusion of two previously published articles in the Appendix. Both of the articles address issues related to the topic of conversion. They are included because of the relevance of the conversion process to participation in Nichiren Shoshu and other such movements, and because in my haste to complete the dissertation - so that I could assume a regular faculty position at the University of Texas at Austin in the Fall of 1976 - I was unable to write the chapter I had planned on the conversion process. Like many, and perhaps most, doctoral candidates in the social sciences and humanities, I recall having reached the conclusion that the best dissertation was a finished one, and thus jettisoned some of my initial plans. This decision was prompted not only by a growing family and a job that was contingent on my having a degree in hand, but also by the understanding that the rich data I had accumulated on conversion could be mined in subsequent work. Thus the inclusion of the two articles on conversion in the Appendix.

The materials on which the book is based were derived from three major sources: my observations and experience as an active participant observer for nearly a year and a half; a systematic examination of the movement's literature over a ten-year period; and a content analysis of members' testimonies appearing in the movement's newspaper and rendered during movement meetings. These data sources are discussed in Chapter 1, which constitutes a research chronicle of the evolution of the study and the problems and procedures that influenced the way it unfolded. It is my aim in this chapter to provide a clear understanding of why I chose to study Nichiren Shoshu rather than some other movement, of how I got involved and the nature of my association with the movement, and of how I went about the business of studying the movement as systematically as possible. One additional factor that influenced the way in which this chapter was written was my desire to make available to members of Nichiren Shoshu an account of how they contributed to the study. Just as they helped me to acquire an understanding of the movement and their perspective, I thought it reasonable to make available to them a documentary account of how and why I proceeded as I did.

Chapter 2 presents a descriptive analysis of the movement's beliefs, goals, ideology, and corresponding ritual practices. My intent in this chapter is to provide a feel for the movement's view of the world or condition of humankind, what it sees as its mission in the world, how it proposes to accomplish that mission, and how action in support of the cause is rationalized and justified.

Chapter 3 traces the movement's historical development and flowering in America. The chapter begins by jumping back in time and across the Pacific in order to provide an understanding of the movement's historical roots and development in Japan, and then chronicles its career and growth in America through 1975.

Chapter 4 considers Nichiren Shoshu's outward-reaching, goal attainment strategies and tactics by examining the following set of questions: what were the major strategic considerations and operational strategies that influenced its propagation and recruitment efforts? How did it reach out and attract potential converts and then secure their nominal conversion? And how did it attempt to carve out a viable niche within its environment of operation? The chapter begins with a discussion of the theoretical importance of these questions, and then systematically examines each. The aim is to provide an analytic description of how Nichiren Shoshu has gone about the business of expanding its ranks, winning support for its cause, and securing its existence as a collective entity.

Chapter 5 turns to the participant or convert side of the recruitment process by examining the issue of differential recruitment: who joined or agreed to give chanting a try? And why some people rather than others? These questions are pursued by exploring the social demographic characteristics of the membership across time, the larger sociocultural context in which the movement flowered, the microstructural determinants of recruitment, and the accounts members invoke to explain their participation.

The final chapter provides a brief summary and integration of the central observations and findings that surfaced in the preceding chapters. This is followed by the Appendix, which includes the previously mentioned articles on conversion.

Although the dissertation was completed more than fifteen years ago, I retain the present tense throughout most of the book, except when discussing my own personal involvement and research. I do so because it lends a greater air of realism to the text, and because Nichiren Shoshu is still a viable collective enterprise. I have not studied the movement since 1975; so I cannot document the extent to which it has changed, if it all, in terms of its goals, beliefs, ritual practices, recruitment activities, and the like. But it is my strong suspicion - based on student reports and papers in Austin and Tucson, and on a 1985 book written by the movement's leader in the United States[2] - that much of what I wrote in 1976 is still applicable today.

In the process of conducting the initial research, writing the dissertation, and then, more recently, transforming it into this book, I have received a good deal of assistance of various kinds from a number of people to whom I am deeply indebted. First, I want to acknowledge the members of Nichiren Shoshu, particularly those responsible for my socialization and integration into the movement as a nominal convert. Much of what I learned about the movement I owe to their persistent vigilance and tutelage. I am also indebted to Ralph H. Turner, the chairman of my doctoral committee and my mentor during my four years at UCLA. He was a patient and constructive critic, a constant source of edification, and an exemplary role model. I am also grateful for the constructive comments and encouragement of Melvin Seeman and Kenneth K. S. Ch'en, both of whom were the other members of my dissertation committee. Gratitude is owed to a number of fellow graduate students as well, particularly Jim Benton, Phil Davis, Bruce Phillips, and Sam Wright. Individually and together they functioned as a useful sounding board, provided valuable encouragement and support, and continuously reminded me of the dangers of "going native."

More recently, I am indebted to Joseph Heirling, for his editorial assistance, and to Barb McIntosh, the manuscript typist in the Sociology Department at the University of Arizona. Barb, in particular, deserves much thanks for her competence and professionalism in helping to produce a desk-top, camera-ready copy of the manuscript.

As noted earlier, the Appendix includes portions of two previously published articles. Accordingly, I am grateful to the Society for the Study of Social Problems and Jossey-Bass Inc. for permission to reprint the following publications: David A. Snow and Cynthia L Phillips, "The Lofland-Stark Conversion Model: A Critical Reassessment," pp. 430-447 in *Social Problems*, Vol. 27, No. 4, April 1980; and David A. Snow and Richard Machalek, "The Convert As A Social Type," pp. 259-289 in R. Collins (ed.), *Sociological Theory*, Jossey-Bass Inc., Publishers, 1983.

Finally, I want to acknowledge the enduring patience and support of my wife, Judy. When I was contemplating prospective dissertation topics nearly twenty years ago, she indicated that she had no strong feelings about what I studied except for one thing. "Don't study a group of offbeat, religious zealots," she said. I did, at least from her perspective, and she paid for it dearly. For the better part of a year and a half she spent many weeknights and most weekends alone as I was out doing my field research. It was not much fun for her, especially when she was badgered about joining the ranks, but she grit her teeth and endured, knowing, or at least hoping, that this preoccupation of mine would pass in due time. It did, of course, but not without her patience and support. Clearly this is her book, too.

David A. Snow
July 1992
Tucson, Arizona

NOTES

1. For thumbnail sketches of these and other such groups, see Charles Y. Glock and Robert N. Bellah, eds., *New Religious Consciousness* (Berkeley: University Press, 1976; Nathaniel Lande, *Mindstyles, Lifestyles* (Los Angeles: Price/Stern/Sloan, 1976); and R.D. Rosen, *Psychobabble* (New York: Atheneum, 1978). For a thorough discussion and synthesis of the social science literature pertaining to this general movement and particularly the "new religious movements," see Thomas Robbins, *Cults, Converts & Charisma: The Sociology of New Religious Movements* (Beverly Hills, CA: Sage Publications, 1988).

2. See George M. Williams, *Freedom and Influence: The Role of Religion in American Society* (Santa Monica, CA: World Tribune Press, 1985).

Shakubuku

1

THE EMERGENCE
OF A CASE STUDY:
A PROCEDURAL HISTORY

A Brief Introduction to Nam-Myoho-Renge-Kyo

In the pre-dawn hours of April 28, 1253, some 1200 years following the death of the great, historical Buddha (variously referred to as Guatama, Siddhartha, Sakyamuni, Tathagata, and/or Bhagavan), a solitary Japanese figure, clad in a priest's robe and enveloped by the still and invigorating mountain air of early summer, made his way to the summit of a hill overlooking the vast expanse of the Pacific Ocean. Having just emerged from seven days of meditative seclusion, culminating twenty years of religious study and search for the absolute truth, the day of revelation, the dawn of a new era, had come.

Standing motionless atop the hill, with his eyes fixed on the eastern horizon of the Pacific, which together with the Atlantic, connected the world into one, he heard neither the singing of the birds nor the roar of the surf far below his feet. His mind was closed to all but the mission to which his years of study and search had awakened him.

As the sun began to illuminate the distant horizon and cut through the haze over the waters below, Nichiren (Sun-Lotus) - a name he had just recently adopted to symbolize his calling and ideals, but which he had not yet revealed to anyone - joined his palms together, with his prayer beads in between, and began to rub them slightly as he uttered, in a loud and sonorous voice that pierced the early morning stillness, a chant which had never been heard before. It was "Nam-Myoho-Range-Kyo," an utterance he considered to be the embodiment of the essence of Buddha's teachings.

After this dramatic proclamation to the heavens and earth, with the sun as his witness, he returned to the monastery below and embarked on his mission to propagate the practice and philosophy that he hoped would bring humankind out of its darkness and usher in a world of harmonious bliss and enlightenment. With a prophetic zeal and determination unique among Japanese religious figures, Nichiren preached that salvation and enlightenment can only be attained through the earnest recitation and propagation of this single invocation and the philosophy it embodies. Nam-Myoho-Renge-Kyo, he held, is the highest law in the universe, the one law that transcends all else and guarantees happiness and enlightenment to those who will invoke and propagate it with great sincerity and vigor.[1]

Today, nearly 750 years later, in corners of the world that even the peripatetic and allegedly omniscient Nichiren could not have envisioned, Nam-Myoho-Renge-Kyo is being chanted and propagated with the same single-minded determination and zealotry that characterized Nichiren.

My first formal introduction to this practice occurred one evening in the Spring of 1973 on the streets of Los Angeles. While I was about to enter a restaurant with my wife and another couple, a neatly dressed, Caucasian female, in her early twenties, approached us and asked if we had ever heard of Nam-Myoho-Renge-Kyo. We looked at her in puzzlement, as if to say, "What are you talking about?"

Noting our confusion, she proceeded to hand us a three-by-five card with Nam-Myoho-Renge-Kyo printed on it, along with the address and telephone number of a meeting place. She then asked if we wanted to be happy and fulfill our dreams. We immediately indicated that we were quite content, to which she responded by suggesting that we could always be happier. At this point she emphasized that we could get whatever we wanted - materially, physically, or spiritually - if only we chanted. And then, so as to objectify this claim, she indicated how chanting had provided her with a greater sense of meaning and purpose, enabled her to get better grades in school, and improved her relationship with her parents. Our response was still largely one of disinterest. Thus sensing that she was not making much progress in luring us to a meeting, she began to invoke the names of various public figures who allegedly chanted, as if to add an air of respectability to the muttering of these strange words. After finally convincing her that we had plans for the evening and were not particularly interested in attending her meeting, she bid us adieu and moved along, apparently in search of other prospects.

While my curiosity had been momentarily aroused, one of the members of the party I was with assured me that it was hardly worth getting excited over, especially since what was being promoted was just another of the many "strange and fanatical religious groups" that grace the Los Angeles scene. "No question about it," another member of the party scornfully added, "those people are really strange, if not downright sick." I nodded, not so much in agreement with my friends' categorical dismissal and denigration of the young lady and the group and philosophy she represented, but in recognition of their response as a fairly typical form of verbal exorcism that is commonly employed when our taken-for-granted world is breached and challenged by an alternative version of reality that forces itself upon our consciousness. Nonetheless, I kept my assessment of the situation to myself. And so the subject of this brief intrusion to our paramount reality was dropped, and we moved inside to partake in a more respectable, but perhaps no more common, Los Angeles pastime - dining out.

Little did I realize at that time that within less than a year not only would I be enmeshed in a study of the movement the young lady represented - Nichiren Shoshu of America - but I would also be vigorously uttering this strange chant and, like this young zealot who had just accosted us, I would be propagating it with other members on the streets of Los Angeles. What follows is a history of how this came to be, a documentary account of the evolution of the study and the methodological procedures on which it is based. But first a brief note on the reasons for writing this procedural history.

Too often social scientists ignore or gloss over, in their final reports, the story behind their studies. For most it is accepted practice to write a brief introductory section outlining the methods or to relegate the subject to a truncated methodological appendix. Most often such discussions describe in a matter-of-course manner the specific sampling and measuring techniques employed or the manner in which entree into a particular setting was negotiated, usually resulting in an account which is meaningful to only the researchers themselves and which usually fosters the impression that a study is simply a matter of following certain logical, scientific canons and adhering to a well mapped-out "game plan."

Although this may be the case with some studies, it certainly did not apply to my experience, and I suspect that it is not really the case with most studies. After all, the nature of a study is really something more than the mere application of specific measuring techniques and adherence to a certain methodological "game plan." For in its own right a study is usually a special kind of sociological event for those who are interviewed and knowingly observed, as well as for the researcher and his or her intimates (i.e., spouse, children, advisors), not to mention a complicated process involving considerable tactical maneuvering, rethinking, and recalculation during the course of the research enterprise itself. Consequently, it seems a mistake to gloss over in four or five pages the story behind the evolution of the study, the procedures, and the resultant product. To do so not only makes replication extremely difficult, but it tends to obscure the extent to which the resultant findings are married to and, in large part, an artifact of the methodological procedures and problematic situations encountered and managed within the context of the evolving study.

One might wish to view this chapter, then, as an attempt to make explicit the nature and aims of this study and the factors which influenced the way it unfolded and evolved. Perhaps in this way the methodological procedures and the trials and tribulations experienced during the evolving study itself will not appear as strange and distant from the findings.

SELECTION OF A TOPIC AND THE EMERGENCE OF A CASE STUDY

It was approximately eight months after the above encounter that I first seriously entertained the idea of studying the Nichiren Shoshu movement in America. A month or so earlier I had decided to explore the possibility of conducting a study of one or more of the seemingly offbeat, religiously oriented cults and movements that began to surface and proliferate in this country sometime in the late sixties.

I was intrigued by both the growth and spread of such phenomena as the Guru Maharaj Ji's following, the Hare Krishna movement, the Nichiren Shoshu movement, what had come to be referred to as the "Jesus movement," and various forms of occultism, and by the extent to which these phenomena seemed to represent - at least on the surface - a striking contrast to the political activism and protest that dominated the sixties and so preoccupied the students of social conflict and change. What socio-historical conditions accounted for the emergence of these offbeat collective phenomena, and who these groups appealed to and why were questions worthy of further thought and investigation. Questions regarding the differences and similarities in their appeal and structure, the configuration of conditions and processes leading to recruitment and participation, the nature of the conversion and commitment-building processes, and the consequences for their adherents and society at large also warranted investigation.

However intriguing and important these curiosities, a no less important question begged attention first: which of these many religiously oriented cults and movements might I study? In some areas of the country this question would not have been particularly troublesome, but in the Los Angeles area, which seemed to be a virtual magnet for the offbeat, there was a plethora of such phenomena. Given the constraint of time and the often ephemeral and secretive nature of these groups, a census, much less a sample, was out of the question. So I turned to the UCLA library and conducted a preliminary search to see what kinds of literature existed regarding these emergent groups. After several weeks of investigation it became apparent that aside from a proliferation of descriptive, and highly speculative, journalistic accounts, little in the way of theoretically-couched, hard-core empirical examinations of any of these phenomena, other than the "Jesus movement" and occultism, existed. To be sure, there was a fairly large body of literature pertaining to the Japanese branch of Nichiren Shoshu, commonly referred to as Sokagakkai,[2] but I had yet to come across any intensive, scholarly examination of Nichiren Shoshu here in America. It was at this point that I vividly recalled my initial introduction to Nichiren Shoshu and seriously began to consider the possibility of studying the movement in America.

Since I thought it would be empirically and theoretically fruitful to conduct a comparative study of several of these recently emergent groups, I was confronted with the task of selecting an additional movement that was situated in the Los Angeles area, that had not yet been the object of intensive, sociological inquiry, and that was similar to Nichiren shoshu in some respects, and yet different. Upon further investigation, the Hare Krishna movement seemed to meet these criteria. Not only was its international headquarters and largest commune located in Los Angeles, but my preliminary library research had not turned up any sociological studies of the Krishna movement.[3] Additionally, and perhaps most importantly, Hare Krishna seemed both sufficiently similar to and different from Nichiren Shoshu to make for an interesting comparative study.

I thus set out in February 1974 to gain entree into and become familiar with these two culturally transplanted eastern religious movements. However, after several months of involvement in each, it became increasingly apparent that the demanding nature of membership in both groups, the demands of the participant observation method of inquiry initially required, and the confluence of a number of additional pragmatic constraints called for a reconsideration of my original intention. In brief, I had reached the point where I was beginning to experience considerable role strain arising out of both the seemingly impossible situation of having to learn and act in terms of two incompatible and highly demanding membership roles and the difficulty of trying to synchronize the membership and observer roles in both situations.

As a consequence, I decided to conduct a more modest and practical examination of just one of these movements, and chose to focus on Nichiren Shoshu for the following reasons. First, my involvement with Nichiren Shoshu had been participatory and much more consistent and intense than my involvement with Hare Krishna, which had been merely observational and occasional. Second, continued participation in Nichiren Shoshu did not require me to drop out, shave my head, and assume an austere, communal lifestyle as would have continued participation in Hare Krishna. And a third and equally important consideration was my marriage, which made the latter course of action a highly untenable proposition.

So in spite of my original intentions, various emotional and pragmatic constraints, which frequently arise only after the researcher has entered the field, forced me to redirect my study. And, as a consequence, a more highly focused case study had evolved.

Methodological Problems and Procedures

Having described how I came to study and focus solely on Nichiren Shoshu, let us now consider the negotiation and management of the three major problems encountered during the course of the study: (1) the problem of gaining entree and becoming a member; (2) the problem of carving out and assuming a participant observer role that lent itself to learning and meeting membership obligations while simultaneously facilitating the accumulation of data regarding additional research interests; and (3) the problem of disengagement and extrication or getting out.

Gaining Entree and Becoming a Member

In considering an examination of a fairly well-bounded and highly organizing group or movement, such as Nichiren Shoshu, the researcher is initially confronted with the problem of deciding at what level contact might be established and entree sought. The answer depends in large part on the purposes of the study. If one is merely interested in the constitutional view or the formally stated ideology and aims of the group under investigation, then such information can be readily ascertained by talking with a few higher-level leaders and by reading the group's literature and sacred texts. If, on the other hand, the aim is to come to know and gain an in-depth understanding of a certain phenomena or social world about which little is known, then it is imperative that the researcher acquires a first-hand knowledge of and familiarity with that particular empirical world.

The first task, then, for surveyors of previously unexplored social terrain is that they immerse themselves in the setting and become intimately familiar with the landscape from the standpoint of insiders or members. Hence, the necessity and problem of gaining entree and becoming a member. What follows is a brief account of how these problems were negotiated and managed.

In the last week of February 1974, approximately nine months after I was first told about Nam-Myoho-Renge-Kyo, I initiated contact with the movement. In the late afternoon of February 28, I stopped by one of Nichiren Shoshu's local community centers to inquire as to where and when I might attend a chanting meeting. Although the Center was closed, a Caucasian female, around age 35, and dressed in a deep ocean-blue suit that appeared to be a uniform of sorts, came to the entrance and asked if I was a member. I indicated that I was not, but that I was interested in learning about Nichiren Shoshu. She smiled, stepped away for a minute, and then returned with a calling card like the one I had received nine months earlier. She instructed me to go to the address on the card at 7:00 that evening, and indicated that she would meet me there.

Upon arriving at the designated address, I found myself standing in front of a small bungalow, situated in a working-class neighborhood undergoing transition. Having expected something out of the ordinary, like a Buddhist temple perhaps, I was somewhat surprised. But this feeling was short-lived; for as soon as I stepped up to the front entrance, I caught the scent of incense and the sound of what appeared to be chanting, accompanied by the dry rustle of beads being rubbed together.

After a few moments passed the chanting stopped, and a Caucasian male, in his early twenties, answered the door, introduced himself, and invited me in. He indicated that he was expecting me, and that the woman I had met earlier in the day would be joining us shortly.

What would have normally functioned as a living room had been converted into a type of shrine-like meeting room. Aside from a wooden altar at one end, a few movement-related pictures and charts on the walls, and an old couch pushed against the wall at the opposite end, the room was literally barren.

No sooner had we situated ourselves on the floor near the altar when I was asked how I had come to learn about Nichiren Shoshu. Since I intended, from the very beginning of the project, to be as open and honest as possible about what I was up to, I used his query as an occasion to explain my interests, indicating that I was a graduate student in sociology interested in studying several religious movements in the Los Angeles area. He smiled, stated it sounded like a good enough reason for seeking out Nichiren Shoshu, and added that I could not have possibly found a more interesting group to study.

About that time the woman I had met earlier that day joined us and immediately asked how I had heard about Nichiren Shoshu. I repeated what I said a moment ago, and then asked how open and accessible they thought Nichiren Shoshu would be to someone with my interests. They assured me that I would not have any trouble getting whatever information I desired, that I would find the members most pleasant and cooperative, and that they would assist me in any way possible.

They then added, however, that it would be impossible to come to understand Nichiren Shoshu and "true Buddhism" (Nichiren Shoshu refers to its version of Buddhism as "true Buddhism") unless I chanted and participated in Nichiren Shoshu activities. After all, they continued, the essence of "true Buddhism" is not in its theory, but in its "effects" on those who practice and believe in it, and the only way to discover and experience this is by chanting and participating in Nichiren Shoshu. Intensifying the sales pitch, both emphasized that I should give chanting a try for no less than one hundred days, and that if I had not received any "benefits" by the end of that period, then I would not have to continue chanting. This was qualified, however, when they added that the chances of not receiving any "benefits" is rather unlikely if one takes chanting seriously.

At this point the male member went into a short testimonial of how chanting "Nam Myoho Renge Kyo" to the "Gohonzon" (a graphic representation of the supreme object of worship which each member has enshrined within his altar) had provided him with an endless number of "benefits."

As soon as he finished objectifying the consequences of chanting, the other member turned to me and asked if I would give chanting a try. I hesitated for a moment and then agreed to do so, indicating that I hoped chanting would not only yield an interesting monograph, but a number of "fringe benefits" as well. They chuckled, shook my hand, and suggested that we chant for a few minutes.

Within less than two weeks after the above encounter, I was formally initiated into Nichiren Shoshu in a conversion ceremony (Gojukai) held at one of its regional temples and conducted by Nichiren Shoshu priests. From the time I left for the temple to when I returned home, I was constantly reminded that not only was this "the most important day in my life," but even more importantly, it was "the beginning of a new life." Three days later my own personal "Gohonzon," which I had received in the conversion ceremony, was enshrined in my place of residence. I was now a new convert and a nominal Nichiren Shoshu member.

Gaining entree and becoming a nominal member clearly was not a particularly difficult undertaking. In fact, it was accomplished with relative ease when compared to the problems encountered in attempting to gain membership in many groups. In contrast to Nichiren Shoshu, for example, some groups tend to be highly exclusive in the sense that gaining entree is dependent on possession of certain ascribed or achieved attributes. For such groups (i.e., Ku Klux Klan, Minutemen, John Birch Society, American Nazi Party, various forms of occultism), gaining entree can be extremely difficult to negotiate and may even require the researcher to conceal his or her intentions, regardless of personal or professional ethical standards. Additionally, membership in some groups, such as Hare Krishna and many utopian communes, is contingent on making certain initial sacrifices, such as surrendering material possessions and giving up one's previous lifestyle.[4] Gaining membership in Nichiren Shoshu was not contingent upon any such initial sacrifices, however. All that was required was that I pay a $5.00 shipping fee for the "Gohonzon," and perhaps be willing to risk a negative reaction by nonmovement significant others.

Gaining entree and nominal membership was only the first step in coming to know and understand the world of Nichiren Shoshu. Still remaining was the more difficult and demanding task of securing and maintaining members' confidence and trust so that they would make available to me, just as they presumably would to any new member, an understanding of what Nichiren Shoshu was all about, of what it meant to be a member, and of how members reasoned, talked, and acted.

Assuming the Role of a Controlled Skeptic: Information-Gathering Strategies and Techniques

As suggested above, one of the basic objectives underlying this study was to come to know and understand the world of Nichiren Shoshu and what it meant cognitively, behaviorally, and experientially to be a member. Before detailing how this was accomplished or, more appropriately, learned, let me first make explicit what has been glossed over - what is meant conceptually by the term "world," and what it means "to know and understand another social world or culture."

Regarding the first concern, the term "world," as used in the context of this study, refers to what George Herbert Mead termed a "universe of discourse" -- that is, "a system of common or social meanings" that "is constituted by a group of individuals carrying on and participating in a common social process of experience and behavior."[5] Although such terms as "meaning system"[6] and "informing point of view"[7] have been used to denote the same idea, and although these terms will be used interchangeably, the basic referent for each is lodged in Mead's conceptualization of a "universe of discourse."

Accordingly, the "world" of Nichiren Shoshu is not merely constituted by the behavior that members engage in (i.e., chanting, proselytizing, giving testimony) or the products of that behavior (i.e., benefits, retrospective motivational accounts), but also, and perhaps first and foremost, it is constituted by what one must know in order to act, talk, and reason like a member.   Or, simply put, it is the information that members use to organize and interpret not only their own behavior but the social behavior of others as well.

From this standpoint, then, to know and understand another world or culture is to have apprehended the information that members use to organize their behavior so that one can "pass" among "them" as, for all practical purposes, one of their own kind. To "know" another "world" is to have thus learned:

> ... whatever it is one has to know or believe in order to operate in a manner acceptable to its members and to do so in any role that they accept for one of themselves.[8]

A clue as to how this might be accomplished was provided when, on the occasion of the previously mentioned entree-gaining encounter, the importance of not only chanting but actual participation was emphasized, and then, again, several weeks later, when I was instructed to develop a "seeking mind": to not only chant and actively participate in Nichiren Shoshu activities, but to seek out and adhere to leaders' "guidance," rather direct or indirect, concerning Nichiren's "life philosophy," the correct practice, the importance of participation, the management of whatever problems I might encounter in my daily life, the correct interpretation of events in the world, and the resolution of whatever conflicts might arise between my daily routines and movement activities. This, I was told, was the only way to experience and understand the nature and meaning of Nichiren Shoshu and its "life philosophy."

What was required, then, from the standpoint of Nichiren Shoshu, was that I immerse myself in the world of Nichiren Shoshu; that I become, rather than just a nominal member, an active member; that I ask not merely "what do I see members doing?" but that I seek to discover both "what I should be doing" and "what they see themselves as doing, and why."

As I quickly came to learn, this called for the devotion of an inordinate amount of time and energy to the movement. Within the limits of job and sleep demands, core members seemed to spend all their leisure time engaged in Nichiren Shoshu activities, and I was expected to do likewise. Unlike members of most voluntary associations and conventional religious denominations, core members seemed to have little, if any, life apart from the movement.

Thus, for a year-and-a-half, Nichiren Shoshu became a preoccupation. Seldom did a day or evening pass when I was not in contact with the movement. What this entailed in terms of actual involvement was daily and nightly phone calls from members, spending an average of three nights a week attending meetings and participating in Nichiren Shoshu activities, subscribing to and promoting movement literature, Shakubuku-ing (proselytizing) with members, giving an experience (testimony) when called upon, visiting other members in their homes, having members visit my home, and constantly explaining to my wife why it was necessary that she spend another evening alone.

Throughout the course of the study my aim was not merely to learn how Nichiren Shoshu went about its work and what participation in the movement involved; I was also interested in discovering what core membership meant cognitively and experientially and in apprehending the information core members used to organize their behavior. I was thus confronted with the task of carving out a role that would facilitate the realization of these interests.

Toward this end, I eventually came to assume and maintain the role of a "controlled skeptic." It can be construed analytically as a derived participant observer role based on a working synthesis of two ideal-type, complementary roles, that of a "controlled elicitor" and that of a "skeptic."

The role of a controlled elicitor was suggested by a methodological technique referred to in cognitive anthropology as controlled eliciting.[9] It is a technique that aims at getting members of a group to verbally manifest their frame of reference, and that therefore shifts the focus of the research from the perspective of the investigator to the discovery of the member's informing point of view. The underlying assumption is that it is well-nigh impossible to ask meaningful questions and elicit meaningful answers until one has begun to tap and know the universe of discourse, meaning system, or informing point of view of those studied. What this entailed in actual practice was to listen patiently to movement members, allowing them to talk about whatever issues and events they had in mind. Whenever I asked questions, the general aim was to help members disclose and articulate their attitudes, feelings, and ideas so as to discover not only what information they possessed, but also what was important to them and what knowledge was necessary in order to talk, reason, and act like a member.

This technique dovetailed nicely with my status within the movement as an overt, rank-and-file convert who routinely took a skeptical stance with respect to movement practices and beliefs. Not wanting to appear overly enthusiastic out of fear that members would not articulate their justifications and rationales for both their own actions and what they expected others to do, I eschewed the role of zealot or "true believer" in favor of the role of the skeptic. The skepticism was tempered and controlled, however, as I acted as if I were a naive, curious, and moderately willing but skeptical member who needed to be coaxed and instructed each step of the way, but who predictably took the next step, thereby reinforcing the entire process. In this way, then, not only was I learning what to do and how to do it as a member, but I was also being apprised of the meaning and rationale behind it.

In assuming the stance of a controlled skeptic, I seldom asked "why?" in response to a particular directive or instruction. Instead, I would couch my curiosity and reluctance in what I thought would have been an acceptable motivational explanation for not doing this or that in the larger everyday world, thereby hoping to elicit not only the rationale for doing what I was reminded or instructed to do, but also the member's interpretation of the particular event or situation that was presumably keeping me from doing what was expected. By way of illustration, consider the following episode from my field notes:

> *Situation*: A member called around dinner time to tell me about a special chanting meeting being held later in the evening and the importance of attending.
>
> *Meaning of event and rationale for participating*: President Ikeda (the current Master and President of Nichiren Shoshu-Sokagakkai) and Mr. Williams (the major leader and prime mover behind Nichiren Shoshu of America) would be chanting to the Dai-Gohonzon (the supreme object of worship) in Japan at 8:00 PM Los Angeles time. So everyone in the Santa Monica area was getting together to chant at 8:00 also. According to my informant, by chanting

together to the Chapter Gohonzon at the same time they are chanting to the Dai-Gohonzon, we will receive their vibrations and special benefits.

My excuse for not attending: I told her that I probably wouldn't be able to make it by 8:00 since I was planning to attend a Weight Watchers meeting.

Informant's interpretation of my excuse, and related guidance: She indicated that it wouldn't do much good, that what I have to do is change my karma. She related that one of the reasons she started chanting was to lose weight, and that through chanting she has been able to change her metabolism so that she can now eat whatever she wants and not gain weight. She then added that this just happened recently, and that it is primarily due to chanting and doing lots of Shakubuku (proselytizing). She went on to say that at first she wasn't losing any weight, so she sought guidance from a leader, who instructed her to hunger for Shakubuku rather than food. Since then, she has been doing more Shakubuku and losing more weight. So on the basis of this, she advised me to seek out additional guidance regarding the matter and not to waste my time going to Weight Watchers.

In summary, the basic methodological strategy was to play the role of a controlled skeptic, a derived role that involved the enactment of a group-specific role (that of a nominal convert) with an air of skepticism and doubt. Although belief was suspended in the Schutzian sense,[10] the will to believe, in William James's sense,[11] was not. It was a role that thus enabled me to cast my informants as teachers or instructors, who, as experts in varying degrees in understanding the world of Nichiren Shoshu, made that world available to me and instructed me how to reason, talk, and act from the standpoint of members of that world.

During the course of my career as an active participant, I was fortunate (which could be construed as a "benefit") to have several equally committed, zealous, and determined informants or "teachers," all of whom I came to have intense alternating feelings toward. While I was usually deeply appreciative of their constant attention and efforts to bring me along as a member and to instruct me in the ways of their world, there were times when I yearned for them to get off my back. Nonetheless, they were teachers par excellence.

What I learned, then, through enactment of the role of a controlled skeptic and associated experiences, observations, and discussions with members was treated as instructions regarding acquisition of the basic membership role, how members talk, reason, and behave, and how members interpret events in the larger social world and see themselves and Nichiren Shoshu in relation to that world.

The Problem of Disengagement and Extrication

Although much of the ethnographic literature addresses itself in some detail to the problem of gaining entree and the confidence of the members of the particular setting or group under investigation, relatively little is said about the process of disengagement and getting out. It often seems as if it is something one just does when the writing deadline nears, when the research funds have been exhausted, when the world under investigation has become taken-for-granted, or when the major research questions have been answered. While the confluence of a number of such factors compelled me to begin thinking about easing out after a year-and-a-quarter of association with the movement, this process of withdrawal and extrication was, in contrast to the problem of gaining entree, an extremely difficult one to manage, as well as an anxiety-producing ordeal. Here there were three factors at work which rendered this process more troublesome than initially anticipated: (1) the attitude and policy of Nichiren Shoshu toward backsliding and disengagement; (2) the intensity of my own involvement; and (3) my own sense of ethics.

Regarding the first, Nichiren Shoshu does not treat backsliding and disengagement lightly (referred to by members as going "taiten" - to lose one's faith and backslide). When disillusioned members begin to backslide and curtail their involvement, the more strongly committed members engage in a type of "rallying action" aimed at turning the straying member back into the fold. As indicated in the following excerpts from my field notes, the initial response to my withdrawal was similarly to rally around me and direct me back into the group and its interpretive schema.

My group leader called around dinner time, just as he does about every evening, to see how things were going and to remind me that there would be a meeting tonight. He asked if I had promoted any *World Tribunes* (Nichiren Shoshu's newspaper) and if I had any guests lined up for tonight's meeting.

Having decided that the time had come to curtail my involvement and begin the process of easing out as an active participant, my response was negative. He then suggested that I try to call some people - anyone I knew - regarding the *World Tribune*, and that I spend twenty minutes prior to the meeting Shakubuku-ing (proselytizing). I indicated that I didn't have time to Shakubuku, but that I would try to make it to the meeting. Well, something came up and I was unable to attend.

Around 8:45 the phone rang again. Just as I figured, it was my group leader. He immediately asked what happened. I told him that something came up which I felt I should tend to. After a pregnant pause I then began to relate my growing disillusionment, emphasizing how my participation was interfering with my home life, that my Shakubuku and promotion efforts continuously met with failure, and that I was deeply distressed with the General Director's refusal to grant me permission to conduct a survey.

No sooner had I finished than he congratulated me, indicating that my efforts and the effect - getting upset - were good signs. He went on to suggest that all of this indicates that something is really happening in my life - that it is the stirring of "human revolution" (profound change within). Rather than getting discouraged and giving up, I was told to chant and participate even more. He also strongly suggested that I should go to the Community Center at 10:00 this evening to get further guidance from the senior leaders.

My reaction to his comments was one of puzzlement and despair. Here I had indicated my growing disenchantment and the factors in which it was grounded. And what does he do? He takes what I had thought to be indicative of failure as a member and grounds for disillusionment, and turns it around by offering a different interpretation. Thus, what I saw as constitutive of failure and reason to defect, he interprets as the stirring of human revolution and reason for greater participation.

This rallying action was indicated again later in the evening. First, my group leader stopped by the apartment at 10:00 - unannounced - to pick me up and rush me to the Community Center to make sure that I received guidance. And secondly, after informing another member of my dismay over the nixing of the survey, this member immediately rallied by leading me over to where a senior leader was giving guidance to several other members and by suggesting that I speak with him about other alternatives. And again, later on, when it appeared that I wouldn't get a chance to speak with this senior leader, she whispered in his ear something about my dilemma, and then related that he indicated I should see him this week at one of the meetings.

While I was thus trying to curtail my involvement and offer what seemed to be legitimate reasons for easing out, I was yet being drawn back in at the same time.

The above instances are but a few of the many that I observed or experienced that are illustrative of the way in which core members deal with incipient backsliding and signs of disillusionment: they mobilize and talk and act so as to turn the straying sheep back into the fold and its problem-solving practices by offering alternative interpretations and by instructing the disenchanted member to seek out leaders for guidance with respect to the problem at hand.

To what extent this rallying action would continue in the face of continued disenchantment and nonparticipation remained unclear. Assuming, however, that it would not be maintained in the face of little response, I failed to respond, as I had done before, to the coaxing and instructions of my informants. After several months this tactic seemed to be working as the daily phone calls and frequent home visitations began to dwindle and, eventually, come to a halt. I should also mention that during this period members were preoccupied with preparation for their 1975 convention, and therefore did not have the time to rally as they had initially done.

A second factor rendering the extrication process somewhat difficult was the nature of my involvement, which was, as we have seen, fairly intense. Erving Goffman once suggested that if an ethnographic enterprise is to be of any quality, then the researcher should immerse her/himself to such an extent that s/he has second thoughts about leaving when the time to exit has come.[12] While I am not certain that I totally concur with this directive, it does, nonetheless, apply to my experience. Having been involved in little else other than Nichiren Shoshu for well over a year, it had, as one would suspect, grown on me and become somewhat of a habit. Additionally, and perhaps even more confounding, I had come to know a number of fellow participants not merely as subjects, respondents, or members of some offbeat religious group, but as very real and personable human beings. As a consequence, I found myself somewhat ambivalent over the necessity of disengagement as an active participant.

I suppose that this could be interpreted as a good sign in the sense that it suggests that not only had I gotten "close" to the world of Nichiren Shoshu but that "this world" had, perhaps, become a part of me. However advantageous this may have been in some respects, it was not without its costs, which manifested themselves in terms of various withdrawal pains and anxieties. One of these came to the fore while in the process of organizing and reorganizing my field notes several weeks after I had initiated the disengagement process. Each time I began to shift my notes from Nichiren Shoshu categories to sociological categories, I found myself questioning the point of it all and asking if I was doing justice to their meaning system, the way in which they organize the world, and so on. And each time I began to resolve this dilemma, I found myself back at another meeting, which only served to exacerbate the problem.

I finally came to the conclusion that my problem was much like that of the fabled family therapist who can help other families work out their problems but who can not do much with his or her own because of being too close to the situation emotionally. I thus decided it was fruitless to continue alternating between the world of Nichiren Shoshu and the world of Sociology. It was at this point, then, that I began to employ the above-mentioned disengagement tactic.

A third troublesome aspect of the extrication process relates to the ethics of the entire research enterprise. Even though I did not announce my intentions and interests to each member I conversed with or in each movement-related situation, I attempted, from the very beginning, to be as overt and honest as possible. For example, whenever I was called upon to give an experience (testimony), I always began by indicating how and why I got involved in Nichiren Shoshu and always finished by adding that I was still too much of a skeptic to attribute whatever "benefits" I mentioned to the power of chanting.

Nonetheless, I still felt somewhat like the con artist who does whatever is necessary in order to set up the "mark," and then, after gaining his confidence, blows the scene with the "take." On the one hand I had assumed the role of an active but controlled and skeptical participant who was treated first and foremost by the "real" members as a fellow human being and participant, and secondarily, if at all, as a sociological investigator; while, on the other hand, I was running off and using what I had learned, the information I had received, in the role of sociologist. As a consequence, not only was I enmeshed in a kind of role conflict situation, but I also found myself in a kind of ethical double-bind that was a source of anxiety that rendered the disengagement and extrication process more difficult than initially anticipated.

Methodological Shortcomings Associated with the Level of My Involvement

As the foregoing discussion clearly illustrates, my contact and association with Nichiren Shoshu was primarily at the level of the rank-and-file membership. Although learning about Nichiren Shoshu from this standpoint was sufficient as far as most of my interests and questions were concerned, it was not without its drawbacks and blind alleys.

One problem was that issues and questions arose from time to time that could be answered only by the upper ranks of the leadership. These leaders were not readily accessible, however. As a rank-and-file member, I could not circumvent the military, chain-of-command-like leadership structure, but had to work through it. As a consequence, my association with those highest in the leadership structure was always indirect in the sense that it was mediated by and through a lower- or middle-level leader.

The ramifications of this dilemma came to the fore when I attempted to gain permission to conduct a survey of randomly selected members shortly after my first year as a member. The final approval had to come from the movement's General Director, but I was never able to communicate with him directly. Rather, my request and rationale, in the form of a formally written letter, was passed up the chain, beginning at the lowest level (District level). A month and a half transpired between the time I first handed the letter to my District Chief and when I was informed, by word-of-mouth, that I was to write to the General Director. Two weeks later I received a letter from one of his assistants, indicating that it was not Nichiren Shoshu policy to approve such surveys.

While the nixing of the survey was not a particularly critical setback for my research, the nature and duration of the process consumed a considerable amount of time and energy that might have been spent in more productive ways had I been able to circumvent the leadership hierarchy and go directly to the top.

An additional methodological shortcoming of entering and participating at the level of a rank-and-file member was that I was not directly privy to the inner workings of the movement from the standpoint of the leadership beyond the District level. Nor was I able to acquire leaders' knowledge and view of the movement in terms of what only leaders know and what leaders do and say when in interaction with each other behind closed doors.

These limitations are not unique to this study, however, since any study that approaches the collectivity under examination from the standpoint of rank-and-file members is likely to gloss over or miss other relevant perspectives and practices. Yet, the blind spots are likely to be even greater when an understanding of a group or movement is sought by only reading the group's literature and establishing contact with higher-level leaders. This is because the researcher has not established her/himself as a member and because of the tendency for leaders to present an idyllic and truncated view of the overall operation. In such situations, then, an insider's view, rather from the standpoint of leaders or rank-and-file members, is never totally apprehended.

Additional Data Sources

Although my understanding of Nichiren Shoshu as both a social world and movement was based largely on my observations and experiences as a member in the Los Angeles area and what I learned through the variously mentioned methodological strategies and techniques, this knowledge was supplemented and complemented by the information obtained from a systematic examination of selected publications from Nichiren Shoshu's voluminous body of literature in both the United States and Japan. However, it was not until I was well into my first year as a member before I was able to read and make use of this material as a sociological source. This was due largely to the fact that I was not exactly sure how I would make use of this material until various serendipitous observations and experiences gave rise to a set of hunches and questions that were neither readily apparent nor well articulated when the research began and which, as I came to discover, could be answered, in part, through a systematic examination of this archival literature.

In time, then, much of the movement's literature - particularly the *World Tribune* and the *NSA Quarterly*[13] - became a valuable source for gaining a greater understanding of the movement's historical development, organizational structure and leadership, formal doctrine and ideology, recruitment channels and practices, core constituencies, patterns of accommodation, and operation outside the Los Angeles area.

Additionally, the content of the *World Tribune* made it possible to collect an array of data that are not normally accessible to ethnographic procedures alone. With respect to the demographic characteristics of members, for example, observational procedures can yield at best information pertaining only to such gross and visible variables as gender, approximate age, and conspicuous ethnicity and socioeconomic status; whereas these and other such information can be ascertained more readily and accurately through a survey instrument or a variant thereof. Since nearly each edition of the *World Tribune* contained several members' experiences (testimonies) - sometimes in first person and sometimes in third - I randomly selected 504 experiences from 1966 to 1974 (six per month), excluding the years 1972 and 1973, which were not available during this phase of the research. Through this procedure I was able to collect systematically an array of quantitative data regarding the demographic characteristics of the membership over time, manner of recruitment, members' retrospective accounts of past life situations, motivational accounts for joining, changes in life situation, benefits received, and length of membership.

I also randomly selected 240 editions of the *World Tribune*, covering the ten-year period from 1966-1975, as the basis for developing an empirically grounded understanding of the movement's historical development and operation.

In sum, the information obtained from systematic examination of the movement literature, particularly the *World Tribune*, functioned as a type of "validity check" for my own observations and experiences, enabled me to examine more closely various preexisting and emergent questions and serendipitous observations, and provided me with a more thoroughgoing understanding of the course and character of the Nichiren Shoshu movement in America.

Summary of General Objectives and Focal Questions

Although it is customary to begin a research monograph with a detailed statement of what questions one hoped to answer or what propositions one sought to examine, I have purposely refrained from making these concerns explicit until now for a number of reasons that are couched in the nature and evolution of both the study and the major questions and issues that will be addressed in detail in the coming chapters.

First, while there were, to be sure, a number of general questions which, as previously discussed, prompted this investigation, they remained just that - general questions - during the first six months in the field. I was concerned that had I entered the field with a set of well-defined questions and propositions, I would - like the determined hunter who, in search of his prey, fails to "see" the forest - structure or impose an order on what I saw to such an extent that I might fail to "see" and come to know the world of Nichiren Shoshu and what is important and meaningful to those who share this world.

Furthermore, even if I had wanted to clearly define and articulate a set of initial questions prior to entering the field, there would have been little point in doing so; for I had no way of knowing whether they were meaningful and relevant to the world and activities of Nichiren Shoshu, much less answerable, until I entered the field and became reasonably familiar with this world. And finally, just as with most studies of this nature, what emerged as most interesting and researchable was often the product of various experiences and serendipitous observations that surfaced only during the course of the research itself.

For these reasons, then, to have explicitly stated at the outset a series of well-defined questions and problems that I sought to examine would have been, it seems, to misrepresent both the evolution and nature of the study and the extent to which my observations and findings were married to and, in part, an artifact of the methodological strategies and techniques employed and the trials and tribulations experienced during the course of the study itself.

Having said this, what, then, were the major underlying objectives that partly structured the research, and the major questions and issues that emerged as the study unfolded and evolved? Regarding the major underlying objectives, let me note first what I wanted to avoid. A common criticism of many participant observation studies is that they fail to go beyond, in their final reports, description of the particular phenomenon, situation, or world under investigation. According to this argument, such descriptive accounts are useful insofar as they introduce us to and provide a basis for apprehending another social world or pattern of behavior, but their scientific utility is limited insofar as they fail to link their findings to other related works and substantive theory. In order to avoid this limitation and tendency to which ethnographers frequently fall prey, I set out from the very beginning to use my investigation of Nichiren Shoshu as an occasion for not only apprehending and making available to others, albeit second-hand, the world of Nichiren Shoshu, but also for considering and conceptualizing, to whatever extent possible, various emergent observations and findings in terms of certain issues and questions regarding social movements in particular and collective behavior in general.

Thus, the underlying objective of this study was essentially twofold: first, to unveil and present a comprehensive picture of Nichiren Shoshu as both a social world and a social movement by discovering and accurately describing what membership entails and means to the participants, and by portraying Nichiren Shoshu in such a way that readers would be able to project themselves into the point of view of its participants and have a basis for apprehending the similarities and differences between Nichiren Shoshu and other religiously oriented cults and movements. And second, I wanted to use Nichiren Shoshu as an empirical referent for examining, extending, and perhaps refining certain relevant issues and questions within the study of social movements, namely those pertaining to differential recruitment, mobilization, commitment-building, conversion, and the strategies and tactics that movements employ in an effort to advance their interests.

Before examining some of these issues and processes, let us take a closer look at the movement's roots and objectives. What is its mission? What are its goals, and how are they rationalized in terms of its ideology? What are its major ritual practices, and how are these connected to its goals and mission? What are its historical roots, and how did it come to flower in America in the late 1960s and early 1970s? These and related questions will be addressed in the next two chapters in an attempt to provide an understanding of both the world of Nichiren Shoshu and its historical development.

NOTES

1. The above account is derived from Masaharu Anesaki, *Nichiren: The Buddhist Prophet* (Cambridge: Harvard University Press, 1916); and Daisaku Ikeda, *The Human Revolution* (Tokyo: Seikyo Press, 1966-1967), and its screen adaptation bearing the same title.

2. This body of literature will be cited extensively later in the text.

3. J. Stillson Judah's *Hare Krishna and the Counter-culture* (New York: John Wiley & Sons, 1974) was published several months after this initial library research.

4. See, for example, Rosabeth M. Kanter's discussion of 19th-century utopian communes, *Commitment and Community: Communes and Utopias in Sociological Perspective* (Cambridge: Harvard University Press, 1972); and Benjamin Zablocki's account of the Bruderhof, *The Joyful Community* (Baltimore, Maryland: Penguin Books, 1971).

5. George H. Mead, *Mind, Self and Society*, edited by Charles W. Morris (Chicago: The University of Chicago Press, 1962), pp. 89-90.

6. Peter L. Berger, *Invitation to Sociology: A Humanistic Perspective* (Garden City, New York: Doubleday-Anchor, 1963), p. 61.

7. Kenneth Burke, *Permanence and Change* (Indianapolis: Bobbs-Merrill, 1965), p. 99.

8. Ward H. Goodenough, "Cultural Anthropology and Linguistics," in Dell Hymes, ed., *Language in Culture and Society* (New York: Harper and Row, 1966), p. 36.

9. See Mary Black and Duane Metzger, "Ethnographic Description and the Study of Law," in Stephen A. Tyler, ed., *Cognitive Anthropology* (New York: Holt, Rinehart and Winston, 1969), pp. 137-165; and Stephen A. Tyler, "Introduction," in S.A. Tyler, ed., *Cognitive Anthropology* (New York: Holt, Rinehart and Winston, 1969), pp. 1-23.

10. Alfred Schutz, *Collected Papers I: The Problem of Social Reality* (The Hague: Martinus Nijhoff, 1971).

11. William James, *The Will to Believe and Other Essays in Popular Philosophy* (London: Longmans, Green and Co., 1896).

12. Goffman suggested this in a session on field work at the 1974 annual meeting of the Pacific Sociological Association.

13. The *World Tribune* is the NSA newspaper. It was first issued in August 1964, and was published five times weekly in Santa Monica during the period of research. At that time, it had over 55,000 monthly subscriptions and constituted a useful record of the growth and history of Nichiren Shoshu in America. The *NSA Quarterly*, also published in Santa Monica, functioned as Nichiren Shoshu's analogue to an academic journal. It was especially useful as a source of Nichiren Shoshu's formal doctrine and ideology and the guidance of its major leaders.

2
TOWARD THE IMPOSSIBLE DREAM: THE GOALS AND IDEOLOGY OF NICHIREN SHOSHU

If we revere the Gohonzon and chant the Daimoku, we will become the Bodhisattvas prophesized to arise from the earth in order to save the world. We have a great mission: to save our fellow men and to propagate true Buddhism.

> Josei Toda, 2nd President of Sokagakkai, quoted in *The Human Revolution*

Dawn is a hope for all mankind. It is similar to a ray which brings hope in the morning after a rain storm at night, and it signifies advancement of the pioneers of today. Therefore a gallant figure of Nichiren Shoshu-Sokagakkai propagating the great Buddhism which appeared in Japan throughout the world by carrying out the will of Nichiren Daishonin is definitely a "dawn" that brings the first ray of hope into the darkness.

> Daisaku Ikeda, 3rd President of Sokagakkai, as quoted in the *World Tribune*, 1966

Wherever you go in today's society, the dark side is prevalent. That is why NSA's movement is really like a torch to light the dark night for all people.

> *World Tribune* Editorial, 1974

The fate of mankind rests on the shoulders of our movement.

> Rank and File Member, 1975

These prophetic and rather apocalyptic statements beg the questions that this chapter will attempt to answer: what precisely is Nichiren Shoshu's view of the world as presently constituted, and what does it see as the proper or ideal aim of humankind? What does it see as its mission or role in the world? What does it hope to accomplish, and how does it propose to do so? In short, what are the nature and content of its goals and underlying ideology, or what has been referred to as a movement's value orientation?[1]

By goals, I refer to the set of valued ideas, changes, and practices that Nichiren Shoshu seeks to promote and institute, and which function, on the surface anyway, as both its raison d'etre and the standards around which its adherents rally. By ideology, I refer to that aspect of Nichiren Shoshu's universe of discourse or meaning system that supports and justifies its objectives and practices, providing the member with a cognitive map containing both a picture of the world as it is and as it should be and a guide for action or statement of the means by which the desired changes and objectives can be best achieved.[2]

Since the aim here is not merely to present a coherent picture of the objectives and changes that Nichiren Shoshu seeks to promote and the underlying rationale that legitimates and calls for action in support of these goals or values, but also to provide a basis for comparing Nichiren Shoshu's value orientation with that of other movements, the following discussion will be organized in terms of the basic structural elements of nearly all movement value orientations. This is not to suggest that movement value orientations are similar in terms of content, complexity, and organization; to be sure, there is considerable variation among movements in the character of their value orientations. Yet, the form or structure of the basic cognitive maps provided by these orientations, and particularly by the ideological aspect, seems to be much the same in that each commonly includes the following elements: (1) a diagnostic statement regarding some aspect of social life that is defined as problematic and in need of alteration or repair; (2) a prognostic statement providing a cure or solution for the problem(s) at hand and frequently including a visionary blueprint of a better world and the way it might be achieved as well; and (3) a rationale for the movement and supportive action in its behalf.[3]

With these prefatory comments in mind, let us then turn to an examination of Nichiren Shoshu's value orientation in order that we might inch closer to the world of Nichiren Shoshu and begin to gain an understanding of what it is all about.

NICHIREN SHOSHU'S DIAGNOSIS OF THE CONDITION OF HUMANKIND

As reflected in the introductory statements to this chapter, for Nichiren Shoshu, just as for most movements that seek to alter the world, whether it be through changing individuals or changing social structures, the world as presently constituted is cast in the image of a large stage on which the same basic themes of misery, unhappiness, and discord are portrayed in one Greek-like tragedy after another. Clearly, there are different scenarios reflecting different problems - one dealing with pollution, another with war, another with inflation, and another with family discord.   There are also different underlying themes that reflect various problematic life conditions - such as greed, animosity, arrogance, meaninglessness, and indifference - that are seen as both the cause and consequence of the more visible problems. But whatever the particular scenario, and whatever the corresponding theme, the basic message, the underlying motif is still the same: the condition of humankind and the world in general is one of suffering, alienation, and unhappiness.

This rather dismal view of life in the world is reflected again and again in Nichiren Shoshu's literature and in the talk of its core members.   Not only is everyone seen as being confronted with numerous problems, and not only is the world seen as being on the verge of disintegration, but those who do not recognize these facts of life are considered to be either blind or living in a fantasy world.

Regarding the generalization of problems and unhappiness to all non-members and all domains of life outside of Nichiren Shoshu, consider the following statments:[4]

In this world, there is no life that is completely free from worry and problems.[5]

Our polluted society is filled with suffering and alienated people.

Regardless of where people may live, whether it be in a small town or a large city, generally speaking, we assume they are coping satisfactorily with their lives if we see no outward signs to the contrary. However, once we step into their homes, we discover that they have financial problems, are suffering from some illness, have an unhappy family or many other troubles. These facts clearly point out that they are not truly happy.[6]

If any of us were really happy before, we wouldn't be here now.

No place in the world, except in Nichiren Shoshu, will you find truly happy people.

And as one of my informants responded after I informed her that I could not attend a meeting because I had relatives visiting: "Oh, isn't it great that you're getting close to your family now" - the assumption being that there was a rift between me and my family prior to my joining Nichiren Shoshu.

As for those who claim they have no pressing problems and that they are truly happy, they are said to be either feigning happiness or living in a fantasy world. As stated in an April 1974 edition of the *World Tribune*:

The man who says he has no problems fools no one but himself. All one has to do is look at his actual life condition. His daily life is bound to contain either family, financial, or physical difficulties. This is true with every human being.

Someone who declares that he is perfectly happy and content with his life is living in a fantasy existence. He might persist saying, 'I have a good job, and I'm in perfect health,' etc. But how long will that happiness last before it is disrupted by an unsuspected event? Those people who have no problems are those who, as soon as something happens to them, lose all composure and assurance. They are the least capable of handling the slightest change. They live in a fantasy existence . . .

Or in the words of one member who, upon seeing a carload of young girls singing and laughing, dismissed it all by suggesting that "they are just pretending to be happy."

But what about those who really appear to have it made, who seem to have all the desiderata symbolic of wealth and good fortune? Here we are told:

> No matter how prosperous some people may appear or how peaceful their family and personal life may be, it is like a fantasy that can disappear without even a trace remaining behind. As cold as it sounds, this is a fact of life without faith in the Gohonzon.[7]

> They are lucky and live affluently, seeming unburdened by problems, but these are only superficial appearances . . . . Fortune is not only financial wealth, but most important, it is a wealth of true happiness gained only from the consistent practice of true Buddhism.[8]

Turning from the individual level and the domains of everyday life to the societal and global level, we catch the image of a smoldering volcano on the verge of eruption:

> Though there exists a True Law in the world, evil overruns and disaster fills the surface. It becomes difficult to make a living in this environment for each has sunk into the last moments of suffering.[9]

> Today's unhappy social atmosphere is beset by moral decay symbolized in the Watergate scandal, unexplainable criminal acts, and the irresponsible egoism which led to the energy crisis. The nation has never before faced such difficult times.[10]

> Our current crisis forewarns of the eventual collapse of our entire material civilization.[11]

> We are living in the dark ages. People know about
> atomic energy and other such things, but they don't know
> how to live happily and peacefully. Unless human beings
> change their destiny within our lifetime, we will either
> become like 1984 or witness our annihilation.

It should be apparent that Nichiren Shoshu's conception of reality
pictures the condition of humankind as being one of general
unhappiness and the condition of the world as spiraling downwards. It
is worth noting, however, that this view is not unique to Nichiren
Shoshu. As indicated earlier, it is a view that is shared by many
movements, both past and present, such as Hare Krishna, the Children
of God, Jehovah's Witnesses, the Oxford Group Movement, also
known as Moral Rearmament, the SDS, and even various versions of
Marxism. Vulgar Marxism, for example, projects a view of life among
all but the owners of the means of production as being similarly woeful
and unhappy or, more appropriately, alienating. And just as Nichiren
Shoshu defines those who do not recognize the problematic nature of
their life condition as being "blind" or as "living in a fantasy
existence," so Marxism defines the non-recognition of one's alienating
life condition as "false consciousness."

Given this tendency for various movements of different
persuasions to cast the world as presently constituted in the image of
a Greek tragedy, we must ask, if we are to gain a clear understanding
of the diagnostic component of Nichiren Shoshu's world view and
differentiate it from that of other movements and philosophies, what
every Greek tragedy begs us to ask: what exactly is the discrepancy
between the world as it is and the world as it should be, between the
real and the ideal, and what is the underlying source or cause of this
discrepancy? More explicitly, if the human condition is defined in
terms of alienation and unhappiness, then it is implied that people must
be alienated from something or unhappy about something. To talk the
language of alienation and unhappiness, then, is to imply a discrepancy
between certain learned expectations, values, or goals and difficulty in
a given society in realizing those values and goals.

The analytic task thus becomes one of ascertaining both the proper
or ideal state from which people are allegedly alienated and the factors
that account for this generalized alienation and unhappiness. If, for
example, one is to gain an understanding of the early Marx's view of

alienation, one must first come to grips with Marx's conception of humans, and secondly with the factors that hypothetically keep us from realizing what the early Marx referred to as our "species-being" or "essence."

Similarly, if we are to come to an understanding of Nichiren Shoshu's conception of the world and what it sees as its role in this world, then we must first examine Nichiren Shoshu's metaphysical view of life, what it considers to be the proper aim of humankind, and what it considers to be the source of the world's woes or the discrepancy between the real and the ideal. For it is on the answers to these questions that the diagnostic component of a movement's ideology hinges. Once we have sketched this diagnostic aspect of Nichiren Shoshu's interpretive system, we can then turn to its proposed solution and prognosis or to what is frequently referred to as the Leninesque question of "What is to be done?".

Nichiren Shoshu's View of Life

Underlying both Nichiren Shoshu's view of life in the modern world and its conception of the proper aim of humankind, and representing one of the cardinal elements of its theological system as well, is its theory of ten worlds (Jikkai). Originally propounded by the T'ien-t'ai sect of Buddhism as one of the three basic elements of the theory of Ichinen Sanzen,[12] and later borrowed by Nichiren and incorporated into his life philosophy, this theory holds that there are ten basic realms of life or sentient existence that can manifest themselves from moment to moment within everyday life, and that the life condition of any given being, at any given moment, is but the present manifestation of any one of these realms. These ten states or life conditions, from the lowest to the highest, include:

> 1) *Hell* - a state of intolerable suffering like that occasioned by the death of a loved one, divorce, loss of job, contraction of a critical illness, and other personal tragedies. It is not an imaginary place where a sinful person descends after death, but, like the other nine worlds, it is a condition of life found within and experienced physically and spiritually at one and the same time.

2) *Hunger* - a condition of life controlled by insatiable desires and greed, especially for wealth, fame, and power.

3) *Animality* - a state in which one is governed by animalistic instincts rather than by reason and morality, and in which the law of the jungle prevails.

4) *Anger* - a state of rage and hostility arising out of competition, unfulfilled desires, egoism, etc., and eventuating in conflict and the externalization of blame.

5) *Tranquility* - an ephemeral state in which a person goes about his business in a peaceful and passive manner.

6) *Rapture* - a fleeting state of ecstasy and joy that results from the satisfaction of a desire or wish, such as that experienced when one falls in love, wins an award, inherits money, acquires a good job, and so on.

7) *Learning* - the state of exploration and inquisitivenss, and the appreciation of increasing knowledge that is common to scholars, professors, research workers, and intellectuals.

8) *Absorption* - a condition in which one is totally engrossed in his labors, appreciating not simple, passive discovery, but the joy coming from creation, like that experienced by artists and writers.

9) *Aspiration for Enlightenment* - the state in which one devotes oneself to helping and improving the condition of others, even at the risk of his own well-being, such as when one risks his life to rescue a child or devotes his life to improving the welfare of all humankind. It is the world of the Bodhisattva.

10) *Enlightenment of Buddahood* - the condition of life in which one is awakened to the true nature of the universe and experiences true, indestructible happiness.

According to Nichiren Shoshu, most people are repeatedly flitting in and out of the first six worlds, which are referred to as "the Six Realms of everyday life." But the worlds of "tranquility" and "rapture" are seen as being terribly ephemeral and constantly subject to instant reversal; so it is maintained that most people are constantly fluctuating among the first four worlds (Hell, Hunger, Animality, and Anger), referred to as "the Four Evil Paths." Since it is also maintained that happiness is an impossibility if one's life is but a manifestation of any one of these "four evil paths," and since Buddhahood alone is the realm of true happiness, it is axiomatic that life in the world as presently constituted would be characterized in terms of misery, unhappiness, alienation, and discord. As we have seen, this is exactly the way in which much of life in today's world is viewed from the standpoint of Nichiren Shoshu.

But what about those whose life conditions are characterized by "learning" and absorption"? Are not these two of the four traditional stages of spiritual ascent? According to Nichiren Shoshu, these two worlds are often misinterpreted as Enlightenment. To be sure, they have to do with partial enlightenment, which some people attain in their respective fields. But just as in the other worlds in which most of human life ranges, true happiness is not available to those in the worlds of learning and absorption either, as illustrated in the following comments:

> In reality, these worlds only discover a small segment of truth, a selfish joy which profits only the individual involved. Since the fundamental spirit of Buddhism is mercy, the self-satisfying worlds of learning and absorption cannot attain enlightenment or absolute happiness.[13]

> They offer only partial enlightenment in a limited area of life. Scholars and noted artists are of no special distinction except in their chosen fields. We often hear about the failure of a famous person to achieve a balance or happiness in his life.[14]

> It is typical of people devoted to Learning to have the illusion that they are authorities of human endeavor, though most of them are specialists in but a narrow field. If a

person persistently sticks to his own ideals and feels that he
has attained a level of "Enlightenment," he is actually
blocking out the teachings of Buddhism. Even Sakyamuni
Buddha denounced and severely warned people in the World
of Learning.[15]

Part of the problem with the world is that too many
people have blind faith in science (or the work of those in
the worlds of learning and absorption).

And as I was frequently reminded, "mere studying or getting a Ph.D.
won't bring you happiness." Accordingly, true happiness cannot be
attained when one's life condition is controlled by the pursuit of
knowledge and ideas. Or, stated differently, Buddhahood cannot be
achieved solely through study, training, and contemplation.

Regarding the ninth world, the condition of aspiration for
enlightenment, many people are said to experience this condition from
time to time, such as when one assists an elderly lady across the street,
or rushes into a burning house to rescue the inhabitants, or altruistically
devotes a sum of money or other resources to the cause of alleviating
the suffering of those in the world of Hell. Yet, just as the realms of
tranquility and rapture are experienced only occasionally and
momentarily, life in this world is equally transient; for in time, most
people are said to regress back to the four evil paths. As a
consequence, the life of the true Bodhisattva, one who constantly has
a "seeking mind" and devotes his or her total being (Ichinen) to
improving the life condition of others and bettering the world in
general, ignoring whatever pain, toil, and abuse incurred along the
way, and who sincerely seeks to attain the condition of absolute
happiness, is seldom achieved or manifested in the lives of most.

The tenth and final realm of existence, the state of Enlightenment
or Buddhahood or Absolute Happiness, is considered, as should be
evident by now, both the ultimate condition of life and the proper aim
of humankind. The problem, however, is that this state is even more
rarely experienced than the state of the true Bodhisattva.

In light of the reputedly elusive nature of this quintessential state
and the contention that most of human life ranges among the "four evil
paths," Nichiren Shoshu's view of the world as but a morass of
unhappiness, misery, discord, and alienation becomes even more

understandable. But within this dismal morass there is also a ray of hope; for the condition of one's life in particular and the world in general is never fixed. Although one always experiences life, both materially and spiritually, in terms of one of the ten worlds, we are not shackled by them for the reason that each of the ten realms contains, according to the "theory of mutual possession," all the other realms. Anyone can thus experience, depending on the cause or stimulus, any of the ten manifestations of existence at any given moment. For example, one might be driving home in a state of rapture after having received a job promotion and immediately descend into a state of anger upon being plowed into from behind. Or one could be living in a state of hell and immediately experience the world of enlightenment upon making the "proper cause."

It is believed, then, that each realm contains, in addition to all the others, the realm of Buddhahood and that all people, regardless of race, gender, nationality, previous creed, and present state of life, therefore have within their life condition the latent possibility of attaining Buddhahood. As Nichiren is said to have written in this regard, "Neither Heaven nor Hell is anywhere outside of us. Both of them are found within our life."[16] Rather than referring to the unattainable state of some transcendental being, Buddhahood, from the standpoint of Nichiren Shoshu, thus refers to an ever-present condition which is inherent in all human beings.

Within the frame of reference of Nichiren Shoshu, what, then, is the meaning of human life? What does it mean to be a sentient being?

As the foregoing has attempted to illustrate, rather than answering this question in the direction that such answers have frequently taken - that we are either good or bad, rational or irrational, benevolent or malevolent, Nichiren Shoshu contends that we can be all of these and much more, that we are fundamentally neither good nor bad, neither rational nor irrational but simply potential, possessing all manifestations of existence within ourselves at any given moment. To be human, from this standpoint, is to be aware that, as Terence said, "Homo sum humani nil a alienum puto" (I am a man and nothing human is alien to me); that each one carries within all the potential manifestations of humanity, both past and future - the classroom dunce as well as the scholar, the beggar as well as the baron, the warmonger as well as the bodhisattva, the despondent and desperate as well as the Buddha.

Given this view of life as a continuous flow of existence in which each being possesses all of these potentialities, including the state of Buddhahood, what then accounts for the "fact" that the life condition of most people, from moment to moment, is but a manifestation of one of the first eight worlds, and particularly the lower four or the "Four Evil Paths"? Why the predominance of these lower realms of existence rather than worlds of the true Bodhisattva and enlightenment? Why all the suffering, unhappiness and discord when the life of Buddhahood is within the reach of all? What, in short, accounts for this discrepancy between the real and the ideal, between the dismal state of life in the world as presently constituted and the state of harmonious unity and true, blissful happiness?

Nichiren Shoshu's Attribution of the Cause of Human Unhappiness and Alienation

According to Nichiren Shoshu, this discrepancy between the real and the ideal is essentially attributable to two interrelated "facts" of life: the first is the ancient Hindu-Buddhist principle of karma, or the law of cause and effect; the second is the "fact" that dominant philosophies in the modern world are partial, incomplete, and one-sided, and therefore are incorrect and leading people astray.

Regarding the karmic principle, Nichiren Shoshu, just as all Buddhist sects, contends that the state of one's present life condition is largely determined by the summation of all of one's past deeds or actions or "causes," as members prefer to say, and that one's future destiny is similarly a function of the causes one makes in the immediate present, coupled with those made in the past that have yet to come to fruition or produce their effect. Thus, our current life condition is not only the heir of our past actions, but we are also the makers of our future; for every act or cause bears its fruit or has its consequences or effects. Accordingly, the state of our life condition or the worlds in which we live are a product of this chain of cause and effect that continues in an endless cycle somewhat akin to a "vicious circle" or "self-fulfilling prophecy." In the words of one core member:

> We all live through this cycle day by day and during our
> entire life. It's all continuous cause and effect. You might
> say prove it, but I can't. This is a theory of life. But if you

look at it from many different angles, it makes real good sense. And most other theories don't. This one at least takes into account and explains why some people are rich and others aren't. It is not because of anything like original sin, but because of the causes one has made. If one gets good grades, it is because he has studied hard, because he has made the proper cause.

Through this idea of karma or the causes you carry with you from the past, you can really explain a lot. If you rob a bank today, you can't wake up the next day and say, 'Well, it's a fresh, beautiful day.' No, the cause you made the day before produces an effect that is still with you and that determines what your day will be like. We often think that if someone has good fortune it is due to luck, but it is not so much luck as the cause one made to acquire that fortune. And if bad things happen to you, it is because of the bad causes you made in the past.

From the standpoint of Nichiren Shoshu, as reflected in the above statement, what is most important to understand about this karmic principle is that each individual is the creator of their own life condition; that humans, as sentient and volitional beings, need not look outside themselves to account for their own destiny or fate; that the world we live in is essentially a world of our own making; and, as a consequence, only we can change it by changing ourselves through making the proper causes.

That most people do not understand this principle, and that they therefore tend to blame others for their woes, is considered to be one of the core factors underlying the dismal state of life in today's world. That this is so, from the standpoint of Nichiren Shoshu, is clearly stated in the thoughts of one informant:

If you think a woman has no fortune or a certain man has no fortune, who do we blame? We look outside and say it's society's fault, or the woman says it's man's fault. The black man says his condition is the white man's fault, and the white man says it is the black man's fault. Russia says it is America's fault, and we say it is Russia's fault.

Somebody at work told me about a TV program on the correctional system in California. The criminals say that they've been in jail too long or for too many times and that this system doesn't work. So they blame the system for their problems and current plight. In other words, it's always someone else's fault - the system's fault, the country's fault, the environment's fault, the spouse's fault. Actually, the only one or thing at fault is ourself.

"But," as this member added, "we can't be too severe on ourselves either, for it is also the fault of the wrong philosophy."

What is being argued here is that although we are creators of our respective fates, our acts and thoughts do not arise in a vacuum but are conditioned, in part, by the philosophy or belief we subscribe to, and so, therefore, is our destiny. Since it is further maintained that all major philosophies and religions in the world, aside from the life philosophy of Nichiren Shoshu, have neither grasped the essence of life (the basic unity between mind and body or spirit and matter [Shiki-shin Funi] and humans and their environment [Esho Funi]) nor provided the means to break through the cycle of migration among the lower worlds and attain the state of true happiness, those who subscribe to these philosophies "will," in the words of one member, "end up with more sorrow for all their trouble."

Accordingly, those who subscribe to the popular belief that we are shaped solely by the environment and the actions of others, will continue to externalize the blame for their misfortunes and the overall state of their life condition, and, as a result, never make the "proper cause" to improve their situation and alleviate their suffering. Likewise, those whose approach to life is either materially or spiritually oriented are also on the wrong road and will continue to flounder in a state of unfulfillment and delusion. As one core member explained:

When you think about the philosophy people have today, it's either materialism or spiritualism. People are either trying to get rich and develop lots of financial power or get close to god or some transcendental being and develop a good spiritual feeling inside.

This philosophy (referring to Nichiren Shoshu) is based on the principle of Shiki-Shin Funi. Shiki means body; Shin means the spirit; and Funi means that there is no difference between the two or that in reality the two are fused. We can't live without spiritual gain, and we can't live without material gain.

This isn't a philosophy of spiritualism where you believe in some spiritual entity and try to identify with it. At the same time, it's not materialism in the sense that you deny all spiritualism and try to pursue just material desires. Rather, it is the perfect union between the two. One without the other is delusion. You can believe in spirits or life after death, but that doesn't make it so, and it doesn't actually improve our life one bit. This is a philosophy of life, of how to live as a human being, not how to die. If you prepare yourself how to live, you won't have to worry about what happens after death because you'll have lots of good fortune.

But what about those who do not subscribe to a particular institutionalized religion or political philosophy, which, according to another member, "don't have the power to bring happiness to mankind," or, in the words of another, "teach us only how to suffer or to get ready for some other world after we die"? Here we are told that everyone subscribes or "Nam's"[17] to something, whether it be a material or spiritual object, an elaborated religious or political philosophy, another person, or whatever. As explained by one core member:

Everybody Nam's to something or the other all the time. Everyone has an object of worship even though you don't call it worship, because we associate that with a formal religion. But everybody in the world worships something, I don't care who it is. You may say there are lots of atheists who don't believe in or worship God as such. But their god could be money, or it could be success, or it could be another person. Young girls, for example, frequently worship a particular boy, and vice versa. Some businessmen worship money. Mothers frequently worship their children. And many housewives worship the television. So this condition exists in everybody, although the object of worship varies from time to time.

When you devote yourself to something or somebody, a very strange phenomenon takes place. You begin to take on the characteristics of your object of worship. Did you ever notice how a man walking a pug dog down the street looks something like the dog? When a husband and wife who have been worshipping each other for fifty years walk together, they often look identical in many ways. Young boys who worship a Honda bike are always revving the motor and are full of oil all the time. They look just like their bikes. And a businessman who worships the almighty dollar begins to look like a greenback. He can only think in terms of money; he makes friends in terms of how much some somebody can do for his financial fortune; nothing is worth anything unless it has monetary value to him.

So no matter what people profess, look at their lives and you will see that they actually do have an object of worship. This goes on and on. This is the law of the universe - that you and your environment are inseparable, that subject and object are one, that you cannot avoid taking on the characteristics of your object of worship.

The underlying implication is that if one devotes oneself to and organizes one's actions and thoughts in terms of the "wrong" object, philosophy, or whatever, one will not only continue to flounder in the lower realms of existence, but true happiness will continue to be elusive; for, according to the karmic principle of cause and effect, one will be following the wrong path and, therefore, making the wrong causes. All of this is brought together and graphically summarized in the following statement of a core member and principal informant.

Even if we don't have a specific organized religion that we belong to, we all believe in a certain type of god, we all have a certain idea about life. Many people today think they don't have a religion, but they actually do. For some people their religion is science, or maybe education. Some people blindly believe in science just like we believe in the light bulb. We don't know how it works or why it works, but we just blindly believe in it. There's nothing wrong with that to a point, because we can't expect to understand everything.

At the same time, so many people have the feeling that knowledge will bring you everything. Or some people believe that money will bring you everything. Or some people believe that love will bring you anything. Actually, all these things have failed many people. Money has never brought anyone happiness, although it doesn't hurt to have it if you have the wisdom to handle it. Otherwise, it can destroy you. The same thing is true of love and knowledge. It took a great deal of knowledge to build the atomic bomb and pollute the air. Whether that is wisdom or not we are still asking ourselves.

So people are walking around not knowing anything about life, but knowing a lot about automobiles, atomic bombs, and so on. But when it comes to how to get along at home and live peacefully in the world, or how to do something constructive with their lives and realize true happiness, people don't have the slightest idea. Why? Because they don't understand the law of cause and effect.

What we're talking about here is that every human being has a destiny or karma that can't be changed by science, education, or mental will alone. People who don't understand this law have no good fortune. This is true of an individual, a society, a race, or an economic group.

Thus, as this member concluded:

If you have the wrong philosophy, no matter how sincere you are, you'll be misdirected. Just as the compass of a ship determines the direction it will take, so a person's philosophy or object of worship will determine the direction his life will take.

If so, then what is the proper philosophy that will free us from the lower realms of existence and guide us along the path toward a life of true wisdom and happiness? What is the proper object of worship to which we should "Nam" or dedicate and devote ourselves, thereby enabling us to change our karma and bring to life that spark of Buddhahood lying dorman within?

In this flow of existence, subject to the workings of karma and other mediating influences and possessing the range of potentialities described above, what does Nichiren Shoshu see as the key to bridging the discrepancy between the real and the ideal, between the dismal nature of life in the world as presently constituted and a flowering of peace and happiness within the hearts and lives of all humankind? Or, stated differently, what is Nichiren Shoshu's answer to the longstanding riddle that all Buddhist sects and movements have addressed in one way or another: how might that ever-present but latent condition of Buddhahood be drawn out and manifested in the daily lives of each? And what, in practical terms, would be the nature of a world based on the manifestation and predominance of this quintessential life condition? What, then, is Nichiren Shoshu's answer to the Leninesque question of "What is to be done?" What is its solution and promise? What, in short, is its prognosis?

NICHIREN SHOSHU'S PROGNOSIS: A BLUEPRINT FOR THE REALIZATION OF THE "IMPOSSIBLE DREAM"

Unlike those movements whose diagnostic component of their value orientation, and, therefore their sense of what is wrong, is much stronger than the prognostic component or their ideas about what is to be done, in Nichiren Shoshu, and especially in the talk of its members, it is the latter rather than the former which is primary. More specifically, it is Nichiren Shoshu's answer to the above dilemma, its clear-cut solution to whatever "problems" one may have, and its vision of and blueprint for not only a better world but a totally different world that constitutes both the most pronounced aspect of its value orientation and its trademark.

Beginning with its answer and solution, Nichiren Shoshu contends that the attainment of "true happiness" is predicated on the creation and maximizaiton of certain values. In the words of Makiguchi, the founder and first President of Sokagakkai,[18] which literally means "value creating society":

The highest and ultimate object of life is happiness, and the goal of life is none but the attainment and creation of

> value, which is in itself happiness ... A happy life signifies
> none other than the state of existence in which one can gain
> and create value in full.[19]

In much the same words, the lead editorial in the Fall 1974 edition of
the *NSA Quarterly* begins by noting that "the ultimate goal of value
creation is to enable the individual to attain absolute happiness, and to
share this with society to the greatest possible extent." And as core
members frequently state, "We are happy because we are creating value
in our daily lives." Simply put, then, happiness and value creation are
obverse sides of the same coin.

But to what does "value" refer, and how might it be created and
maximized?

According to Makiguchi, value is constituted by three interrelated
elements - beauty, gain, and good; whereas anti-value refers to their
opposites - ugliness, loss, and evil.[20] *Beauty* refers to an emotional
and temporary value derived through one or more of the five senses.
Gain (or benefit) refers to anything that contributes to the maintenance
and development of an individual's life. It may be a good night's
sleep, a college degree, a job, good health, and so on. Gain, just like
beauty, is relative in that whatever constitutes gain varies according to
one's needs, desires, and overall life condition. Whereas beauty and
gain pertain to an individual's development and personal happiness
from moment to moment, *goodness* refers to value that is created and
experienced only when sharing beauty and gain with others. More
specifically, goodness is public or collective gain that results when
individuals contribute to the formation and development of a unified
and peaceful community, society, or world.

Of the three values or goals of the value creation process,
goodness or public gain is considered to be the ultimate and, therefore,
takes precedence over the others. Yet, it is important to note that since
goodness is predicated, in part, on individual gain or benefit, we cannot
be expected to contribute to the welfare and betterment of whatever
collectivity we belong to until we have realized a certain degree of gain
in our own day-to-day life. Hence, the importance of attaining
individual gain or "benefits" in the immediate here and now.

In short, then, the attainment of true happiness - the ultimate but
elusive objective of life - is predicated, on the one hand, on the

avoidance and minimization of ugliness, loss, and evil, or the anti-values that characterize life in the lower realms of existence, and, on the other hand, the creation and maximization of value - beauty, gain, and good - in one's daily life.

As to what all this means from a rank and file member's standpoint, it is usually interpreted in terms of the various things which collectively yield a sense of personal satisfaction and well-being in one's everyday life in the immediate here and now. For most, happiness or value creation is thus constituted by the attainment of a semblance of material well-being, family harmony, friends, good health, inner security, and a sense of meaning, purpose and direction.

Regarding the connection between this fairly mundane and utilitarian conception of the quintessential aim and state of life and the more traditional Buddhist conception of enlightenment as breaking away from the cycle of karma into a state of horizonless consciousness, the latter, from NSA's vantage point, is defined in terms of the former. A cheerful, harmonious home, success in one's line of work, a secure and vigorous spirit or "life force," a sense of self-actualization, a sense of internal control or mastery, a life condition bursting with joy, confidence, and enthusiasm - all of this, according to Nichiren Shoshu, is the stuff of value creation that indicates a change in karma and the winning of enlightenment or what members more commonly refer to as "human revolution."

But from where does the power come to create such value? Just how are these values to be created and maximized and their opposites avoided? What, in short, is the "proper cause" that one must make in order to control or neutralize their past karma and start anew (Hon'in-Myo) on the road to human revolution?

It is in response to this question that the practices and teachings propounded by Nichiren and Makiguchi's theory of value were laced together in an answer that is unequivocal and explicit: the power to create value, and therefore to achieve true happiness in everyday life, is available only to those who sincerely embrace and propagate the philosophy and practice of True Buddhism as embodied in the phrase *Nam-Myoho-Renge-Kyo*, the first and most important of Nichiren's "three great secret laws" (San-Dai-HiHo).

Since *Nam*, as indicated earlier, means dedication or devotion to, those who earnestly and consistently invoke or chant this phrase are devoting themselves to "Myoho-Renge-Kyo." Decoded, *Myoho* signifies a mystical or universal law; *Renge*, which literally means "lotus flower," symbolically stands for the simultaneous nature of cause and effect;[21] and *Kyo* refers to sutra or sound. *Nam-Myoho-Renge-Kyo* is thus translated as "Adoration be to the Scripture of the Lotus of the Perfect Truth,"[22] or "I devote myself to the inexpressibly profound and wonderful truth embodied in the *Lotus Sutra*,"[23] or, as most core members seem to prefer, "Devotion to the mystical, universal law of cause and effect through sound."

However translated though, it encapsulates into small compass and makes available to those who invoke it the wisdom of the *Lotus Sutra*, the essence of which, according to Nichiren and others, is the revelation and exaltation of the historical Buddha as an omnipotent, omnipresent, and eternal entity or condition that is immanent in every respect of reality and is therefore available to all humankind. It is for this reason, as well as others that will be discussed later, that Nichiren concluded that the *Lotus Sutra* is the greatest of the Buddha's teachings, the kernel of all the sutras, and that Nam-Myoho-Renge-Kyo is the embodiment of its essence.

To chant Nam-Myoho-Renge-Kyo, then, is to devote oneself to the essence of all phenomena, to the ultimate condition of life, to the state of Buddhahood inherent within each. Accordingly, the invocation of this single phrase, in conjunction with Gongyo,[24] is considered to be not only the proper but the ultimate cause that one can make in order to control or neutralize past karma, to create value in one's daily life, and to achieve human revolution. All of this is illuminated further in the following comments:

> Nam-Myoho-Renge-Kyo is the law of life. It underlies all of life. So somehow when we chant Nam-Myoho-Renge-Kyo, it is the cause of chanting that produces the effect of a happy life. ... Just like the law of gravity, it exists eternally. Somehow gravity exists in the universe. It is a universal law. And so is Nam-Myoho-Renge-Kyo. But it is even the basis of the law of gravity .... There is a lot of information you can get from reading about this, some of which is over my head; but the main thing is the members' experiences ... For the best explanation of what Nam-

Myoho-Renge-Kyo is ... is the experience people are able to have when they chant Nam-Myoho-Renge-Kyo - they are able to enjoy their lives more and more. What it promises is that we will eventually become absolutely happy in our daily lives, not just in our minds, but in our day-to-day lives.

By devoting ourselves to Myoho-Renge-Kyo - this highest condition within us - we begin to take on and exhibit its characteristics. And that's why we get so happy, so confident, and feel so good all the time - because we Nam to "Myoho-Renge-Kyo."

There is no greater power than that of Nam-Myoho-Renge-Kyo. For the disheartened young man, the financially troubled businessman, the estranged family or anyone with any type of problem, sincere Daimoku (the invocation of Nam-Myoho-Renge-Kyo) brings a solution.

Daimoku is the key to human recognition. Whether it be work, school, recreation, or NSA activities, it is the basis for victory ... It is our most important activity; it determines the outcome of the entire day ... If we don't have time to chant, we should make time. It's like breathing - we can't do without it.

By chanting Nam-Myoho-Renge-Kyo you wake up the life of Buddha inside. When you do Gongyo in the morning and evening, it's like feeding the breakfast of champions to our Buddha nature. You become a hopeful, happy human being. That is the meaning of Nam-Myoho-Renge-Kyo. It doesn't mean that I'm a religious person in the sense of believing in some transcendental god - that's just another crazy type of philosophy. This philosophy says you have a Buddha condition inside of you, that you have a vigorous, wise, happy, fortunate, hopeful type of life condition inside of you. So as you chant to the Gohonzon you may not become a millionaire overnight - which isn't true happiness anyway, but your life will gradually begin to take a path toward gain. And then you can look back - like myself, as I look back over seven years of practice - and see how your life has changed.

Nam-Myoho-Renge-Kyo is the thing that we've been looking for our entire lives. It is the source of our happiness. It is the actual thread that pulls us into a world of absolute, complete joy and security. You know, it's an unusual and strange thing in today's world to be able to say, 'I'm a secure person, I'm an absolutely happy person.' Very few people can make this statement. But the people in NSA can unequivocally make this statement regardless of how long they have been chanting, because everybody gets benefits whether they've been chanting one day or twenty years. Why? Because Nam-Myoho-Renge-Kyo is the key. Chanting Nam-Myoho-Renge-Kyo to the Gohonzon is the key or catalyst to open the treasure chest - that life of Buddha that you and I have within - and let out this condition.

Underlying the member's faith in the power of chanting is the existence of the *Gohonzon* and the *Kaidan*[25] - the other two elements of Nichiren's "three great secret laws" which, in addition to chanting, are considered essential to the faith and practice. The Gohonzon is the object to or before which one usually chants. It is a small scroll (6 to 7 inches in width and 12 to 14 inches in length) with Nam-Myoho-Renge-Kyo inscribed down its center and the names of various Buddhas and Bodhisattvas mentioned in the *Lotus Sutra* inscribed on its periphery, all in Japanese characters. It is said to be a graphic representation of the true object of worship and, as such, it is revered as a sacred object. Each member is thus required to have one enshrined in his or her home altar. In actual practice, it functions as an object of focus and visual complement to the audial expression of Nam-Myoho-Renge-Kyo.

Beyond its appearance and functional utility is a far greater and deeper level of meaning. For what it actually symbolizes is the fusion of person, in the form of the true Buddha nature or Nichiren, who represents the embodiment of this nature, and the fundamental law of the universe, Nam-Myoho-Renge-Kyo. In effect, then, there is a sense of "real presence" in the Gohonzon - the presence of the true Buddha nature as embodied in Nichiren himself and as inherent within each one of us. As such, to chant to the Gohonzon is to attempt to fuse with and bring to the surface (Kyochi Myogo) this condition and power embodied within the Gohonzon and latent within ourselves. This is clarified further in the following commentary of a middle-level leader attending a rank-and-file meeting:

> As you devote yourself to and fuse with your Gohonzon by chanting Nam-Myoho-Renge-Kyo, the most positive and beneficial characteristics come out and manifest themselves in your daily life, whereas your negative characteristics subside. So if you fuse with the Gohonzon, you bring out and create value in your daily life.
>
> Depending on what you fuse to, you create value or anti-value. If this were vodka (referring to a glass of water), it might be of value for the first ten minutes, but then it would be anti-value.
>
> Life is made of Kyochi Myogo, you know. If you go home and do not Kyochi Myogo with your bed, you will not sleep. In order to sleep you have to fuse with your bed. So the point is that you have to get the highest object to fuse to in order to bring out the most value in your life. And this Gohonzon is the highest object you can fuse to.
>
> In Nichiren Shoshu we Nam to the Gohonzon. That is our object of worship. In other words, we Nam to Myoho-Renge-Kyo, which is the law of the universe and our ultimate life condition. When we chant Nam-Myoho-Renge-Kyo and look at the Gohonzon, we are fusing our lives with this universal law and the life force of Buddhahood, which are embodied in the Gohonzon. And just like a person who looks at and Nams to the television and becomes like the TV, we become like the Gohonzon.

But the Gohonzon is more than just the true object of worship and the embodiment or mirror of our ultimate but latent life condition. It is also considered a source of unlimited power, knowledge, protection, and benefit such that all problems and domains of life in the immediate here-and-now are believed to be manipulative by earnest prayer and chanting to the Gohonzon.

If so, then what is the source of its power and how might this ultimate power be activated and harnessed? Here the answer is again explicit: the main power-source is the Dai-Gohonzon, the ultimate and most sacred object of worship which Nichiren supposedly inscribed on October 12, 1279, to save all humankind from misery and unhappiness, and which is currently enshrined in the Sho-Hondo, the High Sanctuary of Nichiren Shoshu-Sokagakkai in Japan.

In an attempt to render understandable to guests, recruits, and other non-believers the nature of the Dai-Gohonzon's power and the way in which this power might be harnessed, core members would often say that it functions much like a large electrical generator or power station, or like a TV or radio transmitter. But unlike most electrical generators or transmitters, the power and energy emanating from the Dai-Gohonzon is considered to be present in all places at all times. Thus, not only is the Dai-Gohonzon considered to be omnipotent and omniscient, but it is also omnipresent.

This ever-present power is not readily available to just anyone, however. For just as one's home must be wired electrically in order to harness the energy flowing from the power station, and just as one must have a TV set and an antenna in order to receive the waves emanating from the large transmitter miles away, so one must have a facsimile of the Dai-Gohonzon in order to harness and receive its power, wisdom, and protection. Hence, the importance of each member having a Gohonzon enshrined in his place of residence.

But, carrying the analogy one step further, possession of a Gohonzon alone is not sufficient; for just as one must plug the TV in and turn it on in order to have the signals and waves floating around in space materialize in a coherent picture, so one must have "their antenna up" and "Gohonzon turned on" in order to tap the power of the Dai-Gohonzon. The switch or key for activating this power in one's daily life is, of course, the recitation of Nam-Myoho-Renge-Kyo and Gongyo.

Since the power emanating from the Gohonzon is present and amenable to activation at all times, it follows that the more one chants, the greater the benefit or gain. Thus, members not only chant Daimoku and Gongyo before the Gohonzon in the morning and evening, but whenever they feel the need to draw upon its power and protection, whenever they are confronted with a problem, no matter how mundane, and whenever they have a spare minute between their NSA activities and daily routines. And on the average of at least once a week, they gather collectively for a Daimoku Toso - chanting Nam-Myoho-Renge-Kyo together from anywhere from an hour to six hours.

The Gohonzon is thus seen as a type of power-source and ally, and Daimoku, in conjunction with Gongyo in the morning and evening, is the magic formula or key which enables the practitioner to tap into and receive the power, knowledge, and protection emanating from the Gohonzon. As one member, whose practice allegedly resulted in his recovery from an "undiagnosed illness," stated:

> Chanting to the Gohonzon is preventive medicine. Your natural life force becomes so strong that every aspect of your life is strengthened. It's not necessary to do one thing for your body and another for your mind. The Gohonzon protects and develops simultaneously.

The extent to which there is a sense of "real presence" in the Gohonzon, and the extent to which it is seen as functioning as a power-source and ally, is illustrated even more clearly in the following comments:

> I never felt that an absolutely true religion existed before I began chanting. I now feel that this practice is absolutely true. It is difficult to express what the Gohonzon means to me except to say that it is life itself. It is truly parent, sovereign and teacher.

> We can challenge all of our sufferings and difficulties with a smile ... because everything is under the observation of the Dai-Gohonzon, who is watching and knows everything. Those who criticize, we don't care. Those who laugh, let them laugh. We don't care. We know the Gohonzon is watching us.

> By chanting to the Gohonzon you acquire this vigorous life force, and you're able to do so much more than anyone

else. You'll find you don't need to sleep so much. You sleep less and do more. You'll find out ... you can get done about three times, if not ten times, more than you ever have before. NSA members live about twenty hours out of the day. About one hour of living in NSA is like a week of regular living.

The Gohonzon knows everything. It knows what's best for you and will protect you. If you chant for something that might harm you or get you in trouble, like a kilo of marijuana, it will keep you from getting it. Sometimes you don't always get what you chant for; but it's not because chanting doesn't work, it's because the Gohonzon knows what's best for you.

From the time a person begins chanting to the Gohonzon in his home, he is, in a sense, born again. He can start his life anew, tapping the power and wisdom of the Gohonzon and the Buddha-like nature embodied within the Gohonzon and within himself.

Returning to the question of "What must be done in order for one to change his karma or destiny, to create value in his daily life, and to bring to the fore that spark of Buddhahood lying dormant within?", Nichiren Shoshu's answer is explicit: one must chant Nam-Myoho-Renge-Kyo to the Gohonzon. Not only are all problems and domains of life seen as amenable to manipulation and control by chanting to the Gohonzon, but the earnest recitation of this single invocation before the Gohonzon is considered to be the "proper cause" enabling one to neutralize past karma, the source of power underlying the creation of value, and the key to human revolution and the attainment of true happiness. From the standpoint of Nichiren Shoshu, there is, in short, no other answer. All of this was brought together and nicely summarized by a principal leader in the Los Angeles area:

As you face the Gohonzon and chant Nam-Myoho-Renge-Kyo, something inside of you responds to it. When you chant to the Gohonzon, something inside starts happening and your life starts to change. It's like taking a shower on the inside and cleaning up all the problems we've acquired through all the bad causes we've made. We're actually able to change our karma or the accumulation of all the bad effects we're suffering from right now because of all the bad causes we've made in the past.

With the Gohonzon and Nam-Myoho-Renge-Kyo, you can start completely fresh. This is called Hon'in-Myo. It means to start from right now! No matter what happened in the past, don't worry about the past; starting from now you can start afresh and eliminate the effects from anything that happened in the past. It means you can start creating value in your life and acquire good fortune now.

The relation between the Gohonzon and you is that of object and subject; the Gohonzon is the object and you are the subject. And by chanting you and the Gohonzon fuse together so that you acquire the power and life condition embodied in the Gohonzon. We have this life inside of us, and that's why it is like looking into a mirror when we face the Gohonzon. But we can't see this life condition without the Gohonzon because it's all dusty and dirty from the bad causes we've made in the past. So when you chant Nam-Myoho-Renge-Kyo, it's like polishing your life inside. And the more you chant, the more you see this sunshine coming from within you, and you start becoming truly happy and confident. You discover that people start reacting to you differently, and everything starts changing. And it's all because of the cause you make by chanting Nam-Myoho-Renge-Kyo to the Gohonzon.

The really big benefit, though, is a complete change in character and destiny. This is called human revolution. You become an absolutely happy person in any kind of situation. Whatever circumstances you're in, you find that by chanting to the Gohonzon, you acquire the power, energy, wisdom, and confidence to accomplish the most amazing things and receive the most amazing benefits.

But the attainment of individual gain, personal happiness, and human revolution are incomplete by themselves. For as Nichiren preached, as the worlds of the true Bodhisattva and Buddhahood imply, and as Makiguchi's concept of goodness or collective gain suggests, no one's happiness is complete until the happiness of all humankind is assured.   Accordingly, Nichiren Shoshu insists that its ultimate objective is not merely to change individuals but to change the world; it seeks not only a revolution in the character of individuals, but ultimately a revolution in the character of the world. Its "unchangeable mission," as President Ikeda emphasized in his 1971 presidential address, is "to advance (the) movement for the cause of peace and for the cause of building a new culture." Or, as core members are quick to point out: "The biggest goal of NSA is Kosen-rufu. It means world peace and happiness based on the philosophy and practice of Nichiren Shoshu." Or, as the *World Tribune* emphatically put it in a November 1974 edition:

> Kosen-rufu is the sole purpose of NSA. We are united
> in a harmonious organization that will be ultimately effective
> in manifesting the dream of humanity - life in a peaceful and
> prosperous world.

Kosen-rufu is a long-range goal, to be sure. It is not something that members believe will materialize tomorrow or in a year or two. But it is, nonetheless, something that they are struggling to attain in their own way, that permeates, as we shall see later, all aspects of the movement, and that members firmly believe is within their grasp and that they will therefore eventually attain. As General Director Williams noted in his 1974 NSA Convention address:

> Kosen-rufu is a long-range goal. It is foolish to think we
> have almost reached this goal. In reality, we have just
> begun. We have a long way to go. But, we will make it.
> We will win. Together with our Master, President Ikeda,
> we have a dream. We have a great dream. Now, let's
> share our dream for the peace and happiness of all mankind.

This sense of mission and expectancy, albeit long-range, is conveyed even more graphically in the words of several rank-and-file members:

Nichiren Shoshu is the wave and hope of the future. It will usher in world peace and happiness - maybe not by tomorrow, but certainly by the next generation.

Nichiren Shoshu is out to create the dream the world has been dreaming. It's the glorious movement for world peace and the development of a humanistic world. I don't know exactly when we will attain this dream, but we will.

I first became sensitized to this overarching, visionary objective quite by accident one afternoon several weeks after I joined the movement. Just as I was entering a local store I happened to run into a member whose acquaintance I had already made. After exchanging pleasantries, she immediately mentioned, while bubbling over with excitement and enthusiasm, how great it felt to be "doing world peace." She went on to indicate how the idea of world peace had always been just dream prior to joining Nichiren Shoshu, that it was something she had thought about but never considered a possibility. Now, however, it is no longer an "impossible dream," she continued, but a dream that is within our grasp and that Nichiren Shoshu is struggling to attain. While I was somewhat puzzled as to the connection between shopping and "doing world peace," I didn't press for further elaboration. Assuming that all of this would eventually become clear, I just nodded, as if I understood, and added that world peace is certainly a worthy goal to be striving towards.

Although I had previously heard members refer to "world peace" and other related global ideals and objectives, I had been so intrigued with the talk of various physical, material, and spiritual "benefits" that I failed to give much significance to any discussion of world peace. Consequently, it was not until this fortuitous encounter that I became sensitized to and actually began to grasp the fact that underlying Nichiren Shoshu was a utopian vision, a millenarian dream of sorts, and a correspondent sense of mission and expectancy that was connected to and yet went far beyond individual human revolution and the more mundane goal of realizing personal gain or "benefits" in the immediate here-and-now.

The nature and meaning of this ultimate, visionary objective, the kind of world it embodies, and the sense of mission and expectancy it evokes are illustrated further and brought into sharper focus in the following statements:

This revolution proposed by Nichiren Shoshu is a total revolution which will allow all mankind to enjoy a happy life, not only individually but socially as well. Unlike other revolutions, this one isn't something just dreamed up by a few leaders at the top and supported just by the finances of a few. Instead, it is a revolution that involves all people and will eventually be supported by all people.

The 'Third Civilization' (the actual manifestation of Nichiren Shoshu-Sokagakkai's visionary objective is often referred to as the Third Civilization) will guide the two main civilizations - spiritual or capitalistic civilization and material or socialistic civilization. This is because all the strifes in the present-day world are due to the philosophies of and conflict between these two civilizations. ... It is not war but peace that all people of the world are looking forward to. What they want is prosperity and happiness. This is all promised to be realized in the Third Civilization led by the supreme Buddhism of Nichiren Daishonin ·... The Third Civilization is full of expectations in the future. It will be realized in actual life as the crystal of human wisdom.

A world of peace and happiness is very easy to understnd when you look at it from the viewpoint of true Buddhism. As an individual, it means being able to live and get along with all different kinds of people, and being able to do something constructive with your life - something that gives more value to yourself and that you can share with others. This is what Kosen-rufu means.

And as stated in "The Declaration of Peace," adopted by 158 members from fifty-one nations during the Nichiren Shoshu-Sokagakkai World Peace Conference held on Guam in January 1975:

We, the delegates of the International Buddhist League, with the awareness that life is the inalienable right of every human being regardless of race, nationality, language, or custom, and with the unwavering determination to uphold the sanctity of life throughout the world, do hereby resolve to unite in the common cause of securing lasting peace for all mankind... In order to secure global peace ... we will exert our utmost efforts in contributing to a joy of life in order to ensure the survival of humanity itself (and) ... we acknowledge our noble mission to make the forthcomng twenty-first century a "Century of Life"; a golden age of humanism and warmth in which all people will cherish the sanctity of life... Therefore we will strive ... to bring forth a renaissance of humanism in the remaining twenty-five years of this century, and to create new waves of peace in the hearts of all men. We hereby affirm our resolution to further these ideals and to establish lasting peace throughout the world.[26]

At this point one might ask how Nichiren Shoshu proposes to create a world in which peace and happiness flourish among all humankind. How might this utopian objective, this millenarian vision, this "dream the world has been dreaming" be actualized in the not too distant future? How does Nichiren Shoshu propose to succeed, where all others have failed, in righting the "unrightable wrong," in reaching the "unreachable star," in realizing this heretofore "impossible dream."[27] What, in short, does it see as the key to the attainment of this "glorious quest"?

Here the answer is implicitly suggested in the foregoing discussion. Since the road to human revolution and all it encompasses is seen as being open only to those who earnestly chant Nam-Myoho-Renge-Kyo to the Gohonzon, it not only follows but is vehemently maintained that universal revolution or world peace and happiness will be realized only when a significant proportion of the world is practicing True Buddhism. Social revolution or profound change at the level of social structures is thus seen as being contingent on human revolution or profound change at the level of individuals. Hence, the millennium or "third civilization" will be ushered in only upon the conversion of much of the world to the life philosophy and practice of Nichiren Shoshu, as embodied in the ritual of chanting Nam-Myoho-Renge-Kyo to the Gohonzon.

That personal transformation and happiness, which can only be attained by the assiduous practice of True Buddhism, is seen as the key to social transformation, and therefore world peace and happiness, is reflected again and again in the movement's literature and the talk of its members. An August 1974 edition of the *World Tribune*, for example, contends that previous attempts to change the condition of humans by concentrating on social revolution or the reform of social systems and social structures have not proven successful because they have failed to address themselves to the greatest problem: "the inner life of each individual human being, who both constructs and controls the social structure." It then goes on to elucidate this contention:

No matter how extensively social structures may be revolutionized, if human life, which controls these structures, is not reformed and elucidated, the social revolution is incomplete and only transitory in value. This is where the relationship of human revolution and social revolution becomes clear. A peaceful society can be established only when the fortress of peace and happiness is strongly founded in the life of man ... What is therefore most urgently needed is the construction of a firm foundation of life force to control the inherent and negative life conditions of greed, empty desires of egoism. In other words, it is clear that for a social revolution to bring true happiness to the lives of people and for it to be permanent, a fundamental revolution in the depths of each individual life must first occur.

In another article it is similarly argued that while the cause for misfortune, war, and the like may be due to the fact that people are guided by the wrong philosophy,

... it would be wrong to denounce the government or individuals and expect changes to come about from our criticism. (For) change will only come about when we ourselves win in everyday life. Through individual victory, the cancer of society will be cured.[28]

Or in the words of a core member during a guidance session:

> If you want to change the world, you can't do it by
> sending letters to your Senators or by marching on
> Washington. It will never happen that way. What you have
> to do is change yourself. The change has to come from
> within individuals first, rather than the other way around.

And again, in an article commenting on the Watergate scandal and
titled "Human Revolution: The Cure for Social Evils," it is noted that
even when the Watergate situation is cleared up,

> ... the underlying cause for the illness will still remain
> ... there is some Watergate always lurking behind the
> scenes, awaiting the opportunity to stick its ugly head out ...
> The key to changing this situation is Human Revolution: an
> inner revolution that polishes a person's character and brings
> to the fore his potential. Such an inner revolution affects the
> undercurrent which runs like a river under the society.
> Eventually, anything similar to Watergate will totally retreat
> from the activities of man's society.
> Society today is in need of such a revolution. It is the
> only one that can change the situation at its cause ... The
> campaign ... (is) to change ourselves and at the same time,
> introduce into society something that is strong enough,
> positive enough, to change the currents of life exemplified
> by Watergate.[29]

Or as succinctly stated by a rank-and-file member:

> Nichiren Shoshu strives to change the present condition
> of the world by changing people. It is the only effective
> way to improve and change the condition of the world.

And as General Director Williams emphasized in a speech before some
3,000 members at the Los Angeles General Meeting in February 1975:

> When we, the people of the world, are able to construct
> true Buddhism within our lives ... then world peace will

slowly but surely materialize. In other words, a happy world can only be created by happy people.

If a revitalization in the character of the world is dependent on a revitalization in the character of individuals, if a happy, peaceful world can only be created by happy, peaceful people, as the above statements suggest, and if the key to human revolution is embodied in the act of chanting Nam-Myoho-Renge-Kyo to the Gohonzon, then the tactical key or means to the attainment of this "glorious quest" for world peace and happiness, it is logically argued, is the propagation of this practice and philosophy to all mankind. "To let every person know the fundamental way of harmonizing his life with that ... epitomized in the Gohonzon - that is, the propagation of the Gohonzon," is, in the words of President Ikeda, the sole road to the construction of a new human society and, therefore, the movement's "eternal mission."

Accordingly, the "greatest cause" one can make for the sake of humanity and the world is to *Shakubuku*[30] or inform others about and bring them into contact with the universal law and the true object of worship; for only when a significant proportion of the world has been so informed and converted to True Buddhism will the "dream the world has been dreaming" materialize.[31] Here, then, Nichiren Shoshu's answer to the question of how to create a peaceful and happy world, and thereby usher in the millennium, is as unequivocal and explicit as is its answer to the question of how to bring about human revolution at the level of individuals: the only way in which this heretofore "impossible dream" will be attained is through the propagation of and conversion of much of the world to the life philosophy and practice of True Buddhism.

As the above statements and discussion amply illustrate, Nichiren Shoshu's ultimate goal is not - as it might appear at first glance to the casual observer - the development of a cult of selfish, egoistic, happy chanters, unmindful of the condition and problems of the rest of the world. Rather, it is the realization of something far more ambitious and global - the construction of a new world order or "third civilization" grounded in the philosophy and practice of its version of Buddhism; a civilization that not only transcends the limitations of the major philosophies and international powers in the world today, but one in which peace, prosperity, happiness, and creative spontaneity are enjoyed by all.

All of this is brought together and nicely summarized in the following statement of a rank-and-file member who functioned as one of my principal informants during the first half of my career as an active member:

> The mission of NSA is to create world peace - not just in the minds of people, but to actually create a condition in this world so that wars and unhappiness are no longer possible. The aim is to crush every cause of human unhappiness. And our mission as individuals is to become absolutely happy and prove to others the power of chanting to the Gohonzon; for a happy world can only be created by happy people.
>
> When I first heard this, I discounted it. I thought that's cool, but any self-respecting organization has to say it's for world peace. So I didn't join because of this, but because I wanted to see if I could receive just one little benefit. Now, one of my greatest benefits is that I have, for the first time, hope for true world peace. If you chant, not only will you become happier than you ever would have believed possible, but this dream and hope will awaken inside of you, and it will no longer be an impossible dream.

The foregoing discussion brings to completion our examination of the nature of the diagnostic and prognostic components of Nichiren Shoshu's value orientation, as reflected primarily in its view of the world as it is and as it should be, and in its guide to action or explicit statement of the means by which this disparity can be bridged and its goals of human revolution on the individual level and Kosen-rufu on the global level can best be achieved. Although these elements constitute the core of both its belief system and value orientation, they should not be mistaken for the whole; for there are several other widely articulated features of its informing point of view that function in an ideological manner by providing further justification for, metaphorically speaking, taking up the sword in quest of the "impossible dream," and which are therefore integral elements of the overall value orientation. The final task of this chapter, then, is to pull together and describe these additional ideological strands so as to round out our understanding of Nichiren Shoshu's world view and value orientation.

RATIONALE FOR BEING ACTIVE IN THE CAUSE

For Nichiren Shoshu, just as for most movements that seek to alter the world, its sense of mission and its call for action in support of this mission are not based solely on its conception of what is and what should be and its means-end schema, but are also predicated on a number of ideological justifications and inducements that are related to and yet go beyond its sense of what is wrong and what can and must be done in order to make it right. Running throughout the movement's literature, its leaders' directives, and the talk of rank-and-file members are five distinct rationales or ideological inducements for becoming and remaining active in the cause.

A Divinely Ordained Mission

The first major rationale is Nichiren Shoshu's contention that its mission is not only preordained, but was divinely given. As one rank-and-file member explained:

> There is a whole history and theory going back 3000 years that points to Nichiren Shoshu as both the orthodox practice of Buddhism and the correct philosophy and practice for this time period (referring to the present).

Regarding the source and nature of this prophecy, this member continued:

> It all comes from the first Buddha who lived 3000 years ago - the Sakyamuni Buddha. In his years of teaching, he taught his disciples various sutras. His final teaching was called the *Lotus Sutra*. In that teaching he made several specific predictions. Number one was that 2000 years after his death his form of Buddhism would fall into decay and lose its power to make people happy. In this period, which is called Mappo, he predicted there would be great

unhappiness and turmoil in the world, and that people would be following the wrong philosophies. The period in which we are living is part of Mappo.

He also predicted that in this period called Mappo, a Buddha greater than he would appear in a land northeast of India and would be known as the votary of the *Lotus Sutra*, which is what Nam-Myoho-Renge-Kyo stands for. In terms of this prediction, Nichiren Daishonin ... appeared in Japan and came to propagate the *Lotus Sutra* or Nam-Myoho-Renge-Kyo in order to bring mankind happiness in the age of Mappo.

And as similarly stated in the words of another core member:

> The correct teaching and practice for this time period, you know, is Nam-Myoho-Renge-Kyo. This was predicted by the Sakyamuni Buddha. He said that during the time of Mappo, which is the third time period after his death and which lasts ten thousand years, his teachings would lose all their power. And when this time came, he said a Buddha greater than he would appear to propagate the *Lotus Sutra*. The *Lotus Sutra* is Nam-Myoho-Renge-Kyo, you know. He also predicted that anyone who practiced other forms of Buddhism in Mappo wouldn't become happy or get any benefits. This is why so many people in much of Asia, and all over the world for that matter, have so much suffering - they practice the wrong philosophy. As Sakyamuni prophesied, the only correct teaching for this time period is Nam-Myoho-Renge-Kyo.

At first glance, one might think that the prophecies referred to in these statements are nothing but an ideological concoction manufactured by the leadership of Nichiren Shoshu-Sokagakkai. Such is not the case, however, as these prophecies, and particularly the theory of Mappo, are grounded in an old, apocalyptic Buddhist legend regarding the course of Buddhism following the demise of the great historical Sakyamuni Buddha. According to this legendary tradition, the Buddha predicted that upon his death the influence of his teachings, and therefore the fortunes of Buddhism, would follow three successive time periods.

The first period, referred to as the age of "Perfect Law" or the era of the "Right Path" (Shoho), was to extend for a thousand years after the Buddha's death, during which time the Buddha's teachings and practices would be strictly observed and have their maximum influence. The next period or second millennium, referred to as the age of "Copied Law" or "False Law" (Zoho), was to be a period of false piety, a period in which the influence of his teachings would begin to decline and eventually remain in form only. And the third and last period, referred to as "Mappo" or the period of the "Latter Law," was to last for ten thousand years or more. In this period, as indicated in the above statements, the Buddha's teachings were to fall into complete decay and the world into a state of strife and misery. Additionally, and most importantly for Nichiren Shoshu, there was reason to believe, on the basis of the prophetic utterances attributed to the Buddha in the *Lotus Sutra*, that a new and true Buddha would appear during this era for the sole purpose of propagating a new form of Buddhism, a new truth, for the sake of human salvation.

This "apocalyptic legend" was not shared by just a few, but according to the late Masaharu Anesaki, in his *History of Japanese Religion*, it

> ... was almost universal in the Buddhist countries, and since Chinese and Japanese Buddhists usually put Buddha's death in 949 B.C., they believed, whether in apprehension or in hope, that the last period was to start in the year A.D. 1052. Indeed, the actual conditions of that time exhibited many signs of degeneration or change; and men in the eleventh century thought that the prophecy was being fulfilled.[32]

Given this climate, Buddhist leaders were preoccupied, according to Anesaki, with the question of what form of Buddhism might be best suited to the needs of the people during this period and in the coming days. It was into this era that Nichiren was born, and it was in response to this burning preoccupation and sense of expectancy that he concluded, after twenty-some years of study, including his unique

reading of the *Lotus Sutra*,[33] that not only had he discovered the
correct teaching or true form of Buddhism for this era, but that he was
also the true Buddha prophesied to appear for the purpose of saving all
humankind.[34]

Had it not been for this apocalyptic prophecy and eschatological
view of history underlying much of Buddhism in both China and Japan,
"there could have been," writes one Japanese biographer of
Sokagakkai, "no Nichiren and no Sokagakkai."[35] For according to
this prophetic legend, a true Buddha was destined to appear in the age
of Mappo with the mission of saving all mankind. And, as the
members' earlier statements indicate, it is Nichiren Shoshu's firm
contention that Nichiren was that savior and, as his heirs apparent, that
it is their responsibility to carry out and complete the divine mission for
which he allegedly appeared.

The extent to which this prophecy provides a sense of a divinely-
given mission that functions as a call to arms or ideological justification
for becoming active in the cause is further illustrated in the frequency
with which the leadership refers to Nichiren Shoshu members as *the*
"Bodhisattvas of the Earth," who are repeatedly mentioned in both the
Lotus Sutra and Nichiren's writings. In the *Lotus Sutra*, for example,
there appear, in Chapter 14 entitled "Issuing of Bodhisattvas from the
Gaps of the Earth," innumerable Bodhisattvas, "eight times equal to the
sands of the river Ganges," who pledge to spread the Buddha's greatest
teaching if only he would reveal it to them.

> If the Lord will allow us, we also would, after the
> extinction of the Lord, reveal this Dharmaparyaya (great
> law, teaching or exposition) in this Saha-world (the last days
> or period of the world beyond); we would read, write,
> worship it, and wholly devote ourselves to that law.
> Therefore, O Lord, deign to grant us also this
> Dharmaparyaya.[36]

Since, according to Nichiren Shoshu, this law is Nam-Myoho-
Renge-Kyo, and since it was made available to mankind by Nichiren,
it follows that the Bodhisattvas of the Earth are none other than
Nichiren Shoshu members, who have, as their divinely-given mission,
the restoration of society through the propagation of this sacred law.

As President Ikeda clearly stated in a speech given in November 1969, and which reappeared in the April 9, 1975 edition of the *World Tribune*:

> We were born into this world as Bodhisattvas of the Earth whose greatest wish is to propagate true Buddhism throughout the world. If we forget this wish, we will find no true meaning in our existence. Therefore, I hope you will advance with me to fulfill our noble goal.

Thus, Nichiren Shoshu's mission and call to arms are not only based on its image of itself as the link between the dismal present and a better future, but they are also rationalized in terms of its contention that it is the link between the distant past and the immediate here-and-now, that rather than being part of a fly-by-night fad or craze, it is the present manifestation of part of a longstanding cosmic plan that was more or less divinely prophesied years ago.

The Only "Proven" Religion

A second frequently mentioned ideological justification for joining Nichiren Shoshu and becoming active in the cause is its claim that it is the only "proven" religion. This claim is grounded in the contention that when the quality of all religions are assessed and compared in terms of Nichiren's "three proofs" - literal, theoretical, and actual, only Nichiren Shoshu meets the test of all three. "Literal proof" refers to written documentation, such as the *Lotus Sutra*, Nichiren's writings, the *Koran*, and the *Bible*; "theoretical proof" addresses the question of whether a religion is logical or self-contradictory; and "actual proof" refers to the actual results that come from practicing a particular religion.

Since literal and theoretical proof "are imperfect without actual proof,"[37] the ultimate criterion for assessing the quality of a religion is simply to observe the extent to which its theories and promises are borne out by reality. Since it is further maintained that all religions promise true happiness, either in the here-and-now or in the world beyond, but that this condition manifests itself only in the lives of Nichiren Shoshu members, it follows that all religions pale beside

Nichiren Shoshu. Hence, Nichiren Shoshu is not only the most valid, but it is also the only proven religion or life philosophy. Or as one core member simply put it in response to a guest's question, during a discussion meeting, regarding the difference between Nichiren Shoshu and other religions: "Nichiren Shoshu works; others don't."

The extent to which this ideological strand is shared and the way in which it is employed as a justification for participation and an inducement to become active in the cause is evidenced in the work of Shakubuku or promotion and propagation. As stated by General Director Williams in his lectures given at various universities and colleges, for example:

> Other philosophies and religions talk about the world beyond, but their theories have never been experienced by anyone. In effect, they are teaching the art of dying ... reaching beyond the grave. As human beings, we are more concerned with how to live, not how to die. When someone tells you that God or Buddha is waiting for you in heaven, tell him to go first. Nobody has come back from heaven yet.[38]

And as one member explained in response to a guest's question concerning the difference between chanting and transcendental meditation:

> The real difference is what's going to happen to you when you start chanting. But you have to try it in order to compare the two. It's like somebody asking about the difference between a crepe and a buckwheat pancake. Now I could explain how they are made and how they differ, but you really wouldn't understand the difference between them until you ate one and then the other. So you have to chant before you can really compare it with transcendental meditation. But when you do chant, the effect it's going to have on you will really astonish you. It's really shocking. They may seem similar, but if you try chanting, you will see the difference. I'm not denying that many practices might have effects on you, but how great is that effect and how far does it go? As you will discover when you chant, the effect

is far greater and far more positive than the effect produced
by any other practice.

Or as another member similarly stated when queried about the
difference between Judaism and Nichiren Shoshu:

> The difference between Judaism, or any other religion
> for that matter, and our philosophy is that these other
> religions don't have the power to bring happiness to
> mankind, to other people. Although I was a practicing Jew
> before I joined Nichiren Shoshu, I'm much more vital and
> alive today. I am a happier and better human being.
>
> The Jews who have joined NSA, the Catholics who have
> joined NSA, the Protestants who have joined NSA, the other
> Buddhists who have joined NSA all realize that our
> philosophy and practice helps them to develop the confidence
> and find the satisfaction and happiness in life that these other
> religions couldn't deliver. I'm not saying that Judaism isn't
> all right, because it does have some of the necessary
> components of a good religion. But it is missing the one
> thing that makes it practical for everyday life, the one thing
> which we have. And that is Nam-Myoho-Renge-Kyo.

Carry on the Pioneer Spirit and Tradition

A third ideological call to arms that is verbalized more and more
throughout the ranks and which is reflective of both NSA's
accommodative flexibility and its efforts to render itself respectable in
the eyes of the larger public is its contention that it is the reincarnation
of America's early pioneer spirit and traditions. More specifically,
NSA has linked its mission with that of this country's founding fathers
and early pioneers, maintaining that the basic values and ideals these
early Americans espoused and sought to attain are the same as those
underlying NSA's struggle and quest.

Since this linkage will be discussed in some detail in a later
chapter dealing with Nichiren Shoshu's management of the systemic
problem of adaptation, let me merely cite here from a speech delivered
by General Director Williams on July 4th, 1974, at the Denver Pioneer
Meeting, so as to bring into sharp focus both the nature of this linkage

and the way in which it functions as a call to arms or specific rationale
for becoming active in the cause:

> ... the true spirit of 1776 is humanism, the same spirit
> which is now alive in NSA and in the teachings of Nichiren
> Daishonin all over the world. The dignity of human life has
> been proclaimed by many philosophers and idealists, but
> who has put it into practice? Our forefathers - Washington -
> Jefferson - Adams, fought for these fundamental human
> rights with the blood of thousands when our nation was
> created. They fought so we could enjoy these precious
> rights today ...
>
> The Virginia Bill of Rights and the New England Town
> Meeting clearly stated the concepts of freedom, equality and
> the dignity of human life ... Our forefathers were great
> thinkers and great humanists. They had a broad vision and
> a big heart. They could feel the sufferings of people. They
> had tender, loving hearts - hearts which loved America.
> Like Emerson, they felt that life was to be found everywhere
> in everything, and that this life or soul was sacred and worth
> preserving. They wished to transform this continent into a
> green oasis of freedom and peace ...
>
> ... as the 19th century progressed, the rapid growth of
> science and technology created a mechanical civilization in
> America, where the machine gained more importance than
> the human being. As a result, the values of humanism were
> slowly destroyed ... This is why it is now time to go back
> to the early days of our nation and try to understand the
> principles upon which this nation was founded ...
>
> Today, as we view the vast spiritual desert of our
> country, we as NSA members should have the same
> determination that our forefathers had ... They were men of
> vision ... who fought with their last ounce of courage to
> create a civilization of, by and for the people. This is the
> true heritage of America. Seven hundred years ago, Nichiren
> Daishonin taught about the absolute equality of every human
> being. He taught about happiness, liberty, and the dignity
> of man's life. In other words, he was teaching the true
> spirit of '76. Strange to say, the spirit of Nichiren

Daishonin's life philosophy is exactly the true American way of life ... Every one of you, as true pioneers of NSA, should carry with me this glorious quest to develop America to be a great and shining example of a golden, happy nation where happy individuals are enjoying life, where the society reflects this happiness, and where we have peace and happiness for all mankind and harmony between man and the universe. ... The eyes of the world are upon us. NSA is the focal point. Upon our shoulders rest the dreams, wishes, and all the hopes of the world. This is our mission, our glorious quest. That is why we must develop first a courageous practice ... second, confidence in the Gohonzon and never quit, and third, harmonious unity and Shakubuku.[39]

Greater Tangible Benefits

A fourth ideological justification for actively participating in this "glorious quest" by means of Shakubuku is the widely articulated belief that those who do so will receive greater benefit than those who just sit on the sidelines and chant. Underlying this contention is the fact that Nichiren Shoshu's overall practice actually encompasses two basic practices, both of which must be enacted in order for the member to receive the greatest possible benefit. The first and most basic practice, as already discussed, is to chant Daimoku (Nam-Myoho-Renge-Kyo) and do morning and evening Gongyo daily. The second basic form of practice, which is done for the sake of others, is Shakubuku or the "merciful act" of "telling another individual about the Gohonzon and starting him on the road to an incredibly happy, meaningful, and exciting life."

Since Shakubuku is considered to be the only way to attain the goal of world peace and happiness, it is regarded as the greatest cause one can make for the sake of humankind. Accordingly, to receive the ultimate benefit of the philosophy and practice, one must not only chant, but must also Shakubuku; for in doing so, one is, according to the karmic law of cause and effect, reinforcing and adding to the positive destiny and happiness that has been accumulating through chanting. "By doing Shakubuku," in the words of one member, "you do something great for others and get benefits at the same time."

In accordance with this belief, members at all levels of the movement, and particularly recent converts and those on the periphery or sideline, are constantly reminded of the importance of Shakubuku in relation to both their own destiny and happiness and the movement's primary mission. Representative of the nature of these instructions, and illustrative of the way in which the linkage between greater benefits and Shakubuku is employed as an inducement to become active in the cause, is the following statement by a Discussion Meeting leader:

> Why do we do Shakubuku? Because we should spread the message about the fantastic results of our practice and philosophy. Our mission is to propagate until world peace is attained. We are the only idealists in the world who have a proven, realistic way to achieve world peace. That is why we are so excited about doing Shakubuku. Through Shakubuku the world will eventually become like this room - happy, secure, enthusiastic. This room is a microcosm of the way the world will be in twenty years. But in doing Shakubuku we are not only doing world peace. We are also gaining greater personal benefit and fortune. By doing Shakubuku you are doing Human Revolution and world peace at the same time. So let's promote world peace by doing Shakubuku and promoting the *World Tribune* together.

Perhaps even more reflective of the extent to which and the way in which this linkage between personal gain and Shakubuku is used as a lever to action is the fact that my key rank-and-file informants constantly drew upon this rationale when attempting to coax me into becoming more active in the cause. By way of illustration, consider this episode from my field notes.

> Member X called around 11:00 AM (Saturday, January 1975) to inform me that he would be Shakubuku-ing this afternoon and that I should join him. I indicated that I wouldn't be able to make it because I had a lot of work to do. Rejecting this as an acceptable excuse, he proceeded to give a number of reasons why I should take time out to Shakubuku: "Daily activities have to be balanced with

chanting and Shakubuku; if you Shakubuku for an hour,
everything else will fall into place and go smoothly; if you
put your practice first and have faith, everything will work
out and get accomplished." He then indicated that January
is the time of year to get your motor going, and that
February is the month to build rhythm for the whole year.
But you first have to get the motor running properly in
January and that's why Shakubuku is so important right
now.

As the foregoing clearly illustrates, to become active in the cause
by engaging in the practice of Shakubuku is not only rationalized in
terms of the movement's mission, but it is also justified on the grounds
that it is a source of greater personal benefit and fortune in one's daily
life.

Status Enhancement

The final frequently mentioned mobilizing strand of Nichiren
Shoshu's ideology addresses the question of what it means in terms of
personal status and identity to be in the vanguard of a movement "upon
whose shoulders," in the words of General Director Williams, "rest the
dreams, wishes and all the hopes of the world" and that "will
certainly," in the words of President Ikeda, "develop into a movement
of mankind, the greatest in its history." The answer is implicit in these
claims as well as in the previously mentioned rationales for climbing
aboard: to become an active participant in this glorious and
unprecedented venture is to not only become a beneficiary of the
Gohonzon's power, wisdom, protection, and good fortune, but it is also
to become a part of an elect group that provides one with the basis for
forging a unique and special status and identity in both the present and
the future.

The way in which this strand of the ideology functions as a
call to arms or lever to action by linking participation with the notions
of electness and special status is readily discernible in the speeches and
guidance of movement leaders. As President Ikeda noted before 500
members on the occasion of the ground-breaking ceremony for the first
Nichiren Shoshu temple in the United States:

The day will come when each of you will appreciate
Nichiren Shoshu and this Buddhism of Nichiren Daishonin
without a doubt. In the coming 10, 20, 30, and 50 years,
you will see proof of this and each of you will come to
realize that you have been very fortunate.[40]

In a similar vein, General Director Williams, in a speech before 700
members of the Santa Monica Youth Division, links participation and
future status consequences, but he is more specific as to what this
linkage might mean for individual members:

We have a mission to propagate the Gohonzon all over
the world. That is why we were born at this time ... The
overwhelming weight of national and worldwide problems
only indicates that now, more than ever, is the time to
accomplish Kosen-rufu. This very moment can be the great
turning point of NSA members as they courageously stand
up to awaken their friends and neighbors to the philosophy
of Nichiren Daishonin and the guidance of President Ikeda
... I hope all of you will become great and victorious people
in society ... Very soon the responsibility of the country
may fall on your shoulders. Some of you may become
governors, presidents of large corporations, educators,
doctors, and so forth. ... It is immeasurably fortunate to
have faith in Nichiren Shoshu at this time.[41]

While the above statements reflect the manner in which the
leadership draws upon the ideas of electness and special status in their
attempts to urge members on to greater action, the following are
illustrative of the way in which some core members have internalized
these ideas, thereby hinting at the efficacy of this mobilizing strand of
the ideology.

I hope you will see me in twenty years. I'll be an
important leader in this country.

The people who laugh at us now will be asking for our
advice and help before too long.

Right now Nichiren Shoshu is in its infancy in the United States, but someday everybody will know about it and want to know about it.

Within the next 15 to 20 years, people will be wanting to know more and more about NSA.

You should feel lucky to be in NSA, for it is those who feel such fortune and who work for world peace who will get the greatest benefit now and in the days to come.

Through its "sole" possession of the key to improving the dismal nature of life in the world as presently constituted, its conception of itself as the manifestation of a longstanding Buddhist prophecy, its linkage to the ideals and values on which this country was founded, and its glorious quest for world peace and happiness, the value orientation of Nichiren Shoshu thus contains the bases for a sense of mission, electness, special status, and pride that are not only necessary for collective action, but that make it next to impossible for those who have internalized these beliefs to stand on the sidelines and watch. In this way, Nichiren Shoshu's value orientation provides a solution to the "free-rider" problem that supposedly plagues all social movements and collective struggles that seek some generalized objective, such as world peace, that benefits all individuals regardless of their contribution to the cause.[42] In the case of Nichiren Shoshu, it is clear that only those who participate fully reap the greatest benefit or reward.

A CONCLUDING CAVEAT

Although it is highly unlikely that most NSA members have internalized their movement's beliefs and principles in the systematic fashion presented in this chapter, I am reasonably certain that the majority are quite familiar with these beliefs and principles and that a sizable percentage have, in fact, internalized them.

The reasons for this assertion are several. First and foremost, what has been presented in this chapter is based primarily on what I heard, what I was told, on the instructions I received, and on my own personal experiences during my tenure as an active member. If, during the course of my perusal of the movement's literature, I happened to run across various pamphlets and concepts that were not commonly bandied about by rank-and-file members themselves, then these principles and concepts were not incorporated into this chapter. Since my primary aim in this chapter was to present, in a systematic and integrated manner, those aspects of NSA's meaning system and value orientation that seemed most salient in the talk of the members themselves, there seemed to be little reason to include anything other than that which members actually referred to and talked about in constructing, organizing, and justifying their lines of action.

To be sure, the theological system of the Japanese Nichiren Shoshu priestly sect, the parent sect of both Sokagakkai and NSA, is much more extensive and complex than what was revealed in the talk of most members and what was therefore presented here. But an understanding of its totality did not seem essential, from my experience anyway, to an understanding of what NSA is all about. In short, then, this chapter represents above all else an exposition of the core of NSA's meaning system and value orientation from the standpoint of the members themselves.

A second factor which suggests that a sizable percentage of the membership is quite familiar with the ideas and principles discussed in this chapter is the fact that NSA places great emphasis upon the study of these ideas and principles and its historical development. Not only does it have a Study Department in which members are ranked according to their familiarity with its lore, beliefs, underlying principles and so on, but members are expected to prepare once a year for a series of exams covering this material.

When this emphasis on study is considered in conjunction with the fact that such concepts and principles as the karmic law of cause and effect, Esho Funi, Shiki-shin Funi, Sansho or the three proofs, the ten worlds, and Mappo are repeatedly mentioned, whether in the context of guidance sessions, mass meetings, discussion meetings or NSA songs, it seems reasonable to conclude that the vast majority of the members are not only quite familiar with all that has been presented here, but probably even know more of the movement's underlying principles and claims than is usual among the followers of many sects and movements, and even churches for that matter.

In summary, the value orientation of NSA represents a curious blend of the old and the new, the Eastern and the Western, materialism and spiritualism, and egoism and altruism; a blend which is based on a medieval version of Buddhism that is updated and mixed thoroughly with western utilitarianism and strands of liberal humanitarianism. Contained within this is the primary goal of Kosen-rufu and the eventual construction of a "third civilization" or new world order: a world in which war is a ghost of the past and international peace and prosperity will flourish; a world in which all individuals have within their grasp the opportunity to attain their highest potentiality or Buddha-like nature; a world in which creativity and self-actualization become taken for granted; a world which, in short, is shorn of all its present ills and constitutes the actual manifestation of that long-awaited heavenly city on earth, that "impossible dream" of not only contemporary times but of centuries past.

Contending that one's life situation as well as the state of the world are but a reflection of one's inner state, NSA holds that the only way the condition of humankind can be altered and improved is through human revolution or the personal and spiritual regeneration of all people. While it is not clearly specified how changes at the individual level will bring about changes at the structural and global levels, this is not seen as problematic; for it is firmly believed that happy, peaceful people will yield a happy, peaceful world.

In this regard, NSA is similar to many other salvationist-like religious groups in that personal transformation is seen as the key to social transformation. However, unlike most salvationist religious sects and movements, such as Pentecostalism, Jehovah's Witnesses, and the Children of God, which see Jesus as the answer or "one way," the answer for Nichiren Shoshu lies in the repetitive chanting of Nam-Myoho-Renge-Kyo to the Gohonzon, the daily performance of morning and evening Gongyo, and in the assiduous practice of Shakubuku or the act of spreading the word and bringing others into contact with the Gohonzon and the key to unlocking its power, Nam-Myoho-Renge-Kyo. Or, as succinctly stated and brought into sharp focus in the highly popular and widely sung NSA song titled "Have a Gohonzon" (to the tune of Hava Negela):

> Have a Gohonzon, Have a Gohonzon,
> Have a Gohonzon, Chant for awhile.
> When day is dawning, Gongyo each morning,
> Keeps you from yawning, and makes you smile.

You'll find that you will be, full of vitality,
    Watching your benefits grow in a pile.

And ---- Do ---- Shak-u-buku
You'll find your days go smoother
    Even though you've been a loser.
Your surroundings may be looney
    Just remember Esho Funi.

Turn it on,
    Karma's gone
And be happy evermore
    Hey-Hey-Hey

Have a Gohonzon, Have a Gohonzon,
---------- (and so on)

With these promises, hopes, ideas, and claims in mind, let us turn to an examination of the movement's historical development in America.

NOTES

1. See Ralph H. Turner and Lewis M. Killian, *Collective Behavior*, 2nd Edition (Englewood Cliffs, N.J.: Prentice-Hall, 1972), pp. 269-288.

2. In elaborating NSA's value orientation, or goals and ideology, the discussion in this and subsequent chapters will focus primarily on those aspects of the philosophy and value orientation that are revealed in the talk and reasoning of members and in the movement's most widely circulated piece of literature, the *World Tribune*. This is because there is frequently a gap between a formally elaborated value orientation - which is seldom if ever static, but instead undergoes modification in response to the vicissitudes of the movement's career - and what adherents actually know and refer to in constructing and organizing their lines of action, and because I am primarily concerned with the extent to which NSA's value orientations manifest itself in the consciousness of the members and functions as a lever to action.

3. For a more detailed discussion of these structural elements of a movement's value orientation, and particularly of its ideology, see John Wilson, *Introduction to Social Movements* (New York: Basic Books, 1973), pp. 89-131.

4. Although many of the statements or comments presented throughout the text are derived from the movement's literature, the majority are those rendered by members during meetings I attended, during activities in which I participated, and during telephone conversations and informal interviews. Whereas the source of those statements derived from the movement's literature is indicated in the text or in a footnote, members' statements are presented anonymously. Therefore, whenever a statement appears without a source, it is to be read as a statement rendered directly by a member. Nearly all of these statements are presented verbatim, since I was allowed to tape movement meetings.

5. *World Tribune* (April 17, 1974).

6. *World Tribune* (August 21, 1974).

7. *World Tribune* (August 23, 1974).

8. *World Tribune* (April 17, 1974).

9. *World Tribune* (January 1, 1966).

10. *World Tribune* (May 8, 1974).

11. *NSA Quarterly* (Winter, 1975), p. 2. It is interesting to note here that Nichiren Shoshu frequently draws on the popular press and on various popular works - such as those of Toffler and Fromm - in order to legitimate and objectify its view and diagnosis of the world.

12. Ichinen Sanzen literally refers to "3,000 worlds in a state of momentary existence." It is posited as the fundamental theory of life, as initially systematized by Chih-i, founder of China's T'ien-t'ai sect of Buddhism, and further elaborated by Nichiren. It elucidates life in terms of the interrelationship of three principles: the ten worlds; the ten aspects of life through which the worlds manifest themselves; and the three realms of life. As a comprehensive scheme of human life and its relationship with the environment, every human feeling, every action, living as well as non-living, that affect man are included in this principle. For a more detailed discussion, see Daisaku Ikeda, *Buddhism: The Living Philosophy* (Tokyo: East Publications, 1974), and Kiyoaki Murata, *Japan's New Buddhism* (New York: John Weatherhill, Inc., 1969).

13. *World Tribune* (June 26, 1970).

14. *World Tribune* (May 10, 1971).

15. Ibid.

16. *Seikyo Times* (April 1971), p. 58. The *Seikyo Times* is a Sokagakkai-Nichiren Shoshu magazine published monthly in Tokyo, Japan.

17. *Nam*, the first word in the chant "Nam-Myoho-Renge-Kyo," is defined as meaning "dedication or devotion to," with the implication of "fusion with," such that one begins to take on the characteristics of whatever the object or philosophy of devotion.

18. Sokagakkai is the Japanese parent organization of NSA. It was allegedly founded as a lay organization for the followers of Nichiren Shoshu (the orthodox sect of Nichiren), but in fact represents a syncretism of the separate philosophies of Nichiren and Makaguchi. Its overseas branches were redesignated Nichiren Shoshu in 1966. The Sokagakkai will be discussed in greater detail in the following chapter.

19. Tsunesaburo Makiguchi, *The Philosophy of Value* (Tokyo: Seikyo Press, 1964).

20. Makiguchi's theory of value is said to have been posited in lieu of the Kantian triad of truth, good, and beauty. According to Noah S. Brannen ["Soka Gakkai's Theory of Value," *Contemporary Religions in Japan*, V. 5 (June 1964), p. 143], one of the few Westerners to have studied Makiguchi's writings: "Makiguchi's theory claims to be a correction of the alleged aberrations of the traditional Platonic values - truth, goodness, and beauty - by the substitution of 'benefit' (or gain) for that of 'truth.' The reason for this is said to be that truth and value are entirely different concepts. Truth reveals that which is; value connotes a subject-object relationship. Truth makes epistemological statements about an object. Value relates the object to man. Truth says, 'Here is a horse'; value says, 'The horse is beautiful.'" Also, see "Makiguchi and the Philosophy of Value," *World Tribune* (July 7, 1975); and Dayle M. Bethel, *Makiguchi: The Value Creator* (New York: Weatherhill, 1973).

21. "Unlike other plants or flowers, the seed pod and the blossom of the lotus are said to be visible at the same time. With most plants, either the seed appears and then the blossoms follow, or the blossoms spring forth, giving way to the seeds. In either case, the show of seed and bloom is staggered, with one being the cause or effect of the other. Only in the lotus, however, are the two simultaneous." *World Tribune*

(March 23, 1970). Also, see the *NSA Seminar Report: 1968-1971* (Santa Monica, Ca.: World Tribune Press, 1972), p. 38.

22. Masaharu Anesaki, *Nichiren: The Buddhist Prophet* (Cambridge: Harvard University Press, 1916).

23. Daisaku Ikeda, *op. cit.* (1974).

24. *Gongyo* refers to a prayer service before the "Gohonzon," the second of Nichiren's three great laws, in the morning and evening. It entails the recitation of parts of two chapters of the *Lotus Sutra* sandwiched in between Daimoku (the invocation of Nam-Myoho-Renge-Kyo).

25. *Kaidan* refers to the sanctuary or proper place of worship. It is actually classified into *Jino Kaidan*, the actual or Grand Main Sanctuary which houses the Dai-Gohonzon - the great and original Gohonzon inscribed by Nichiren (the current Jino Kaidan is called the Sho-Hondo and is located in Japan); and *Gino Kaidan*, which refers to the nominal sanctuary or home altar that enshrines each member's own personal Gohonzon. The term *Butsudan* also refers to the home altar, and is, in fact, the term most commonly used.

26. *NSA Quarterly* (Spring 1975), p. 15.

27. In case the reader should wonder why I have couched these questions in terms of the lyrics of "The Impossible Dream," the popular theme song of *The Man of La Mancha*, I should emphasize that this song was adopted by NSA as one of its theme songs and was seen as symbolizing the nature of its mission or "glorious quest," as General Director Williams put it. More specifically, it was the theme song of the 1973 Sho-Hondo Convention; it was recited at the 1974 Convention; and it is frequently sung at various movement activities and meetings, not to mention the fact that core members frequently draw on its lyrics when describing what NSA is all about.

28. *World Tribune* (May 8, 1974).

29. *World Tribune* (June 10, 1974).

30. The term "Shakubuku" refers to the "merciful action" of introducing others to the Gohonzon and Nam-Myoho-Renge-Kyo, and therefore encompasses all of the various recruitment and promotion strategies and tactics employed in Nichiren Shoshu's propagation effort. Since Shakubuku will be discussed in greater detail later on in this chapter and in the chapter dealing with recruitment, let me merely note that next to chanting it is the most important NSA practice and activity, and, in many ways, symbolizes what NSA is all about.

31. Numerically speaking, it is believed that Kosen-rufu will be attained when one-third of the world is practicing True Buddhism, when one-third knows about the practice and is sympathetic but unconverted, and the remaining one-third is still ignorant of the faith. This idea was introduced by President Ikeda in 1965 in order to make Kosen-rufu - which was previously equated with conversion of the entire world - a more plausible goal. For a discussion of the doctrinal basis of this idea, see K. Murata, *op. cit.* (1969), pp. 129-132.

32. M. Anesaki, *History of Japanese Religion* (Rutland, Vermont: Charles Tuttle Co., 1963), p. 150.

33. On this point, see M. Anesaki, *Nichiren: The Buddhist Prophet* (Cambridge: Harvard University Press, 1916).

34. Since the *Lotus Sutra* is the sacred source of Nichiren's theology, which, in turn, is the sacred source of much of Nichiren Shoshu-Sokagakkai's philosophy and practice, it should be noted that just as the Old and New Testaments of the Judeo-Christian tradition are ridden with countless phrases and parables which can and have been read and interpreted in different ways, such is also the case with the *Lotus Sutra*. And just as numerous cults and sects in the Christian tradition have drawn on various passages and parables as a source of inspiration and rationalization for their existence, so Nichiren drew upon certain passages in the *Lotus Sutra* not only as a source of prophetic inspiration, but also as pointing to him as the "true Buddha" in the age of Mappo.

35. K. Muruta, *op. cit.* (1969), p. 34.

36. From H. Kern's English translation of the *Lotus Sutra: Saddharma-Pundarika or The Lotus of the True Law* (New York: Dover Publications, 1963), p. 281.

37. *World Tribune* (April 7, 1971).

38. As quoted in the *NSA Seminar Report, 1968-1971* (Santa Monica: World Tribune Press, 1972), p. 2. This pamphlet is a compilation of General Director Williams' lectures given during NSA seminars hosted by various colleges and universities throughout the country. More will be said about these seminars in a later chapter dealing with recruitment and promotion.

39. *World Tribune* (July 10, 1974).

40. *World Tribune* (January 1, 1966).

41. From a speech delivered by General Director Williams before 700 members of the Youth Division in Santa Monica on May 3, 1974. Also reprinted in the *World Tribune* (May 8, 1974).

42. The seminal statement of this "free-rider" problem is provided by Mancur Olson, in *The Logic of Collective Action: Public Goods and the Theory of Groups* (Cambridge: Harvard University Press, 1965).

3
THE HISTORICAL DEVELOPMENT
OF NICHIREN SHOSHU OF AMERICA

The Dai-Gohonzon that we worship is for all mankind.
There is no way to attain happiness other than chanting
Daimoku to the Gohonzon. I strongly believe that it is the
mission of the Sokagakkai to let people know of the power
of the Gohonzon which Nichiren Daishonin inscribed for the
happiness of the human race. From that view the United
States is just like a garden ... Every human being, whether
he is American, Chinese, German or English, thirsts for the
Dai-Gohonzon in the depths of his life. As a member of the
Sokagakkai, I'll run across the globe to drive a wedge of
happiness into the world's people for the sake of Kosen-rufu.

President Ikeda, just prior to
launching the Sokagakkai's first
overseas propagation tour in
1960.

On a cool, autumn day in the first week of October, 1960, a
Japanese jetliner touched down at San Francisco's International Airport.
Among the passengers was Daisaku Ikeda, the newly inaugurated
President of Sokagakkai, and an entourage of followers. Not only was
this the occasion of Ikeda's first visit to the United States, but more
importantly, it marked both the beginning of Sokagakkai's propagation
efforts abroad and the formal establishment of Nichiren Shoshu of
America (referred to as Sokagakkai of America up until late 1966). At
the time of this historic occasion, there were fewer than five hundred
members in the U.S. By the mid-1970s, nearly sixteen years later,
Nichiren Shoshu of America claimed a membership of over 200,000.

In this chapter we will trace the historical development and
flowering of Nichiren Shoshu of America, and examine in detail its
membership claims. We will begin by jumping back in time and across
the Pacific so as to acquire an understanding of its historical roots and
development in Japan.

HISTORICAL ORIGINS

Nichiren Shoshu and Sokagakkai in Pre-World War II Japan

Although the practice of chanting Nam-Myoho-Renge-Kyo to the Gohonzon and much of the doctrine on which it is based extends back in time to 13th Century Japan and the person of Nichiren Daishonin, it was not until the second third of this century that Nichiren's revelations and teachings began to command a significant following. At the time of Nichiren's death on the morning of October 14, 1282, his band of devout followers reportedly numbered less than three hundred, six of whom he had previously entrusted with the mission of carrying on his work.[1]

In the years after his death, the sect Nichiren founded was weakened further by factionalization over different disciplic interpretations of his teachings, thereby giving rise to a number of divergent sects, collectively referred to as the Nichiren sect of Japanese Buddhism. This marked the beginning of a schismatic tendency characteristic of the Nichiren sects as a whole. A survey of Japanese religions indicated, for example, that as of December 1970, there were thirty-seven sects associated with some aspect of Nichiren's work.[2] Of these, the Taiseki-ji subsect,[3] which renamed itself Nichiren Shoshu in 1912, claimed that it was the only true and legitimate Nichiren sect because of its close association with Nichiren's most trusted disciple and because of its alleged possession of Nichiren's major writings, his Dai-Gohonzon, and other relics, such as one of his teeth.

In spite of these claims and the conviction of its superiority over other Nichiren sects, Nichiren Shoshu, which is translated as Nichiren's true teaching or the orthodox sect of Nichiren, was primarily a priestly sect that, throughout much of its history, neither commanded a sizable following nor wielded considerable influence in Japan. All of this changed dramatically in the years following World War II, however. With an estimated membership of around twenty million by the early 1970s, Nichiren Shoshu, through its association with its lay organization called Sokagakkai, had become not only the largest of the Nichiren sects, but also one of the largest and most influential religious groups in modern-day Japan.

Much of the ideological and organizational groundwork underlying its modern upsurge dates back to 1928, when a fifty-eight year old educational philosopher, teacher, and headmaster from Tokyo called Tsunesaburo Makiguchi was fortuitously converted to Nichiren Shoshu, along with a younger friend and protege named Josei Toda. Disappointed with the lack of favorable response to his pedagogic work and ideas, Makiguchi retired from teaching in 1929. A year later, in November 1930, he and Toda organized a study group called Soka Kyoiku Gakka (Value-Creating Educational Society), which was renamed Sokagakkai (Value-Creating Society) after the war.[4]

It was not, however, until December 1937, when sixty people who had become responsive to Makiguchi's ideas met at a Tokyo restaurant, that Soka Kyoiku Gakkai was formally organized. During this meeting, Makiguchi was named as the organization's first president, Toda as its first general director, and the decision was made to launch propagation activities, using as its basic promotional appeal or line the realization of value, and particularly the value of personal gain or benefit in one's daily life, by means of the Nichiren Shoshu practice of chanting. Prior to this organizational meeting, Soka Kyoiku Gakkai was primarily a small, informally organized discussion group consisting mostly of frustrated teachers interested in educational reform or Makiguchi's philosophy of value as it pertained to education. In the years following the 1937 meeting, the linkage between Makiguchi's ideas and the Nichiren Shoshu doctrines became more pronounced, and the membership began to expand and change, as people from other walks of life were now being drawn into the organization.

Both of these changes were reflected, in part, in the testimonials appearing in *Kachi Sozo* (The Creation of Value), a monthly periodical that Soka Kyoiku Gakkai began publishing on July 20, 1941. In these testimonials, members claimed to have realized various spiritual, physical and material benefits as a result of adhering to President Makiguchi's guidance and the Nichiren Shoshu practice of chanting. In the first issue of this periodical, for example, there appears a group testimonial of twenty-seven mothers who collectively attest to experiencing painless childbirth after joining Soka Kyoiku Gakki. In addition to such testimonials, this periodical included articles dealing with the philosophies of Makiguchi and Nichiren Shoshu, as well as articles encouraging members to engage in Shakubuku or propagation and recruitment activities, all of which differed markedly from the content of Soka Kyoiku Gakkai's earlier publications.[5]

It was not until around 1937, then, that the teachings and philosophy of Nichiren, as interpreted by the Nichiren Shoshu sect, began to have a pronounced effect on the orientation of Makiguchi and Soka Kyoiku Gakkai; and it was not until around this same time that this incipient movement began to take on the characteristics of a religiously-oriented one.

In spite of its propagation efforts, Soka Kyoiku Gakkai remained an incipient religious movement that never numbered more than a few thousand members in the years prior to its wartime dissolution in 1943. Its eventual, temporary demise was first heralded in 1940, when the imperial government enacted the Religious Organization Law in an attempt to unify all of Japan under Shintoism in order to provide the Emperor with a kind of divine right to wage war and to facilitate the prewar mobilization effort. In due time, all sects that refused to announce their allegiance to state Shintoism were either driven underground or suppressed. But Makiguchi and his followers remained undaunted by the government's demands and suppression. Since praying to the Shinto sun goddess was seen as an act of blatant heresy, they not only refused to relent, but they continued to propagate their beliefs and preach that Japan's only salvation was in adherence to Nichiren's teachings and practice, all of which only further infuriated the authorities.

With increasing suppression, the intensification of the war, and the eventual Allied air raids, Gakkai activities came to a halt. The final blow came in July of 1943, when Makiguchi, Toda, and nineteen other core leaders were arrested. Subjected to intensive interrogation and the fear of torture, all but Makiguchi, Toda, and one other recanted and were released. A year-and-a-half later, in November 1944, Makiguchi passed away while still imprisoned in Tokyo. For all practical purposes, it seemed as though Soka Kyoiku Gakkai had been effectively wiped out.

Postwar Reconstruction

At the end of World War II, there occurred in Japan a phenomenal flowering of an astonishing diversity of religious sects and movements. With the defeat of the imperial regime and the concomitant discrediting of state Shintoism, there was a spiritual-political void which these emergent beliefs were presumably trying to fill. When this void was coupled with the guarantee of complete religious freedom as one of the new constitutional principles of postwar reconstruction, "the way was open," as one Western observer put it, "for innumerable captive and incipient religious movements to become independent sects and for new 'prophets' to let their voices be heard."[6]

One of the first Occidentals to address this phenomenon was a Father W. Shiffer, a professor at Sophia University in Tokyo. At the twenty-third International Congress of Orientalists at Cambridge in 1954, Schiffer presented a paper dealing with this religious resurgence.[7] A year later, in an article addressing the same topic, Schiffer reported that no fewer than 120 new religions had emerged toward the end and immediately after the war.[8] Another observer, who aptly characterized this period of religious proliferation as "the rush hour of the gods," noted that by 1952, at the end of the American occupation, there were approximately 600 new religions.[9]

Most of these emergent faiths were created around some charismatic leader or divinely inspired founder who either rediscovered a vital religious element from some previous tradition or allegedly received what was felt to be a new revelation. The general religious content of many of these faiths was thus supplied by some version or aspect of Buddhism, Shintoism, Confucianism, and even Christianity. The majority, however, seemed to be based on a syncretic blend of these more traditional philosophies or various and sundry ideas infused with religious significance, some of which seemingly stretched the limits of even the religious imagination.

One emergent faith, for example, cleverly combined the appeals of faith-healing and sex, offering faith cures through sexual intercourse. Another was based on the belief that its founder contained within his abdomen an energy-radiating pearl that provided him with the power to cure the ill and bring forth a rich harvest by merely passing his hand over the stricken individual or a farmer's unfertilized field. One sect paid homage to some eight hundred gods, while another had its followers worshipping one god during official collective ceremonies and different clan gods during private, individual worship. There was also a Perfect Liberty Sect, proclaiming that people must practice whatever their first inspiration dictates; a dancing religion; a sect organized for the purpose of tax evasion; and even a religion founded by an electrical appliance dealer that had Thomas Alva Edison elevated to the status of a deity.

It was during this "rush hour of the gods," this post-World War II period of societal transformation in which old and new religions blossomed like flowers after a spring rainfall, that Soka Kyoiku Gakkai was virtually reborn as Sokagakkai and began to gain ascendancy over the rest.[10]

Its resurrection and phenomenal growth was largely attributable to the energetic and inspirational leadership of Makiguchi's main disciple, Josei Toda, who was believed to have achieved enlightenment during his two years of imprisonment. With a renewed and deepened faith, Toda set about the task of reconstructing the Value-Creating Society shortly after his release from prison on July 3, 1945. In the years 1945 to 1950, Toda contacted and reassembled as many of the prewar members as possible; renamed the organization the Sokagakkai, to signify that it was an organization for all people and not merely educators; stressed the importance of doctrinal knowledge and discipline, giving greater emphasis to the teachings of Nichiren; engaged in limited propagation; and began to build the organizational infrastructure and develop the ideological weaponry for later propagation and expansion. In May of 1951, Toda was installed as the Gakkai's second president and launched its great propagation drive by vowing to convert 750,000 families before his death. Although this target must have seemed like the visionary goal of an idyllic dreamer, it was, in fact, achieved several months prior to his death in April 1958.[11]

Since Toda was seen as the guiding flame behind Sokagakkai's phenomenal growth, many expected the movement to collapse after his premature death at the age of fifty-eight. But the movement's membership and influence continued to grow. By the end of the decade, the Gakkai claimed nearly ten million adherents and boasted that it was the fastest growing religious force in the world. Spearheading the Gakkai's propagation efforts and meteoric growth was one of Toda's organizational creations known as the Youth Division, a militaristically organized and highly disciplined corps of youthful zealots. It was also from the ranks of the Youth Division that Daisaku Ikeda, Toda's successor and the movement's next president and master, was to emerge.

In retrospect, Ikeda's rise through the ranks and eventual assumption of the presidency seems to have been almost foreordained. At the 1951 inaugural meeting of the Young Men's Division, Toda made the following prophetic speech:

> I am certain that the next president of Soka Gakkai is among those of you who have assembled here today. I am convinced he is among you. Kosen-rufu is a mission which I must accomplish. I want every one of you to realize the sacred position you have. The youth is the motive force for any revolution ... In Nichiren Daishonin's days, too, his followers were all young men.
>
> I want you young men to accomplish this great, holy mission. Our aim is not so small as to cover only Japan, but Nichiren Daishonin has ordered us to spread the Lotus Sutra to Korea, China, and India. Today I take this opportunity to greet the person to be our next president and congratulate you with all my heart on the inauguration of this young men's group. [12]

Among those in attendance was the then twenty-four year old Ikeda, who joined the Sokagakkai in 1947, at the age of nineteen. Less than two years following his conversion, his commitment to the cause seemed to be total. "In this turbulent age," he wrote in his diary in 1949, "who is it who will restore peace and purity to society?" "It is," he answered, "the Soka Gakkai! Herein lies our great mission. Revolution demands death," he continued. "Our death, however, is our devotion to the Mystic Law. Death is truly significant only when it serves as the foundation for the eternal salvation of our fellow human beings." [13]

So with this firm determination and commitment, Ikeda became Toda's most trusted disciple and began his move through the ranks. In 1954 he was appointed the Chief of Staff of the Youth Division, and, in effect, became the operational head of the Gakkai's successful propagation and recruitment efforts. Just after Toda's death in 1958, Ikeda assumed the role of General Director, and in 1960 he was named the Gakkai's third president.

Under Ikeda's leadership, the Sokagakkai's membership continued to expand. By the end of 1970, it claimed around sixteen million adherents, a membership which embraced approximately fifteen percent of Japan's total population. In addition to overseeing this continued growth, Ikeda expanded the range of the movement's activities. In May 1964, for example, he officially moved the Gakkai into the political arena with the formal establishment of its own full-fledged political party called the Komeito or Clean Government Party. Although this fusion of religion and politics (obutsu myogo)[14] created a public furor, the Komeito was remarkably successful, so much so that it has often been referred to as Japan's "third force."

While the Komeito constitutes Ikeda's most prominent and widely publicized creation, of greater importance to the development of Nichiren Shoshu of America was Ikeda's establishment of Sokagakkai's Overseas Branch on July 15, 1960. It was with the founding of this branch that Sokagakkai began to spread its wings and propagate abroad in an organized manner.

THE DEVELOPMENT AND FLOWERING OF NICHIREN SHOSHU OF AMERICA

In October of 1960, less than three months after the formation of the Overseas Branch, Ikeda visited the United States and formally established the Los Angeles Chapter of Sokagakkai, the first formally organized branch of Sokagakkai outside of Japanese territory.[15] Although the practice of chanting Nam-Myoho-Renge-Kyo to the Gohonzon was initially brought to America by a handful of Japanese war brides of American GIs and a few Japanese students, it was not until Ikeda's historic visit that the movement which would eventually become known as Nichiren Shoshu of America got going on a regular footing.[16] The importance of this visit in the development of NSA and the sense of mission and expectancy it fostered is graphically reflected in a widely quoted statement allegedly made by Ikeda as he stood before the statue of Christopher Columbus on Telegraph Hill in San Francisco shortly after his arrival:

> Just like Columbus, we now stand here and set our first step on the continent of America. Our trip is more historic and greater than that of Columbus. In 50 or 100 years, the greatness of this day will be understood.

Although the hope and vision of successful propagation and expansion was foremost in the minds of Ikeda and his entourage of assistants, a more pragmatic and requisite objective was the development and formation of a highly committed and organized cadre that would eventually function as the springboard for future expansion. Here Ikeda turned to the Sokagakkai members living in the U.S. At that time, however, there were fewer than five hundred Nichiren Shoshu-Sokagakkai members in the U.S., nearly all of whom were Japanese war brides scattered about the country and reportedly leading lonely, isolated and miserable lives. As one of Ikeda's assistants noted in a magazine account of her initial encounter with these war brides during the 1960 visit:

> At that time, I accompanied President Ikeda on his trip to the United States and met many of the war brides who were Soka Gakkai members there. I had heard that these women were leading lonely and isolated lives, and one purpose of my trip was to see what could be done for them.
>
> There to greet us at the Los Angeles Airport were about twenty or thirty war brides, many of them accompanied by their husbands. Because their husbands were GIs, their lives were not very good. There was no one who owned a car, and it was necessary to rent one just to get President Ikeda to his hotel. Thus I could see that their standard of living was not very high. Of course, as war brides, their lives were miserable and they were isolated from society. I felt that they needed even greater faith than they had in Japan.
>
> And yet, these war brides had been separated even from each other. When they saw one another at the airport, they said in surprise, 'Are you here too?' The situation was of course intolerable, and it was necessary to organize at once. Thus, the (initial) purpose of the organization was not to engage in missionary work, but rather it arose naturally in response to this situation.[17]

In a 1975 *World Tribune* article reconstructuring the birth of NSA, George M. Williams, NSA's General Director, offers a similar account of the situation of these transplanted Gakkai war brides at the time of Ikeda's initial visit and also alludes to their eventual role in the development and spread of NSA. The article begins with a discussion of the tranquil 50s and the volatile 60s, a period Williams refers to as "an age of darkness," and then turns to the Gakkai war brides:

> The 50s ended with hopeful signs. At the same time Daisaku Ikeda was assuming the presidency of the Sokagakkai in 1960, John F. Kennedy was inaugurated as President of the United States ... Kennedy was the symbol of rising youthfulness and vitality... . There was a real feeling of hope and upward development as the torch was handed to a younger generation ...
> With the violent death of Kennedy in 1963, the torch exploded with youthful fury. The young struck out at the complacency of the once tranquil society, opening up the problems of the nation for all to see... .
> As the curtain fell on America's tranquility, a new group of players emerged on the scene. Unnoticed by the general public, they were to play an important role in the nation's history nonetheless. They were scattered in every corner of the country, but they all had something in common; they were Japanese in origin and had come to America as 'war brides.' They had left their island country dreaming of a rosy life overseas. But the new world was so different, so harsh. They were forced to face reality... . At that time, I was an ordinary student in a foreign land... . Seeing those war brides in desperate longing for home, I empathized with them; I too was homesick, but I had the encouragement of President Ikeda to give me hope. I encouraged them through reading the *Gosho* (Nichiren's writings) with them and dreamed with them of the day when we could see Japan once again. With the encouragement of President Ikeda as a springboard, one person after another began to practice.

The first step on the road to propagation and expansion in America, then, was the unification and organization of these culturally transplanted Sokagakkai war brides. As implied at the end of the above account, the responsibility for this task fell largely on the shoulders of

George M. Williams, a naturalized American citizen of Japanese parentage and the central figure behind the development and growth of Nichiren Shoshu of America.

Born Masayasu Sadanaga in 1930, in Seoul, Korea, Williams returned with his family to Japan at the end of World War II. In 1949, he enrolled in Meiji University in Tokyo, and worked his way through school by acting as an interpreter and teaching English to Japanese. In 1953, a year prior to his graduation with a B.A. in Law, a most important event occurred in his life. During that year, Williams' mother, who was in poor health, had decided to convert to the Nichiren Shoshu-Sokagakkai faith. Worried about her declining health, Williams accompanied her to the temple and followed in her footsteps, renouncing his former Methodist faith and becoming an ardent follower of and participant in Nichiren Shoshu-Sokagakkai.

Through his active role in the Gakkai's Young Men's Division, Williams had the opportunity in 1955 to meet President Ikeda, who was then the head of the Youth Division. During this meeting, Williams is said to have expressed the desire to study and propagate in the U.S. Two years later, in 1957, this desire became a reality as Williams came to the U.S. and enrolled at U.C.L.A. to study political science. Two years later he moved to Washington, D.C., where he attended classes at George Washington University and formed the first Gakkai discussion group in the U.S.

In 1962, Williams received a Master's in political science from the University of Maryland, and shortly thereafter returned to Los Angeles to devote all of his time and energy to the propagation of the Nichiren Shoshu-Sokagakkai philosophy and practice in America. In 1967 he received his permanent residence status; and in 1972, a year prior to his naturalization as an American citizen, he had his name changed from Masayasu Sadanaga to George M. Williams, apparently to strengthen the American identity of both himself and NSA.[18]

During Williams' tenure as a student in this country, his studies were reportedly secondary to his passion for Shakubuku. When not studying or supporting his family through various odd jobs, such as working nights in a bowling alley, he is said to have devoted every possible moment to uniting and encouraging other Sokagakkai members living in the U.S. Through personal visits or encouraging correspondence via mail, Williams put isolated members in touch with each other, attempted to strengthen their faith and resolve, and began to develop a nucleus of committed followers.

When President Ikeda visited the U.S. in 1960, Williams was among the first to greet him as he stepped off the plane. During this visit, Williams renewed a promise he made to Ikeda prior to departing for the U.S. three years earlier: to spread the True Buddhism of Nichiren Shoshu-Sokagakkai in America and eventually return to Japan on a pilgrimage with thousands of fellow American members. Considering that only several hundred Gakkai members were scattered about the country at that time, this vow must have seemed just as idyllic and unrealistic as the one made by Toda when he was named the President of Sokagakkai in 1951. Yet, just as Toda fulfilled his promise, Williams also made great strides toward fulfilling his vow.

In 1961, for example, only sixty-eight members accompanied Williams on a pilgrimage (Tozan) to the main Nichiren Shoshu temple housing the Dai-Gohonzon at the foot of Mount Fuji. By 1967, ten years after Williams initially vowed to return to Japan with thousands of Americans, this pilgrimage contingency had expanded to some twelve hundred. And in 1973, three thousand made the trek across the Pacific, making it the largest NSA pilgrimage to date. Even more significantly, NSA's membership had expanded from only several hundred in 1960 to around 200,000 by 1970, with the greatest period of growth occurring in the latter third of the sixties.

A Change in Course and Character: From a Sokagakkai Outpost to an Active Proselyting and Expanding Movement

Prior to NSA's fantastic growth between 1967 and 1971, and especially in the first half of the sixties, the movement functioned primarily as a Sokagakkai outpost or spiritual aid station for Japanese war brides experiencing a variety of marital difficulties and adjustment problems associated with migration to a strange and alien land. The specific nature of the problems experienced by many of the war brides, and the extent to which NSA initially functioned to alleviate these problems and facilitate the adjustment and strengthen the resolve of their bearers, is all nicely illustrated in the personal accounts of many of these early members appearing in the *World Tribune* in the form of testimonials. One Japanese female, in her forties and married to an

American GI, offers, for example, the following account in a 1966 edition of the *World Tribune*:

> As I think back to what I had been nine years ago, I shudder to think how close to eternal life of hell I was in. I had been in America for nine years, yet I did not have enough respect for my husband to even try to learn or speak his language. Always sick and whining, too tired to appreciate the children, till everything became a burden.
>
> April, 1964, through the mercy of a Gakkai member, I accepted the Gohonzon as a last straw. To my surprise, I regained my health and learned to appreciate my beautiful children, and became more thoughtful of my husband. My two older children had been reared Catholic, my husband's religion, but when they saw me read the Sutra they joined me and learned in two weeks. To my astonishment, my husband, who had been a devout Catholic for 35 years, saw the tremendous change in me and voluntarily attended the meetings and became a member.
>
> How wonderful life now is to be able to chant and do Gongyo with my four children and my husband in complete unity. My husband and I are campaigning strongly as district leader and assistant district leader... As a true disciple of President Ikeda, I will rear my four daughters to become strong members of the YWD that need never be ashamed to face President Ikeda ... I will revolutionize my character and be No. 1 as a member, as a wife, as a leader, and as a disciple of President Ikeda. I will beat a path to the senior leaders, wherever they may be, and receive guidance after guidance until we achieve world Kosen-rufu.

And another Japanese female, married to an American GI, relates, in another 1966 edition of the *World Tribune*, how having the Gohonzon and being in close contact with the Los Angeles Chapter eased her adjustment to America.

> My how time flies. It is now six years since I received the Gohonzon on October 15, 1959. Through the power of

the Gohonzon I came to America five years ago and since
then there have been numerous incidents. Being close to the
North American Headquarters, I have been able to receive
much guidance. Through this, and following my leaders
very closely, although my husband has been assigned
overseas for the last eight months, I have experienced no
hardships. Instead, I have received many divine benefits...
I realize how fortunate I have been to receive the
Gohonzon... I resolve to chant more Daimoku and work
towards my goal of faith as a family. As a leader I will
fight to the very last for the Kosen-rufu of America.

It was from the ranks of these culturally transplanted war brides and
their families, then, that NSA drew its early adherents and began to
develop a highly committed and organized corps of devotees that
functioned as the springboard for propagation and expansion.

For several years, however, the movement remained oriented to
this initial constituency. Not only was the work done by and for these
women and their families, but most meetings were conducted in
Japanese. It was not until late 1963, in fact, that enough Americans
were practicing to warrant a few English-speaking discussion meetings,
the first being led by Mr. Williams in Los Angeles.[19] Moreover,
propagation and recruitment were directed primarily towards the
Japanese community. As one Japanese female member living in the
San Francisco area reported in a 1966 edition of the *Seikyo Graphic*:

> For the first two or three years, shakubuku and other
> Soka Gakkai activities were performed mainly by the
> Japanese. We would look up Japanese-sounding names in
> the telephone book, take a bus out to the area, find the
> house, and begin shakubuku. I remember those days
> well.[20]

Even as late as 1964-1965, little concerted effort was yet being
made towards recruiting and converting non-Japanese Americans.[21]
Although the membership grew, allegedly numbering 20,000 by 1965,
the movement had yet to attract a sizeable number of Occidentals. To
be sure, the proportion of non-Oriental members had increased from

around four percent in 1960 to twenty-three percent in 1965,[22] but most of these Occidental members were the husbands or male friends of Japanese females, with the majority being associated with the military. As noted in a 1966 *World Tribune* article pertaining to the growth of Sokagakkai in America, "the largest percentage of male members in the Sokagakkai in the United States are either former service personnel or presently in the military service."[23]

By the middle of the decade, then, NSA still appealed primarily to Japanese females and secondarily to their American husbands and male friends associated with the military. Within the next several years, however, all of this began to change; for by 1970, not only had the movement reportedly expanded its ranks by 180,000, but the membership was now around seventy percent non-Oriental,[24] the greatest percentage of whom were Caucasian, single, under thirty, and students or lower-level white-collar workers rather than military personnel or housewives.[25]

Although the movement's leadership was initially attuned to the importance of relating to American history and values and of having Americans recruit Americans if the movement was to broaden its membership and become something more than an outpost for Japanese Gakkai members living in this country and their American kin, it was not until 1966 that the "Americanization" of the movement, including the broadening of its constituency, was in full swing. During this year, for example, not only were Japanese members being encouraged to master the English language, attain American citizenship, and the like, but most meetings were now being conducted in English. As the Sokagakkai newspaper, *Seikyo Shimbun*, reported in a 1966 article dealing with activities in America:

> Group meetings are held once a week. District and
> Chapter meetings are also held. In spite of the fact that
> many of the women here have trouble with English, all of
> these meetings are held in English. Nowadays, only the
> lectures on the *Gosho* (Nichiren's sacred writings) are in
> Japanese.[26]

Perhaps even more reflective of this shift in course and character, and of the resultant attempt to broaden its appeal, was the 1966 decision to change the name of the movement from Sokagakkai of America to Nichiren Shoshu of America. Although the reasons underlying this decision were not spelled out in the official announcement of the name-change in the last 1966 edition of the *World Tribune*,[27] I suspect that the decision was based on two interrelated considerations: to provide the movement in America with an identity separate from that of Sokagakkai in Japan, and to strengthen its American identity. Regarding the first consideration, Sokagakkai of Japan had been on the receiving end of a barrage of public criticism concerning its allegedly high-pressured recruitment and conversion tactics, its fusion of religion and politics, and its alleged fanaticism ever since the days of Toda's great propagation drive, all of which could taint the image and impede the operation of its overseas branches. Thus the tactical importance of separating the Sokagakkai of Japan from the Gakkai of America in name if not in fact. Hence, the change in name.

Regarding the second and perhaps most important consideration, it seems reasonable to argue, given the movement's attempt to broaden its appeal and strengthen its American identity, that it would be tactically important to acquire an American-sounding name. Thus the name NSA, which has more of an American ring to it than does Sokagakkai.

By the end of 1966, NSA was thus becoming more than a Sokagakkai outpost and spiritual aid station for Japanese females and their American husbands and families. Both the Americanization and expansion of its membership continued, although not as dramatically, throughout the first half of the seventies, as the movement claimed over 200,000 adherents, ninety percent of whom were said to be of non-Oriental descent.[28] Within the span of fifteen years, then, NSA not only expanded its ranks from several hundred to some 200,000, but there was also a corresponding change in its orientation and membership composition. Before examining in greater detail such intriguing questions as "Who swelled its ranks, and why?" and "How was this rather remarkable growth accomplished?", let us first take a closer look at its membership claims.

TOWARDS A REASONABLE RECKONING
OF NSA'S MEMBERSHIP CLAIMS

How large, in fact, is NSA in terms of sheer numbers? Although this is a question certainly worthy of consideration if we are to gain a fair fix on the scope of the movement's appeal and spread, it is by no means an easy one to answer; for determining the actual membership of any movement is a most difficult and often speculative task.

Unlike formal organizations and most voluntary associations, social movements seldom maintain a precise membership listing. Furthermore, movements seldom have a well-defined, objective criterion for determining membership, much less for distinguishing gradations and levels of membership. Take the Women's Liberation Movement, for example. Is membership determined on the basis of sympathy with the cause; by occasional, intermittent action in support of the cause; or in terms of continuious communication with significant others in the movement and continuous supportive action in behalf of the movement? Similarly, is membership in the Hare Krishna movement determined by the mere chanting of the Krishna mantra or by renunciation of the larger culture's conventional lifestyle and affiliation with and residence in a Krishna commune?

An additional confounding problem is the tendency for most movement leaders and activists to exaggerate the size of the movement's membership in order to foster and sustain morale among its variously defined adherents and to impress upon the general public that "this movement" is by no means an inconsequential, fly-by-night happening, but it is rather the wave of the future or at least something that more and more people are coming to understand and support.

For these reasons, then, when one speaks of the membership of a social movement, the referent is seldom, if ever, a monolithic entity with a stable, well-defined, similarly committed body of adherents, but is more typically a collectivity that is loosely defined, varies over time, and within which different grades or levels can be discerned. As a consequence, when one sets out to gauge the size of a movement's membership, it is imperative to proceed with the understanding that whatever the final reckoning, it is most likely a speculative inference that rests heavily upon the meandering estimates and claims of those insiders most conversant with the movement.

These caveats also hold when considering the quantitative and qualitative dimensions of NSA's membership. Although NSA differs from most movements in that it has at least one objective determinant of membership - receiving a Gohonzon at the conversion ceremony called Gojukai, its total membership is not reckoned merely on the basis of the number of Gohonzon distributed. Instead, it is the product of several confounding practices.

Frequently following the practice of its Japanese parent organization, as well as the practice of many Japanese religions, NSA's membership is often reckoned by counting families or households rather than individuals. This practice is predicated on the assumption that if a married woman joins Nichiren Shoshu-Sokagakkai, then her husband and children will eventually join also, or vice-versa. As a consequence, NSA frequently considers immediate members of a new convert's household as being within the orbit of the faith, regardless of whether they have gone thorugh the conversion ceremony.

While this is confusing enough, it is further complicated by two additional factors. First, there is usually only one Gohonzon per household, no matter how large the household may be or how many family members are actually practicing the faith. And secondly, the movement's total membership is sometimes announced in terms of individuals and sometimes in terms of households, without indicating precisely the size of the family unit being used as the multiplier. The total number of individuals in NSA can thus vary considerably depending on whether the family unit is multiplied by 2, 2.5, 3, or whatever figure is taken as the index of family size. Consequently, it is seldom clear as to the exact number of Gohonzon distributed or the actual total membership.

A final factor which tends to further inflate and obscure the total membership given at any particular time is that the count not only commonly includes the family members of those who have actually received a Gohonzon, but usually those individuals who have renounced their faith and ceased to participate in NSA activities as well. For these reasons, then, exact statistics regarding membership size and grades or levels of membership are just as difficult to determine for NSA as for most movements.

In spite of these confusing and inflationary reckoning practices, I have attempted to reach an informed estimate of NSA's membership by comparing several of its membership reports and announcements. In

TABLE 1

Approximate Size and Growth of Membership
1960 to 1974

Year	(1)* Membership in terms of Individuals (1960-1970)	Absolute Increase	(2)* Membership in terms of Households (1962-1968)	(3)* Scattered Membership Claims (A) Indi- viduals	(B) House- holds
1960	500			300(a)	
1961	1,500	1,000			
1962	5,000	3,500	2,500		
1963	10,000	5,000	5,000		
1964	15,000	5,000	7,500		
1965	20,000	5,000	10,000		
1966	30,000	10,000	16,000	25,000(a)	
1967	50,000	20,000	30,000		
1968	80,000	30,000	44,000		
1969	140,000	60,000			
1970	200,000	60,000			
1971					
1972					
1973				200,000(b)	100,000(b)
1974				220,000(c)	
				250,000(d)	

*Sources: (1) "NSA Demographics," *NSA Seminar Report, 1968-1971*, Santa Monica: World Tribune Press, 1972.

(2) From report on membership growth in *World Tribune*, March 19, 1968, p. 4.

(3A) (a) and (b) *Mainichi Daily News*, October 15, 1973, p. 19.
(c) *Mainichi Daily News*, April 6, 1974, p. 14.
(d) Personal communication with a *World Tribune* staff member.

(3B) (a) Stated in article written by General Director Williams in the *World Tribune*, January 1, 1966, p. 5.

(b) *Mainichi Daily News*, October 15, 1973, p. 19.

Table 1, which is based on published membership reports and various membership claims, the size and growth of the movement's membership is shown in terms of both individuals and households. The figures in columns 1 and 3A represent individuals or the total membership claimed for each year; whereas the figures in columns 2 and 3B indicate the number of households or family units claimed within the orbit of the faith. Upon comparing the figures in these four columns, the overall membership picture comes into clearer focus. In comparing the total membership figures with the household figures, it becomes reasonably apparent that the total number of claimed adherents is a multiple of the number of households times an index of two persons or believers per family.

Although this correspondence is not perfect for each of the years in which both total individual and family membership are indicated, it is close enough to suggest that a good rule of thumb for reaching a reasonable estimate of both the number of Americans with Gohonzons and the number of active practitioners is to divide total membership claims in half. While core members will probably object to this reckoning procedure, it seems reasonable in light of the movement's confounding and inflationary counting practices and the fact that the majority of the movement's active members are single.

Even though this calculation suggests that NSA's membership claims have been exaggerated, two significant facts still stand out. First, it has attracted a considerable number of non-Oriental Americans for a culturally transplanted movement with a set of beliefs and practices that must appear strange to most Americans. And second, whatever the reckoning procedures used, its ranks expanded phenomenally during the latter third of the sixties. Moreover, when a movement is able to muster 3,000 adherents for a transoceanic pilgrimage to its holy see, when it is able to assemble 3,000 to 5,000 members and guests for a weeknight general business meeting and mass rally month after month, when it is capable of attracting 10,000 to 15,000 followers to its annual conventions, and when it is able to conduct several hundred discussion meetings four evenings per week, with anywhere from ten to fifty members in attendance at each, it is clearly not some inconsequential, fly-by-night fad or happening, but a well organized, highly orchestrated collectivity with a sizable number of strongly committed core activists and a larger number of less ardent and variously committed followers who are, nonetheless, readily available for periodic mobilization.

In light of these observations and findings concerning NSA's development and flowering, several intriguing questions call for further examination and analysis. First, how has this rather phenomenal growth been accomplished? How does NSA reach out, make contact with, and bring in potential converts and secure their nominal conversion? What are the major strategic considerations and operational strategies and tactics underlying its propagation and recruitment efforts? In short, how has NSA gone about the work of expanding its ranks and winning support for its cause? And secondly, who has swelled its ranks? From what social-demographic categories have most of its membership been drawn? And why have some individuals been drawn into the movement and not others? Who, in short, has joined the movement and why? Each of these questions will be dealt with in the following two chapters.

NOTES

1. Kiyoaki Murata, *Japan's New Buddhism* (New York: John Weatherhill, Inc., 1969) pp. 40-41. For a more detailed discussion of Nichiren's life, teachings, and influence, see, in addition to Murata's account: M. Anesaki, *Nichiren: The Buddhist Prophet* (Cambridge: Harvard University Press, 1916) and his *History of Japanese Religion* (Rutland, Vermont: Charles Tuttle, 1963); and D. Ikeda, *Buddhism: The Living Philosophy* (Tokyo: East Publications, 1974).

2. Agency for Cultural Affairs, *Japanese Religion* (Tokyo: Kodansha International Ltd., 1972).

3. Taiseki-ji refers to the first temple founded by Nikko, Nichiren's closest disciple. It is located at the foot of Mt. Fuji, the site of Nichiren Shoshu-Sokagakkai's Grand Main Temple called the Sho Hondo.

4. For a detailed account of Makiguchi's life and value-creating philosophy, see Dayle M. Bethel, *Makiguchi: The Value Creator* (New York: John Weatherhill, Inc., 1973).

5. The foregoing discussion of *Kachi Sozo* and its content is derived largely from the discussion of this periodical and related material by Dayle M. Bethel, *op. cit.* (1973), pp. 89-98.

6. H. Neill McFarland, *The Rush Hour of the Gods: A Study of New Religious Movements in Japan* (New York: Harper and Row, 1967), p. 4.

7. W. Schiffer, "Shinko-Shukyo: A Social and Religious Phenomenon in Post War Japan," *Proceedings of the Twenty-third International Congress of Orientalists*, Cambridge, August 21 to 29, 1954 (Cambridge, London: W. Heffer & Sons, 1954).

8. W. Schiffer, "New Religions in Postwar Japan," *Monumenta Nipponica*, V. 11, No. 1 (April 1955), pp. 1-14.

9. H. Neill McFarland, *op. cit.* (1967), p. 65.

10. There is a fairly large body of literature pertaining to this religious resurgence in Japan in general and to the development and operation of Sokagakkai in Japan in particular. Regarding the former, see, in addition to the work already cited by Schiffer (1954; 1955) and McFarland (1967): *Contemporary Religions in Japan*, a quarterly journal published by the International Institute for the Study of Religions, Tokyo, from 1960; Clark B. Offner & Henry Van Straelen, *Modern Japanese Religions* (New York: Twayne Publishers, 1963); Harry Thomsen, *The New Religions of Japan* (Rutland, Vermont: Charles E. Tuttle, 1963); and H. Byron Earhart, "The Interpretation of the 'New Religions' of Japan's New Religious Movements," in R. J. Miller, Ed., *Religious Ferment in Asia* (Lawrence, Kansas: The University Press of Kansas, 1974), pp. 169-188. Regarding the Sokagakkai in particular, see, for example: Noah S. Brannen, *Soka Gakkai: Japan's Militant Buddhists* (Richmond, Va.: John Knox Press, 1968); James A. Dator, *Soka Gakkai: Builders of the Third Civilization* (Seattle: The University of Washington Press, 1969); Kiyoaki Murata, *op. cit.* (1969); Hirotatsu Fujiwara, *I Denounce Soka Gakkai* (Tokyo: Nisshin Hodo Co., 1970); James W. White, *The Sokagakkai and Mass Society* (Stanford, Ca.: Stanford University Press, 1970); and Daisaku Ikeda, *The Human Revolution*, Vol. I, II, III (1966-1967), *The Nichiren Shoshu Sokagakkai* (1966), and *Nichiren Shoshu and Soka Gakkai: Modern Buddhism in Action* (1972), all published by the Gakkai's own Seiko Press in Tokyo.

11. For a moving and informative account of Toda and his work, see D. Ikeda's *The Human Revolution*, *op. cit.* and/or its screen adaptation bearing the same title.

12. Quoted in K. Murata, *op. cit.* (1969), pp. 98-99.

13. Quoted in *Nichiren Shoshu and Soka Gakkai*, *op. cit.* (1972), p. 133.

14. For a discussion of the philosophy and reasoning behind Sokagakkai's fusion of politics and religion, see Ikeda's lengthy essay titled "Politics and Religion" in the *Complete Works of Daisaku Ikeda*, Vol. 1 (Tokyo: The Seikyo Press, 1968), pp. 13-192.

15. During this first overseas tour, Ikeda visited Hawaii, San Francisco, Chicago, New York, Washington, D.C., Los Angeles, Canada, and San Paulo, Brazil, where he also established the Brazil Chapter of Sokagakkai.

16. NSA was referred to as Sokagakkai of America up until December 20, 1966, when it was officially renamed Nichiren Shoshu of America.

17. From a Japanese women's magazine, *Shukan Myojo* (Deember 20, 1964), as reported in James A. Dator, *op. cit.* (1969), p. 22.

18. Williams is said to have received his first name, George, from President Ikeda, who then instructed him to choose his own last name. Apparently wanting a common American surname, he scoured through the Los Angeles telephone directory. Seeing pages and pages of "Williams," he decided that this was about the most common name he could take as his own. According to the October 15, 1973 edition of the *Mainichi Daily News* (a Nichiren Shoshu-Sokagakkai newspaper published in Tokyo and Osaka), Williams said, upon choosing this name: "He was the 11th George Williams in the telephone book."

19. *World Tribune* (August 15, 1974), p. 6.

20. Also reported by James A. Dator, *op. cit.* (1969), p. 23.

21. Reported to me in private conversation with a core NSA member and middle-level leader.

22. "NSA Demographics" (Appendix 3) in *NSA Seminar Report, 1967-1971* (Santa Monica, Ca.: World Tribune Press, 1972).

23. *World Tribune* (March 31, 1966), p. 1.

24. "NSA Demographics," *op. cit.* (1972).

25. Based on the demographic data compiled from my own analysis of 504 randomly selected testimonies appearing in the *World Tribune* from 1966 to 1974. This data base will be discussed in more detail in Chapter 5.

26. *Seikyo Shimbun* (April 10, 1966). Also reported in James A. Dator, *op. cit.* (1969), p. 23.

27. *World Tribune* (December 24, 1966), p. 1. Although the headlines of this edition read "H.Q. Renamed Nichiren Shoshu," all that followed were two brief sentences: "The Sokagakkai of America, a religious organization, has changed its name to Nichiren Shoshu of America as of December 20, 1966. We would appreciate your cooperation and assistance as in the past." Signed, "Nichiren Shoshu of America, M. Sadanaga, Headquarters Chief."

28. *Mainichi Daily News* (April 6, 1974), p. 14.

4

DOING SHAKUBUKU:
NSA'S PROPAGATION AND
RECRUITMENT EFFORTS

Shakubuku early in the morning
Shakubuku late at night
Shakubuku when the sky is storming
Shakubuku is the way to Kosen-rufu
Twenty years will see Kosen-rufu
Keep chanting, keep chanting
We've got just twenty years to go.

Do your Gongyo early in the morning
Daimoku late at night
We will follow President Ikeda
To make this planet peaceful and bright
Shakubuku is the way to Kosen-rufu
Twenty years will see Kosen-rufu
Keep chanting, keep chanting
We've got just twenty years to go.

(Shakubuku campaign song,
to the tune of "Breakin'
Rocks on the Chain Gang")

Social movements are commonly defined and differentiated in terms of their change-oriented objectives and attendant ideologies.[1] However important these factors, to treat them as the crucial determinants of a movement's course and character can yield a truncated understanding of a given movement in particular and social movements in general. For a movement is constituted by more than an aggregate of individuals subscribing to a particular set of beliefs and objectives; it is also a relatively organized collectivity acting upon the larger society or some target group in order to promote its beliefs and realize its objectives.   As one approach to social movements emphasizes, "whatever the goals and ideology of a movement, influence must be exercised over persons or institutions outside of the movement if the values are to be more than the daydreams of a small band of devotees."[2]

A thorough and balanced understanding of a social movement is thus contingent on giving equal consideration to the strategies and tactical practices developed and employed for the purpose of acting upon its social environment so as to advance its interests. In order to understand the course and character of NSA as a movement, then, it is necessary to consider not only its beliefs and goals, but also the question of how it has sought to promote these beliefs and realize its goals. Having discussed the former, we now shift our attention to the latter, as we examine in this chapter how NSA has gone about the business of expanding its ranks and winning support for its cause.

MEANING AND IMPORTANCE OF SHAKUBUKU

As implied in the above song, the means by which NSA acts upon its environment so as to further its interests are symbolized in the word and practice of "Shakubuku." Shakubuku is allegedly one of two traditional methods of propagating "True Buddhism," and, as learned earlier, refers to the process of bringing outsiders into contact with and informing them about the Gohonzon and Nam-Myoho-Renge-Kyo.

Traditionally, however, Shakubuku refers to a much more aggressive form of propagation and recruitment employed for the purposes of refuting heretical religions and incorrect views of life and supplanting them with the correct views of "True Buddhism." This is reflected in its literal translation - "to break and flatten or subdue," although I never heard a member refer to it in this manner. Rather, Shakubuku was always talked about in such glowing phrases as "merciful action," "the greatest cause one can make for the sake of others," and as "the most compassionate act one can perform," phrases that are more descriptive of the other traditional form of propagation and recruitment called "Shoju."

In contrast to the traditionally aggressive nature of Shakubuku, Shoju is much less combative and imperative, and merely involves telling non-members about the benefits that flow from chanting to the Gohonzon, without denying the sect or religion to which the non-member belongs. In short, Shoju is a soft-sell approach to propagation and recruitment, whereas Shakubuku represents more of a hard-sell approach.

Although the propagation and recruitment strategies and practices employed by NSA come closer to approximating the Shoju method, especially when compared to the highly aggressive and ultramilitant recruitment tactics reportedly employed by Sokagakkai members in the fifties and early sixties in Japan[3], NSA has retained the term Shakubuku to refer to its propagation and recruitment activities and efforts. Although the reasons for this are unclear, the NSA literature suggests that the term is used because of its popularity. But that only begs the question further. I would guess that the answer is lodged, in part, in the greater mobilizing power of the word Shakubuku. In contrast to Shoju, Shakubuku is not only a more catchy word, but it is also has a harsher, more vigorous and combative sound, a sound that not only catches one's attention but which evokes the imagery of action as well. From a strategic and symbolic standpoint, then, the word Shakubuku has the sound of a more effective coordinating and mobilizing symbol. Metaphorically speaking, Shakubuku sounds much like a call to arms, a call to action, which, in fact, it is.

Whether this explanation is correct is not terribly important, however. What is important to our overall understanding of NSA, though, is the emphasis placed on propagation and recruitment or the doing of Shakubuku. A sense of its importance to NSA's overall operation and character is graphically captured in part of a speech delivered by General Director Williams before more than 4,000 members and guests on the occasion of a mass rally held at the Santa Monica Civic Auditorium in May of 1974:

> We must never forget the prime point of our practice, the act of Shakubuku. Shakubuku is the only method to accumulate the great fortune our country needs to become the leader of world peace. 'There is no doubt,' President Ikeda says, 'that NSA is destined to lead the construction of a new civilization. Pride yourselves on your mission and

pave the way for the prosperity of not only your beloved
America, but also of the rest of the world ... Make it your
mission to plant millions of flowerbeds of happiness
throughout the vast continent of America.'

This is why NSA has now begun a tremendous
Shakubuku campaign. Only through Shakubuku can we
change our poor destiny and gather great fortune. Only
through Shakubuku, the altruistic act of helping others ...
can we establish true freedom and true independence. Only
through Shakubuku can we reply to our Master's
expectations for peace in the world and happiness for all
mankind. This is our quest, our glorious quest.

This same message and directive regarding the importance of
Shakubuku is manifested again and again in the movement's literature,
its songs, in members' talk, and in its varied activities and campaigns.
Seldom does an issue of the *World Tribune* roll off the press, for
example, wherein Shakubuku is not a topic of discussion. In fact, a
content analysis of 240 randomly selected editions of the *World Tribune*
over a ten-year period revealed that a greater number of articles were
thematically related to Shakubuku than to any other single activity.
Some articles state Shakubuku goals and results, some discuss the
doctrinal basis for doing Shakubuku, others stress the personal benefits
that emanate from Shakubuku, and some provide directives on how to
do it. But thematically running throughout all of these articles is the
underlying message that Shakubuku is NSA's primary collective
activity. This theme is reflected and captured again and again in such
recurring phrases as:

Shakubuku is the most important of all NSA activities.
Shakubuku is the key to everything.
Shakubuku is the ultimate cause a man can make.
Shakubuku is the greatest cause for all mankind.
There is no greater action for humanity and the world.
The way a person fulfills his purpose in life as a
   Bodhisattva is by doing Shakubuku.
In every action and conduct, members carry out the
   practice of Shakubuku.

Several of the movement's campaign songs also emphasize the primacy of doing Shakubuku, stressing the importance of Shakubuku in relation to the attainment of personal benefits and the larger goal of world peace through the recruitment and conversion of outsiders. In addition to the song cited at the beginning of this chapter, there were two others that I heard repeatedly - sometimes two or three times an evening - during the course of my membership. One, called the "Song of Shakubuku" and sung to the tune "I've Been Working on the Railroad," goes:

> I've been doing Shakubuku
> All the live long day
> I've been chanting Daimoku
> To get me on my way.
>
> The eyes of the world are upon me
> And I shall never stray
> Can't you hear the members calling
> And happiness is on your way.

And the other song, sung to the tune of "The Notre Dame Fight Song," directs members to:

> Go - Go - Go Shakubuku
> Spread the word, get benefits too
> Do someone a favor now,
>   Take them with you to Gojukai
> Da - Da - Da - Da
>
> Whether the odds be great or small
>   Shakubuku wins over all
> And a chanting we will go
>   Onward to victory!
>
> Go - Go - Go Shakubuku
> Chant Daimoku to help you through
> Invite strangers, invite friends
>   Invite your neighbors, invite your kin.

> Whether the odds be great or small
> Shakubuku wins over all
> And a chanting we will go
> Onward to victory!

Shakubuku is not only a most important and time-consuming activity, it is also the one activity that arches over and ties together all NSA activities and campaigns. "In every action a member makes and in every activity he participates, he is or can be," in the words of one informant, "carrying out the practice of Shakubuku." Shakubuku thus refers to all lines of action, whether they be individual or collective, conducted for the manifest purpose of advancing NSA towards its goals. And, as such, it is the one major activity that renders NSA a true social movement; for it is through the variety of activities and practices that constitute the doing of Shakubuku that NSA reaches out and acts upon the larger society in order to promote its interests and extend its span of influence. Shakubuku is, then, as one perceptive member succinctly stated, "the lifeblood of the philosophy and movement," for "without it," he added, "there would be no NSA."

Strategic Considerations Underlying the Doing of Shakubuku

In light of NSA's preoccupation with Shakubuku and the deployment of members in this work, the question arises as to how the movement actually goes about this business in a relatively organized and strategic manner. Up to this point we have discussed the emphasis NSA places on the doing of Shakubuku as the general means to advancing its interests, but we have yet to examine the underlying strategies guiding this work, the various organizational mechanisms and tactical lines of action constituting this work, and the problematic considerations on which these strategies and lines of action are based. Before delineating the major strategies and practices constitutive of Shakubuku, let us first consider what is logically prior: the set of problematic considerations impinging on and influencing NSA's choice of strategies and tactics.

In attempting to make sociological sense of the means by which NSA has sought to act upon its environment so as to advance towards its objectives, it seems huristically useful to begin by considering this matter of outward-reaching strategies and tactics from the standpoint of a recently emergent approach to collective phenomena variously referred to as the resource mobilization or management perspective.[4]

From this vantage point, social movements are generally seen as relatively organized and instrumentally oriented collective enterprises engaged in the process of resource appropriation, mobilization, and management for the purpose of promoting or resisting a change within the society of which they are a part. While all movements, as well as all voluntary associations and formal organizations, are seen as being confronted with this problem of resource appropriation and management, it is axiomatic that the way in which it is handled will vary with differences in group goals and ideology, with differences in the scarcity or availability and elasticity of the resources deemed as most important to the realization of group goals, and with differences in societal or public reaction to movement goals, values, and tactical practices.

It thus follows that the outward-reaching strategies and tactics developed and employed by social movements can be conceptualized as instrumental procedures calculated to deal with two interrelated and ongoing problems: 1) the problem of resource appropriation, whether the resource be manpower, money, votes, the support of community influentials, legitimacy and respectability in the public eye, or a combination thereof; and 2) the problem of establishing some kind of working relationship with the larger environment so as to facilitate the resource appropriation effort. Accordingly, the success of a movement's outward-reaching goal attainment efforts is largely dependent on the extent to which the strategies and tactics it develops and employs enables it to appropriate from the social environment those resources deemed as most vital to its interests and enables it to foster a viable relationship with its community or society of operation in order to expand its resource appropriation opportunities and secure its existence as a collective entity.

Although this view of the operation of social movements is, perhaps, overly rationalistic, it does provide a useful point of departure for considering the means by which NSA has acted upon its social environment.

Regarding the question of resources and their mobilization, the strategies and tactics developed and employed by NSA are aimed primarily toward the mustering of manpower or recruits and public respectability and legitimacy. While nearly all movements value these resources to a greater or lesser extent, they are of greater importance to NSA than to many movements for two basic reasons. First, NSA is exceedingly more expansionistic than most movements and voluntary associations. Although not all movements are equally concerned with attracting an ever-increasing number of adherents, a good many, being convinced of the appropriateness of their cause and of the uniqueness and veracity of their message, set few, if any, limits on their recruitment designs. And some are even more aggressive and expansionistic than most in this regard, seeing recruitment and multiplication of their ranks not only as a sign of success and as a means to one or more ends, but even, at times, as an end in itself. As already suggested, such has been the case with Sokagakkai and NSA. Second is the related fact that NSA is a proselyting movement, a movement that seeks to modify the larger social world by incorporating an ever-increasing number of people within its span of influence and by remolding them in accordance with its ideals. In light of these considerations, NSA is confronted with the strategic problem of how best to lure outsiders into its fold in order to expand its ranks and move toward the realization of its primary objective of Kosen-rufu.

But here NSA is confronted with another problem: the fact that it is a culturally transplanted movement with an underlying philosophy and set of ritual practices that are rather off-beat in comparison to conventional religious beliefs and practices in this country can function to encumber its recruitment efforts by rendering it somewhat strange and suspect in the public eye. Hence, the strategic problem of how best to render itself respectable in the eyes of the larger society in order to facilitate its recruitment efforts.

Given these two valuable resources - people power or converts and legitimacy within the public eye - in conjunction with the fact that NSA is a culturally transplanted movement whose existence is not common knowledge, it is confronted with a third major problematic consideration: how can it best reach out and gain the attention of those not yet aware of its existence, much less its promises, practices, and the like. If it is to make any headway in its resource appropriation efforts, then it must also consider the ongoing strategic problem of how best to bridge the access or information gap between itself and the outside world.

In light of these strategic considerations, not only does NSA's preoccupation with Shakubuku and the deployment of members in this work become more understandable, but it is clear that certain organizational strategies and mechanisms have to exist that enable NSA to reach out and make contact with outsiders for the purposes of facilitating its recruitment efforts and bringing in potential converts and, once this is accomplished, that enable it to win over those brought in by promoting and securing nominal conversion.

How, then, has NSA gone about this work of information dissemination and resource appropriation, or what it refers to as "doing Shakubuku"? More specifically, (1) how has it dealt with the problem of outreach and information dissemination? What kinds of organizational mechanisms and practices has it developed and employed for the purpose of reaching out and making contact? And in what domains of social life has it channeled its efforts in this regard? (2) How has it strategically sought to establish a viable relationship with its community of operation? To what extent has it attempted to render itself respectable and legitimate within the public eye, and how has it gone about this face work? And (3) how has it dealt with the problem of securing recruits and nominal converts? What kinds of communicative lines and interpersonal tactics do members employ for the purpose of luring outsiders into the fold. And once recruits have been secured, how does the movement go about the business of promoting and securing nominal conversion? These problematic considerations and the strategies and tactics NSA has employed to deal with them obviously merge and overlap in actuality, but they will be examined separately for descriptive and analytical purposes in the remainder of this chapter.

REACHING OUT AND MAKING CONTACT: TOWARD BRIDGING THE INFORMATION GAP

Whatever the interests or values a movement seeks to promote and advance, some attention must be initially given to the problem of reaching out and establishing contact with those outsiders who constitute the target group or constituency that the collectivity in question is attempting to appeal to and influence. In fact, this problem of how best to gain the attention of those not yet aware of the information or values in question must be dealt with prior to, if not apart from, the problem of how to stimulate interest once contact is established. In military parlance, for example, the question of when and where to engage the enemy must be addressed prior to strategically mapping out the details of the attack.

In considering the possible strategies and means through which this problem of engagement can be dealt with by any collectivity whose viability is partially dependent on successful information diffusion and promotion, it seems reasonable to begin by asking two general questions. First, what are the variety of accessible socio-spatial settings in the larger society in which contact can be established?   And secondly, what are the variety of generally available modes of communication through which information can be imparted?

Regarding the first question, most spatial settings or domains or social life can be conceptualized in terms of a continuum ranging from public places to private places.[5] "Public places" refers to those regions or areas in a community or society that are freely and officially accessible to most members of that community or society.   "Private places," on the other hand, refers to those spatial domains that are off-limits to all but acknowledged members and guests, and in which uninvited outsiders are considered as actual or potential intruders or invaders.   Examples of the former would include shopping malls, community sidewalks, airports, bus stations, and the like; whereas country clubs, one's personal office, a sorority or fraternity house, and one's apartment or home are illustrative of the latter.

Regarding the modes or channels of information dissemination, it would seem as though all such means can be conceptualized most generally in terms of a continuum ranging from direct to indirect communication.[6] By direct communication, I refer to all information, whether it be verbal or non-verbal, that is imparted during face-to-face interaction or when two or more individuals or groups are physically co-present. In contrast, indirect communication refers to information dissemination by means of institutionalized mass communication mechanisms, such as radio, television, and newspapers, or by means of institutionalized but individualized and privatized communication mechanisms, such as the mail and telephone.

The cross-classification of these two dimensions suggests four general and fairly distinct possibilities that are more or less available to most groups interested in gaining the attention of outsiders or a target constituency for the purpose of promoting and selling a particular product or message, whether it is a political candidate or program, a religious doctrine or practice, a self-help formula, or a new line of clothing or automobiles. Figure 1 schematically summarizes these possibilities, each of which is distinguished by the spatial domain of social life in which contact can be established and by the general means through which contact can be initiated and information imparted.

Given these alternative outreach and information dissemination possibilities, the question arises as to which of these NSA has typically employed. That is, in what spatial domains of the social world has it typically sought to establish contact, and by what means or mechanisms has it generally attempted to do so?

Direct Information Dissemination and Promotion in Public Places

One need not be a longstanding member of NSA to come to the realization that it has concentrated its outreach and information dissemination efforts in public places by direct means. Before and during my tenure as a member, public places constituted the one major crack in the larger society into which the movement constantly sent its members to spread the word about chanting, to enhance public awareness of its existence, and to lure outsiders into its fold. The direct outreach and promotion mechanisms and practices it has employed include sidewalk proselytizing, promotion of movement literature, holding seminars on college campuses, participating in ritualized public events, and sponsoring and staging events for public consumption. I will briefly examine each of these in order of the relative frequency with which they have been employed.

Face-to-Face Proselytizing in Public Places. I noted earlier that Shakubuku refers to all lines of activity, whether they be individual or collective, conducted for the manifest purpose of acting upon the outside world in such a way as to advance NSA towards its goals. Of these varied lines of activities, the one that first comes to mind when the word Shakubuku is mentioned and the one that is most frequently employed is face-to-face proselytizing in public places.

Seldom a day or evening goes by in which some members do not spend at least fifteen to thirty minutes beating the pavement in search of prospects. Before and frequently after movement meetings, for example, members are instructed to spend some time foraging for recruits and spreading the word. Since meetings of one type or another

DIRECT MEANS

| Direct Information Dissemination and Promotion in Public Places (face-to-face, leafleting, petitioning and proselyting on sidewalks; participation in public events; staging events for pubilc consumption) | Direct Information Dissemination and Promotion in Private Places (door-to-door leafleting, petition- ing and proselyting; information dissemination along the lines of promoter's interpersonal networks) |

PUBLIC_____PRIVATE
DOMAIN   DOMAIN

| Indirect Information Dissemination and Promotion through Institution- alized Mass Communication Communication Mechanisms (advertising and campaigning via radio, television, and newspapers) | Indirect Information Dissemination and Promotion through Institution- alized but Individualized and Privatized Communication Mecha- nisms (advertising and campaigning via mail and telephone) |

INDIRECT MEANS

FIGURE 1: Schematic Classification of General Outreach and Engagement Possibilities for Information Dissemination and Promotion.

are commonly held at least six nights a week, excursions into the public domain of the social world for the purpose of recruitment are thus common practice. During these forays, members will work sidewalks, shopping malls, and the like in teams of two or three, or they will situate themselves near the entrances of grocery stores, liquor stores, laundromats, the like, initiating contact with whoever passes by or happens to enter or exit from such places of business. Not only are nearly all public places seen as fair hunting ground, but all outsiders who happen to be moving about in these places are seen as fair game. The issue of the kinds of communicative lines and interpersonal tactics employed once contact is established will be discussed later in the chapter.

Face-to-Face Promotion of Movement Literature in Public Places. In addition to approaching strangers in public places for the purpose of luring them to a meeting, they are also frequently approached in hopes of getting them to subscribe to or at least purchase or take a single copy of NSA's newspaper, the *World Tribune*. Its appeal, according to

Mr. Williams on the occasion of its 10th anniversary on August 15, 1974, is that unlike so many other papers which carry articles about miserble distrust and confusion all over the world,

> ... the pages of the *World Tribune* are like flower gardens containing the experiences of those NSA members who are leading a beautiful way of life. The *World Tribune* has gradually become a glorious record of mankind, like a burst of happiness that will remain for all posterity.

The newspaper is thus seen as an important vehicle for enhancing public awareness of and stimulating interest in the movement. As a consequence, the movement sponsors *World Tribune* promotion campaigns at the end of each month.

During these campaigns, which usually ran for a week, recruitment seemed to take a back seat to promoting the newspaper and attempting to increase its circulation. Even though the vast majority of subscribers are members, and even though I never observed a stranger shell out three to five dollars for a yearly subscription, members would still take to the streets to push the paper during these promotion campaigns. Whether members were actually able to get strangers to subscribe to or even buy a single copy of the paper did not seem terribly important, however; for the mere act of attempting to do so was seen as a mechanism for enhancing public awareness of the movement and for "planting," in the words of several members, "seeds of curiosity and interest." This and other reasons for engaging in such seemingly unproductive work will be discussed in more detail in a later chapter.

Conducting Public Seminars on College Campuses. Of the various public and quasi-public institutions in American society, the institution of higher learning has probably come closest to constituting a true marketplace for the dissemination and discussion of various and sundry ideas and philosphies. With a relatively high degree of commitment to the circulation of ideas and the freedom of argumentation and debate, American universities and colleges have been more open to the purveyors and promoters of new ideas and philosophies or old ideas with a new twist than have most other institutional domains of American life. And, as a consequence, not only have the campuses of higher education constituted a virtual magnet for such promoters, but they have also frequently constituted the seedbed for the germination and spread of new ideas and movements.

It is therefore no surprise that NSA, as a proselytizing movement scanning the horizon in search of fertile soil for planting seeds of curiosity and interest, would turn to the university and college campuses of America during the turbulent and change-oriented atmosphere of the latter sixties and early seventies. Beginning in late 1968, NSA formally entered this quasi-public "world of disillusioned hopes" by launching a seminar program consisting of one- to two-hour lectures conducted by Mr. Williams and occasionally President Ikeda. With the goal of promoting and spreading "the humanistic teachings of Nichiren Daishonin's life philosophy" and of awakening students "to new dreams for their own future and that of the world," Mr. Williams would explain to students:

> ... the 'Philosophy of Happiness,' relating Buddhist terms directly to their own daily life. 'Hell is how you feel when you get all D's and heaven is when you get A's ... 'Heaven and Hell are not waiting for you when you die, but rather are conditions in your life right now. So why don't you work hard to change your life of hell into heaven?' Then he (would) give them the key to this happy life - Nam-Myoho-Renge-Kyo.[7]

The first such seminar was held on November 8, 1968, at UCLA. Since then, Mr. Williams conducted these promotion seminars at more than eighty colleges and universities across the country, including such well-known universities as Harvard, Princeton, Cornell and Berkeley, as well as at many smaller and lesser-known schools, such as Western College in Oxford, Ohio, Pierce College in Los Angeles, Temple Buell College in Denver, and Eastfield College in Dallas. Considering that over eighty percent of these seminars were conducted in the years between late 1968 and the beginning of 1972, a period in which the mood of the campuses was relatively turbulent and exploratory, it appears that the seminars represented a strategic attempt to exploit this fertile campus soil until its potential yield began to wane. NSA thus began to conduct fewer and fewer campus seminars. Twenty-six such seminars were held in 1971, for example, but only six in 1972, four in

1973, and only one or two in 1974 - a pattern of response that hints at NSA's accommodative flexibility and strategical ingenuity.

Participation in Conventional, Ritualized Public Events. The extent to which NSA is constantly on the look out for openings in the larger society through which it can impart information and stimulate interest, and the extent of its accommodative flexibility in this regard, is nicely illustrated by its practice of participating in various public events sponsored by the communities in which it is operating or by various groups within these communities.

In each of the larger urban areas across the country in which NSA has mustered a sizeable following and developed a viable organization, such as in Los Angeles, San Francisco, Chicago, the Washington, D.C. area, and New York, it has also organized and developed a Young Women's Division Fife and Drum Corps, a Young Men's Division Brass Band, and a Men's Division Pipe and Drum Corps, as well as various dance teams and singing groups. Much like combat troops standing-by for deployment to the front, these various performance teams are readily available for mobilization whenever an opportunity arises, whether it be marching in holiday parades, performing at a noonday concert series at a public park or shopping mall, or putting on a pre-game or half-time show for public consumption at an athletic event. Illustrative of the movement's eagerness to participate in such events and of the extent to which its performance teams are standing-by on ready alert is the following episode described in the April 7, 1975 issue of the *World Tribune*:

> March 29. Lake Arrowhead, Ca. - A Parade: the call went out from the American Headquarters Building less than 24 hours before it was to begin - 130 miles away.
>
> The Golden Eagle Bagpipe Band responded immediately. Leaders contacted the band members into the late hours of Saturday night. 'Tomorrow we have a parade. Get ready!'
>
> The Blue Jay, California, Chamber of Commerce needed help, and it turned to NSA for assistance. Groups were cancelling out of their Easter Day Parade pell mell, and they had heard they could count on NSA in any emergency. 'NSA can do the impossible - call them.'

They did. Sixteen hours later, 85 pipers gathered for
Gongyo at the American Headquarters Building in Santa
Monica ... Like the Minutemen of the Revolutionary War,
the Men's Division was ready for anything at a moment's
call. Many of them didn't even know where the parade was
to be held, or what uniform to wear. Some had been
members of the band less than two weeks. But they all
came to help in any way they could.

Following a vigorous Gongyo, rides were quickly
arranged, directions to the resort area near Lake Arrowhead
were given, and in 10 minutes the room was vacant. The
bagpipers were on their way ...

This eagerness to use public events as occasions for promotion
and the pains to which NSA will go in this regard is illustrated even
more graphically by the extravagant and enthusiastic show it put on
before 33,000 spectators at Dodger Stadium prior to the September 21,
1974 game between the L.A. dodgers and the San Diego Padres.
With an Hawaiian theme, the show consisted of over 1000 costumed
members singing and dancing amidst a backdrop of artificial palm
trees, grass huts, two mountains and a large smoke-belching volcano.
The show lasted for around thirty minutes and, judging from the
applause it provoked, favorably impressed the spectators. As the
Dodger radio broadcaster commented following the show:

Amazing. Must have been the most impressive show
I've ever seen at Dodger Stadium or any any ball park, for
that matter. I wish more of you had been here to see it. It
was really beautiful. NSA deserves to be congratulated for
all the effort that went into it. It was every bit as good as
the half-time shows at the Hula Bowl in Hawaii and at the
Super Bowl. And the enthusiasm which was displayed
seemed to rub off on the fans. It pepped everybody up.
What a way to start a ball game.

Such extravagant public performances are somewhat atypical,
however. What is more common is for one or two of NSA's bands
and drill teams to march, along with other bands, in ritualized public
parades commorating some important date in the country's history or

in deference to some religious or national holiday. During my tenure as a member, for example, NSA bands could be seen marching in Thanksgiving Day Parades across the country, and seldom was there a local parade in which at least one NSA band was not among the marchers.

Participating in such public events, whether they are ritualized parades or shows sponsored by some local organization, represents, then, an additional strategic means for reaching out, establishing contact, and stimulating awareness of and interest in NSA. As one member of the YWD Drill Team told me, "The Fife and Drum Corps, the Drill Team, the Brass Band, and the Bagpipe Band are all very good means for doing Shakubuku."

Sponsoring and Staging Events for Public Consumption. In addition to participating in conventional, ritualized public events for the purpose of information dissemination and promotion, protest groups and movements, as well as politicians and the news media, often create and stage events or happenings for public consumption.[8] Although these two strategic maneuvers may seem quite similar, there are several important differences between them.

First, the former is usually an event or occasion that is in keeping with a cultural tradition or that is sponsored by the larger community or some longstanding and respectable organization within that community, such as the Shriners or the L.A. Dodgers; whereas the latter is an event or happening that is usually sponsored by some emergent grouping or association that is outside of the mainstream. Secondly, the former is an event or occasion that is repetititve and anticipated - it is on the calendar so to speak, and is therefore more or less institutionalized; whereas the latter is relatively novel and usually unanticipated, at least initially anyway. And third, in the case of the former, many of the participants are usually members of associations other than the sponsoring group, which has either solicited or approved their particpation; whereas in the case of the latter, not only are the sponsors and participants one and the same, but the event or happening is frequently one that is neither solicited nor sanctioned by the larger society or community in which it is being staged. In short, the differences between the two are much the same as the differences between the politics of order and the politics of disorder.

As implied in the foregoing, such events are normally staged for the purpose of enhancing a group's visibility, dramatizing a particular plight or cause, and/or conveying a particular message. Furthermore, such events are most often sponsored and staged by a protest group for whom many of the more conventional engagement and promotion possibilities are frequently foreclosed for a variety of political, legal, and monetary reasons. But as NSA exemplifies, such events are also frequently manufactured and staged even when alternative engagement possibilities and means of influence are available and, in fact, employed.

The way in which NSA has employed this less conventional outreach and promotion tactic is through its annual General Meetings, which are commonly referred to in everyday life, as well as by NSA, as conventions. Although "conventions" are a common and ritualized feature of the bureaucratized, corporate world, NSA conventions consist of much more than a gathering of people who have congregated in order to listen to speeches, to nominate or elect leaders, to renew acquaintances and socialize, and to get reinvigorated and make individual determinations for the year ahead. Although some of these characteristic features of conventions typified NSA's first two conventions, held in 1963 and 1965, these annual affairs have since been expanded to include parades, fireworks, cultural festivals or shows, and the like.

This shift in format began with the third general meeting, held in New York in August 1966, the same year in which NSA began to actively Americanize its operation and expand its constituency to include more than disgruntled Japanese war brides and their American husbands and families. This particular convention marked the debut of what the movement refers to as its cultural festivals or shows: extravagant performances on stage or in the middle of an arena consisting of dancing, singing, and various skits reflecting the theme of the convention. These shows are organized and performed solely by members, and frequently resemble, on the surface anyway, such well-known shows as the IceCapades or Follies. In 1967, a parade was added to the format, and at the 1968 convention in Hawaii, both of these were brought together - a parade along Waikiki Beach and a show depicting the culture of the Islands - "to create a huge mass movement which the entire community could see."[9] This was the first convention that was actually called a "Convention" rather than a "General

Meeting." Since 1968, each convention became noticeably larger and more extravagant and flamboyant than the preceding one. As members would often say in anticipation of the 1975 convention, held again in Hawaii:

> You've just gotta go. The whole world is going to be watching, and this one is going to be bigger and better than ever - even bigger and better than the San Diego Convention.

The San Diego Convention was held during the first weekend in April 1974, with between ten to fifteen thousand members from all over the country in attendance, all of whom were attired in the convention uniform: a white shirt, a sky-blue pullover sweater with a San Diego Convention insignia over the left pocket area, and white trousers. This two-day production included a one-and-a-half-hour parade through the streets of downtwon San Diego, a fireworks display promoted as the largest ever in North America, a cultural show on ice at the San Diego Sports Arena, and a General Business Meeting featuring President Ikeda at the helm.

Since this weekend affair was staged not only by and for NSA but also for the purpose of reaching out and promoting NSA to the larger community, the question arises as to how effective was NSA in this quest. Although it is difficult to provide a conclusive answer, the manner in which the convention was portrayed by the local media suggests that NSA was at least partially successful in promoting itself in a positive way. One San Diego television station, for example, reported the following on its 11:00 p.m. news broadcast on the evening of the first day of the convention:

> Today was an ideal day for a parade, and there was one. Fifty thousand people lined Broadway between 9th and Columbia Street for the Nichiren Shoshu Buddhist parade. At the head of the parade was Daisaku Ikeda, president of the 20 million Nichiren Shoshu members. In the parade were more than 3,000 people, with the line stretching a mile. There were bagpipe bands, fife and drum corps, and brass bands. The parade came on the first day of the

Buddhist's convention here in San Diego, with some 10,000 people in attendance.

Now I must admit that parades don't fascinate me as much as they used to, but fireworks still do. And tonight, those same folks who brought the parade gave us a spectacular show in the sky. It started with a massive traffic turnout. The call for police direction came a half-an-hour before the fireworks started. Crowds by the thousands (mostly NSA members) flocked to the MIssion Bay Park area, and at exactly 8 o'clock the first explosion of fireworks lit up the sky.

The more than 10,000 members of the Nichiren Shoshu Buddhist sect financed the giant fireworks display. A spokesman said that the display cost the Buddhists $20,000. In all, that means that it cost the Buddhists a penny apiece, since the cult boasts 20 million members ... Those holding the convention will wind up ceremonies tomorrow with a general meeting at the Sports arena. But for tonight, it was fireworks on a giant scale. This fireworks display is a gift to the people of San Diego from the more than 10,000 members of the Buddhist sect holding their convention in this area.

And to the members of the Buddhist sect, we say thank you.

The following morning, the *San Diego Union* devoted a full page pictorial to the parade, as well as a one-column article titled "Buddhists Celebrate Happiness."

Nichiren Shoshu Academy members expressed their philosophy of joy and happiness yesterday by parading it downtown on Broadway.

For 1½ hours, 3000 participants marched and danced down the street. The parade was sponsored by the Buddhist sect that brought 11,500 delegates to a two-day meeting that ends here today.

The parade preceded a $20,000 fireworks display fired from Fiesta Island in Mission bay and billed as the most spectacular show ever seen on the West Coast.

San Diego Police Department estimates put the parade crowd at 40,000.

One of the most popular units in the parade was the Washington D.C. Brass Band and Eagle Buglers. The dancers and marchers in their hot-pink and green costumes with turquoise cummerbunds got the crowd's applause as they performed 'Get it On'...

Marchers came from 30 major cities in the United States, Panama, Puerto Rico, Venezuela and Mexico. The parade included three floats. The Mexico float featured an animated bullfighter and snorting black bull. There was a 'world peace float' and one constructed from 40,000 flowers flown here from Hawaii for the parade ...[10]

The following year, in July 1975, NSA held a three-day convention in Hawaii. With plans for a cultural show atop a floating island stage off Waikiki Beach and a night parade with synchronized flashing lights attached to the participants marching along Kalakaua Avenue, this production was to be the most expensive, extravagant, and flamboyant one to date. The theme song of the convention - "Pearly Shells, Pearly Shells Shining in the Sun" - was selected to symbolize "the coming of world peace, with all the shells representing people embracing the Gohonzon and the sun representing President Ikeda's guidance and compassion for the members."[11] More importantly, every event and happening was planned to be held outdoors so that "the general public will be able to view the extravaganza."[12] As one member, who was bubbling over with excitement and anticipation, related:

This one is really going to be special. It's going to be the biggest Shakubuku event ever. Everybody knows about it, and the whole world will be watching.

This sponsoring and staging of extravagant events for public consumption thus represents another tactical means through which NSA has attempted to exploit the accessibility of public places in its ongoing effort to reach out and gain the attention of the larger social world.

Direct Information Dissemination and Promotion in Private Places

In addition to engaging outsiders in public places by various face-to-face means, outsiders can also be contacted and brought into a state of direct information flow on their own turf. Since it is commonly understood that private places, such as one's residential domain, are off-limits to all but acknowledged claimants and guests, and that uninvitees, and particularly total strangers, are not normally welcome, even on the doorstep, it is often assumed that the claimants or occupants are less vulnerable to being confronted by promoters and solicitors than when scurrying about in public places. But, as most homeowners and apartment residents will testify, as well as many solicitors, this is an erroneous assumption; for many collective enterprises engaged in some type of promotion work do, in fact, attempt to reach directly into the private sphere of social life in order to enhance awareness of and sell or solicit support for a particular product, message, or cause.

For those individuals or groups attempting to promote by face-to-face means in private places, there are several general tacks that can be taken: contact can be attempted and information disseminated by means of door-to-door canvassing; or promotion and recruitment can be channeled along the lines of promoters' interpersonal networks; or both tacks can be pursued.[13]

While many promoters follow the door-to-door route - Fuller Brush salesmen, political campaigners, and members of the Jehovah's Witnesses movement, to name a few, NSA has generally eschewed this possibility. Although in the early years of the movement Japanese members attempted to gain entree into the homes of non-members who were strangers, a selective process was at work in that such attempts were structured by the fact that the target population was usually of Japanese descent. Hence, promotion and recruitment were being channeled along lines of ethnicity.

While it is reasonable to assume that some NSA members attempt to promote by means of door-to-door canvassing among strangers, I neither participated in nor observed this practice during my tenure as a member. Moreover, I cannot recall hearing members being instructed to promote in this way. To be sure, members will knock on the doors of homes and apartments, but it was my experience that the occupants were never total strangers. That is, if they were not inactive members, they had at least previously subscribed to the *World Tribune* or were usually acquaintances, friends, or kin of one or more members.

Although the invasion of the private residential domains of strangers by means of door-to-door canvassing does not seem to be formally prohibited, the point to emphasize is that NSA, in contrast to many groups whose viability is partially dependent on successful promotion, does not actively promote and recruit in this way. The reasons for not exploiting this outreach and engagement possibility seem to have little to do with manpower considerations, but seem to be based more on NSA's accommodative orientation and its acute sensitivity to the image it provokes among outsiders. Since these concerns will be discussed a bit later, let me merely note here what NSA seems to know well: that private space is relatively sacred in comparison to public space; and, as a consequence, that rapping on strange doors and intruding into the private spatial domains of outsiders can often be more counterproductive when it comes to promotion and image-building than propagation in public places.

In addition to promoting in private places by means of random door-to-door canvassing, Figure 1 notes that promotion in the private sphere of social life can also be channeled along the lines of members' extra-movement interpersonal networks. As suggested earlier, NSA actively exploits this possibility. Not only are the doors that are knocked on usually the doors of acquaintances, friends, or kin, but members are commonly instructed to promote and recruit among those outsiders with whom they have interpersonal ties. During recruitment and *World Tribune* promotion campaigns, I was constantly asked, for example: "Don't you know someone who would be interested in coming to a meeting?" I was also constantly badgered about my wife: "When are you going to bring her to a meeting?" "Isn't she interested in practicing with you?"

Although it is reasonable to assume that the members of most movements and groups engaged in some type of promotion work will channel some of their efforts along the lines of their interpersonal networks, it is important to bear in mind that not all movements can exploit this possibility to the same extent for the reason that not all movements share the same network attributes. That is, since core membership in some movements is contingent on the severance of all or most extra-movement interpersonal ties, whereas other movements are less demanding in this regard, it follows that movements can vary in the extent to which they are linked to or isolated from other groups and networks within their respective communities of operation.

Since movements can vary in the extent to which they constitute open or closed networks or systems of social relations, it follows that movements' outreach and engagement opportunities can also vary considerably. Accordingly, it seems reasonable to suggest the following propositions regarding a movement's network attributes and the channeling of its promotion and recruitment efforts:

> Movements which are structurally more exclusive, closed, and isolated, but which can operate above ground - such as the Hare Krishna movement - will have to concentrate their promotion and recruitment efforts in public places to a greater extent than will movements which are linked to outside networks via members' external interpersonal ties.

And obversely:

> Movements which are structurally more open and inclusive - such as NSA - will be able to channel their recruitment efforts along the lines of members' preexisting social networks to a greater extent than movements which are structurally more exclusive and insulated.

Whether such differences in network attributes and corresponding differences in outreach and promotion opportunities make any significant difference in the success of a movement's recruitment efforts, as measured in terms of the number of outsiders actually recruited, is hypothetically dependent not only on the movement's value orientation, but also on whether recruitment among extra-movement acquaintances, friends, and kin typically yields a greater return in terms of actual recruits than does recruitment among strangers in public places or in private places by means of door-to-door canvassing. If the latter is more productive, then not only are movements' network attributes of little relevance to their spread and growth, but recruitment along the lines of members' extra-movement networks would be, from a cost-benefit standpoint, largely a waste of time, energy, and manpower. But if recruitment among strangers, whether in public places or on their own turf by means of door-to-door promotion, is not as productive as recruitment among acquaintances, friends and relatives, then a movement's network attributes constitute a significant and important structural variable in relation to the movement's growth and spread. In the following chapter we will attempt to shed empirical light on this problem and the foregoing propositions by examining the recruitment channels from which NSA members have been drawn.

Indirect Promotion through Institutionalized Mass Communication Channels and/or Individualized and Privatized Communication Mechanisms

In addition to engaging outsiders by reaching directly into the public and private domains of social life through the various means discussed above, outsiders can also be contacted and brought into a state of information flow by various institutionalized but indirect communication mechanisms - such as the newspaper, radio, television, telephone, and mail - that are officially accessible to nearly all individuals and groups interested in information dissemination and promotion.

Although many movements, as well as most large corporate and institutionalized religious denominations and political parties, commonly advertise via one or more of these indirect means, NSA has generally refrained from exploiting these possibilities. To be sure, some of its activities are occasionally covered by the local media within the communities in which it operates,[14] as well as by nationally circulated magazines such as *Newsweek* and *Time*.[15] And undoubtedly the hope of media coverage is in mind when the movement's performance units are on stage. But being the subject of media coverage is different from taking out newspaper ads or purchasing radio and television advertising time, neither of which is a common NSA practice. Nor is NSA in the habit of plastering advertisements on telephone poles, store windows, billboards, and the like.

But what about the promotion campaigns associated with the *World Tribune*? As noted earlier, this newspaper is clearly seen as an important means of information dissemination. However, it is seldom, if ever, mailed directly to total strangers. Instead, it is peddled face-to-face in public places and is circulated via mail primarily among members or their extra-movement acquaintances. Insofar as promotion via telephone is concerned, this communication mechanism is used primarily for disseminating information from one member to another and not for contacting strangers or bringing them into the movement's span of influence.

As the foregoing suggests, NSA has not generally sought to reach out and promote through the various institutionalized but indirect means of communication officially accessible to most individuals and groups.[16] Nor, as we learned earlier, has promotion in private places by means of door-to-door canvassing figured significantly in NSA's outreach and engagement efforts. Rather, it has channeled its outreach and promotion efforts primarily in public places by various face-to-face means and along the lines of members' extra-movement interpersonal networks.

Accordingly, NSA's outreach and engagement strategy can be characterized as follows: face-to-face promotion in public places, including occasional participation in ritualized public events and periodic staging of events for public consumption, coupled with concentrated promotion among members' extra-movement acquaintances, friends, and kin.

This general outreach strategy points to the accessible cracks or openings in the environment in which NSA has concentrated its promotion efforts and provides us with an understanding of the means through which NSA has attempted to gain the attention of outsiders and disseminate information. But the nature and content of "doing Shakubuku" once contact is established still remains somewhat problematic. Once a stranger is stopped on the street, for example, what is he or she told and how are members instructed to conduct themselves during such encounters? Or when in the presence of extra-movement acquaintances, friends, or family members, whether at work, school, or home, how are members to go about the work of Shakubuku? How, in short, does the movement go about the business of getting outsiders to do, think, or feel what they want them to do, think and feel once contact has been established, and what are the major considerations underlying the choice of the strategies and tactics employed. Or, in the language of the resource appropriation and management approach, by what means has NSA sought to extract from its social environment, once contact has been made, those resources deemed as most necessary to advancing towards its objectives.

As indicated earlier, NSA's outward-reaching goal attainment strategies and tactics have been directed primarily towards the appropriation of two basic resources: (1) public legitimacy and respectability; and (2) recruits or potential converts. In the remainder of the chapter we will delineate and discuss the strategies and tactics by means of which NSA has attempted to secure these two resources.

DRAMATIC INGRATIATION: SECURING RESPECTABILITY IN THE PUBLIC EYE

That NSA sees the success of its recruitment efforts and its collective viability as being partially contingent on its ability to foster and maintain a favorable and respectable public image is continuously reflected in the *World Tribune*, in leaders' directives or guidance, in the speeches and ventures of President Ikeda and Mr. Williams, and in various movement practices, including some of the outreach and engagement mechanisms and practices outlined above - such as its practice of participating in ritualized public events, the kinds of public events it stages, and its disinclination to invade the private domains of strangers by calling them on the phone or by rapping on their domicile doors. As illustrative of this concern with its public image, consider the following guidance based on a 1968 speech delivered by President Ikeda and reported in the October 7, 1968 edition of the *World Tribune*:

> As members of Nichiren Shoshu we should have good common sense so that people will get an accurate impression of the meaning of Kosen-rufu and of our Shakubuku activities. It is a pity to have to admit that some members act foolishly and cause misunderstanding of this organization and President Ikeda's spirit. When we explain Nichiren Shoshu and the life-philosophy of Nichiren Shoshu to

someone,they listen to our words, but at the same time they watch our behavior. What we say, how we say it, our manners, our dress are all under scrutiny.

On many occasions President Ikeda has said that 90 percent of the people are watching us, not listening to us. As a result, our behavior in society is directly influential on the outcome of the Kosen-rufu campaign. Even one careless word can cause great misunderstanding. One indiscretion will make a potential member misunderstand Nichiren Shoshu and keep him from accepting the Gohonzon ...

A more recent *World Tribune* editorial similarly expressed this concern by noting that the movement "is coming more and more into the public eye" and that members should always make a conscious effort to conduct themselves so as to "prove the high value of the Gohonzon" and not "tarnish the name of NSA" or "inhibit our movement for peace."[17] Or as a middle-level leader put it one evening during a discussion meeting:

The point to keep in mind is that many non-members judge NSA by the way each member presents himself. If anyone of us conducts ourself in an obnoxious and disrespectful manner, all people who come into contact with us are going to think all of NSA is like we are. We should therefore be aware of how we look and sound to the general public and strive to make a good impression. This is a subtle but very important form of Shakubuku.

Given this sensitivity to the way in which the movement is perceived by the general public and the premium that is apparently placed on securing a favorable public image, the question arises as to how NSA has strategically gone about the business of attempting to render itself respectable and legitimate within the public eye, without, at the same time, totally undermining its alleged ideological and problem-solving uniqueness. Based upon my experiences and observations as a member and on my content analysis of the *World Tribune*, it seems as though NSA has strategically attempted to deal with this problem by means of a type of accommodative strategy that I think can be best conceptualized as "dramatic ingratiation."

By an accommodative strategy, I refer to the process of strategically taking note of and adapting to various perceived societal values, traditions, and normative constraints; the process of "fitting-in" or deferring to certain traditions, values, and situations by adjusting one's lines of action accordingly. And by dramatic ingratiation, I refer to the process of strategically attempting to gain the favor and blessing of others by conducting and presenting oneself in a manner that projects an image that is reflective of fitting-in and deferential regard for certain values, traditions, and proprieties perceived to be important to those whose favor is being courted.[18] At the group or movement level, dramatic ingratiation thus refers to a type of instrumental accommodative strategy aimed at controlling the environment for the purpose of attaining the movement's objectives by means of fostering the impression that its values, aims, and conduct are in conformity with certain values, traditions, and normative standards within its community or society of operation.[19]

The relevance of this strategy to NSA is manifested in four discernible practices or tactics that it has employed in its effort to render itself respectable and legitimate in the public eye: (1) the tactic of articulating a linkage between its mission and values and the values and traditions of the larger society; (2) the practice of instructing members to be "winners" in all domains of social life; (3) the practice of celebrity ingratiation and endorsement seeking; and 4) the practice of instructing members to conduct themselves with propriety and deference when in the public eye. Each of these tactical practices will be elaborated in turn.

Value Congruence as a Means to Building Respectability and Legitimacy

One tactic of dramatic ingratiation is to impress upon others that you are in agreement with them by attempting to convince them that you share their views or values and that your interests are in accord with theirs. One way in which NSA has employed this tactic is by acknowledging and deferring to certain national traditions and ritualized public events commemorating some important date in the country's civic or religious history. The practice of participating in various public parades, the kinds of events it stages - with fireworks, parades, and the like, and the fact that it prominently displays the American flag at its Community Center and Headquarters Building are illustrative of such deference behavior. Along these same lines, NSA joined in the celebration of the nation's Bicentennial. Not only was a segment of the cultural show at the 1975 Hawaiian Convention devoted to the American Revolution, but the movement sought and received permission from the American Revolution Bicentennial Commission to emblazon the front page of the *World Tribune* with the official Bicentennial symbol whenever it ran an article relating to America's founding. Accordingly, the *World Tribune* announced on May 1, 1974, that it would devote several columns a week "to exploring the traditions of America and the great men who made these traditions."

In addition to these practices, NSA has attempted to link its mission with that of this country's founding fathers and early pioneers by contending that the basic values and ideals these early Americans espoused and sought to attain are the very same as those underlying NSA's struggle and quest. It thus comes as no surprise that NSA proclaims it is the reincarnation of that early pioneer spirit and tradition, and that its members are the new pioneers carrying out the unfinished work of America's forefathers. The April 26, 1974 edition of the *World Tribune* notes, for example, in an editorial titled "Pioneer's Struggles are Backbone of Freedom," that:

> We are the pioneers of a new age of freedom. For that reason we have a formidable task ahead ... Like the pioneers of this great country, we are etching out a new way of life. The American colonists are good examples for us to follow ...

And a few days later, in a talk before the NSA headquarters staff, Mr. Williams emphasized that "people today have forgotten the pioneer tradition" and "it is" therefore "the mission of NSA to reawaken this spirit." This linkage between NSA and America's early pioneering spirit is even more clearly stated in a September 1974 *World Tribune* editorial based on a speech given by Mr. Williams:

For the American pioneers who opened up the West, the trip across the nation was like suicide. It was a tremendous challenge and very dangerous. Indians were everywhere and water was scarce. Like NSA members, these pioneers felt a sincere sense of mission. Even with no water for days on end, they traveled on and tried to continue their journey to reach their goal. Everyone who felt the urge to go West did so because they felt a sense of mission. Our quest for world peace has the same pioneering spirit as these people.

Although this value linkage is most frequently articulated in the *World Tribune* and in the speeches and guidance of Mr. Williams, it is also expressed from time to time among rank-and-file members and during discussion meetings. A case in point is the following extemporaneous guidance given by a lower-level leader during a district discussion meeting on July 5, 1974:

As you know, many of the members from this district and chapter are in Estes Park at Ft. Pioneer tonight. Along with 1500 other members and Mr. Williams, they are sharing the experience of life in the wilds. They have built a fort from scratch - a fort that looks exactly like Ft. Apache. They're not just having a vacation or playing cowboys and Indians. Rather, Mr. Williams is giving continuous guidance and encouraging members to develop a pioneer spirit - the spirit which characterized our forefathers and made possible their accomplishments. To celebrate July 4th - the birth of our nation - Mr. Williams led the members in morning Gongyo at 5:00 a.m.

What Mr. Williams is stressing is that the early pioneer spirit is seemingly lost in the U.S. today, but that the philosophy of Nichiren Daishonin is exactly in the same spirit of the founders of our country - the spirit to develop ourselves and make something great out of our society. This is the philosophy of True Buddhism. And Mr. Williams stresses that the mission of NSA is to keep alive that pioneer spirit and awaken many, many people to the values of such a high philosophy.

Not only has NSA attempted to establish a linkage between its values and mission and those of early America, but it has also seen fit to suggest that its Shakubuku-Discussion meetings are in keeping with the "town meetings of old" and epitomize what Democracy is all about. In fact, one 1974 edition of the *World Tribune* notes that "our discussion meetings are the epitome of a democratic society," and then adds that:

> Democracy seems to have become a mere formality, an abstract idea. Democracy retains its meaning only in our discussion meetings where every participant who plays a major role finds true equality and can freely express himself.

And in another edition, it is maintained that discussion meetings are

> ... continuing the tradition of America. Ideas are shared, new determinations are made, and each person pursues his dreams of happiness. What is unusual about a discussion meeting is that, more than any other gathering, it is a reflection of America. That is so both because every kind of American is there and because the means to fulfilling the American dream of freedom and happiness is there, ready for everyone to try ... NSA is the heart of America because it is bringing to life the ideals it has written into law. For a true picture of this, a person must visit a discussion meeting.[20]

Although this alleged congruence between what NSA's mission and what this country is ideally all about became more pronounced in the mid-1970s, it is a tactic that has been employed for a number of years. A November 1967 *World Tribune* editorial, titled "Pioneers of Happiness Observe Thanksgiving," refers to the original pilgrims, for example, and suggests that the members of NSA are the new pilgrims who are reviving the true spirit of Thanksgiving. And a July 1971 editorial succinctly states and summarizes this articulation with its title: "America's Heritage: Our Mission for Peace and Happiness."

"Winning" in Daily Life as a Means to Gaining Respectability and Legitimacy

In a society that glorifies winners and places a premium on competence and success, another way in which one can attempt to secure the favor and respect of others is by conducting oneself in a manner that is suggestive of competence and success. Simply put, one can attempt to act like a "winner." In keeping with this so-called "Protestant ethic" or strand of Calvinistic Protestantism, NSA's leadership and literature constantly encourages members to be winners in every domain of life and in whatever endeavor they undertake. Consider, for example, the following directives appearing as article titles in the *World Tribune*:

Become a Victorious Person, Doing the Utmost at Work
Become a Winner in Your Own Realm
Obligation to Excel at Work
Seek Perfection in Work and Daily Activities
Be a Winner in Every Facet of Life
Become Best Examples in Contemporary Society
Become a Model Worker at Place of Employment

But not only are members given general directives to "be winners in every aspect of daily life," they are also provided with instructions on how to be winners and with the rationale for becoming one. Students, for example, are instructed to have a diligent attitude toward their studies and to never miss their classes; they are reminded to be alert, attentive, and responsive in the classroom, and to never let their homework slide. Sons and daughters are instructed to do their chores, and are cautioned about missing dinner and arguing with their parents, so as not to give their "parents the wrong impression of NSA." Housewives are reminded that they should strive to create a happy, tidy, and respectable home. As explained in an October 1974 guidance article:

A woman may practice the teachings of Nichiren Daishonin and may be proud that she is a member of NSA. However, if unnecessary noise blares from her home late at night, if her home is always untidy, laundry never tended to, and if her household chores are never fulfilled, what will her neighbors think? She would be a nuisance. People in general would not only have little respect for her, but their thoughts of the teachings of Nichiren Daishonin would also be influenced.

And those members who are regularly employed are instructed never to take time off unnecessarily or arrive late to work, to complete whatever tasks they are assigned enthusiastically, to volunteer eagerly to do whatever tasks other employees ignore or refuse to carry out, and to gain the respect and trust of their fellow workers and superiors.

Why? What difference does it make insofar as NSA is concerned? The difference it makes, according to the following statements, is that NSA sees its reputation, its image, as being on the line.

> If we slack off on our job, act irresponsibly or unkindly, we will tarnish the name of NSA and only inhibit our movement for peace and happiness.[21]

> Those who are fired from their jobs ... or who are distrusted by fellow employees are creating anti-value and are slowing down the progress of Kosen-rufu.[22]

On the other hand, by heeding the above instructions and becoming a "winner" at work, not only will the member gain respect and admiration, but so will NSA. As one leader explained in response to a member's query about doing Shakubuku at work:

> By doing the best possible job in whatever our line of work, we will gain respect from people around us, and they will be impressed with NSA. And the amazing thing is that you won't even have to give them a *World Tribune* or ask them if they know about Nam-Myoho-Renge-Kyo, because by being a winner they will want to know what makes you stand out. And then you can tell them it's because you chant.

One time when I was selling clothes a customer kept complaining about the many problems he had. I told him not to worry, that at least he had some new clothes and looked good. I kept saying encouraging things to him ... So when the guy was leaving he said, 'I really like your philosophy.' Then he turned around and asked, 'What is your philosophy anyway?' I told him I was glad he asked, and then told him about chanting.

So this is a good way to do Shakubuku at work - by example, by becoming the most remarkable employee on the job. Being a winner at work is a subtle form of Shakubuku, but as Mr. Williams says, 'It is one of the most effective means of Shakubuku.'

This emphasis on "winning" or doing Shakubuku by example, as it is sometimes called, was related to me in a very personal way one evening when chatting with a key informant. She had asked me how my studies were going at UCLA. I indicated that things were progressing, and then added that I had received a dissertation fellowship. She responded with a big smile, congratulated me, and then proceeded to link this reward with Shakubuku and chanting. "Gee, you are really a winner," she said. "You know by being so successful in school you are doing Shakubuku." While anticipating what might follow, I acted as if I was baffled by her comment, and asked her to elaborate. She then explained:

By winning this reward all your fellow students will become curious and want to know how you did it and why. So they will eventually ask you about it. And you can tell them it's because you chant.[23] And then they will probably want to learn all about it. So by being a winner you are doing Shakubuku.

Given the emphasis that is placed on being a "winner," it is reasonable to wonder to what extent are members actually "winners" in their respective lines of work. That is, to what extent do they adhere to the directives and instructions outlined above when engaged in the mundane activity called work?

This is obviously a difficult question to answer, for it was well-nigh impossible for me to observe members at work. And even if I had attempted to do so, my observations would have been suspect in that my mere presence and their knowledge of what I was up to would have probably functioned as a cue that they were in a movement-related situation (any situation in which two or more members are knowingly in the presence of one another) and thereby compel them to attend in part to their membership role. As a consequence, it would be most difficult to generalize about the behavior of members beyond movement-related situations without relying on various subterfuge and perhaps unethical techniques. There is, however, another possibility: that is when the participant observer accidentally comes upon another member or presumed member engaged in work, but who has no knowledge of the participant observer's membership. This opportunity presented itself to me quite by accident one afternoon during my tenure as a member, and was described in my field notes as follows:

> My wife and I stopped at a McDonald's establishment in Santa Monica for an early dinner. While waiting for our order, I mentioned to her that I bet the fellow waiting on us was an NSA member. Even though I had never seen this fellow before, I sensed that he was in NSA because of the way he conducted himself. That is, he looked, acted, and talked as if he were in NSA. He spoke in short, choppy and exuberant sentences - a parroting of Mr. Williams' style of speaking. He worked at a frantic pace, moving around in an exceedingly quick manner. To be sure, most everyone at McDonald's scurries about when busy, but this guy was ahead of the pack. NSA members also scurry about, always making haste. He was also exceptionally pleasant and well-mannered. And he wore an enormous grin and seemed most happy - again like many NSA members.
>
> So upon returning with my order I asked him if he was in NSA. Sure enough. He extended his hand, flashed an even more radiant smile, and asked what chapter I was in. We spoke for a minute and then parted.

Although one might question whether this outward appearance and behavior - the super smile, exuberance, and excessive animation - are reflective of an inner state or merely reflective of an attempt to project a certain image, an image suggestive of competence, happiness, and "winning," the important point is not whether it was a sincere or insincere presentation. Rather, what is significant is that this fellow's behavior suggests that at least some members take the above directions and instructions seriously and do, in fact, attempt to act like "winners," presumably in hopes of furthering both their own interests and those of NSA. And this is especially significant in light of such additional directives as the following:

> To practice True Buddhism means to develop the attitude and ability to become the best worker, the best student, the best son or daughter.[24]

> For an NSA member to be truly worthy of the title, he should strive to be victorious and successful in society. Through this purpose, he shows other people the power of the Gohonzon.[25]

NSA, just as good Calvinists, thus places a premium on "winning" in one's daily life. But unlike the followers of Calvin, it is not to win the favor or good grace of God; rather, it is to win the favor and respect of the larger public within its society of operation.

Celebrity Ingratiation and Endorsement Seeking

A related tactic that NSA has employed in its quest for respectability and legitimacy is that of directly courting the favor and seeking the endorsement of various celebrities or public figures, all of whom have achieved the status of a "winner" in their own respective occupations. Especially illustrative of the application of this tactic was a dinner party NSA conducted in behalf of a Los Angeles city councilman and several members of the Los Angeles Dodgers, all of whom were to attend a forthcoming Nichiren Shoshu-Sokagakkai General Meeting in Japan as guests of President Ikeda. During the party the guests were told about the development and purpose of NSA, shown a 50-minute film of NSA accomplishments, and treated to a live NSA show consisting of dancers, singers, and musicians. The evening ended with the guests, performers and audience singing an NSA song.

As to whether all of this yielded a public endorsement, there is no need to speculate.   Several months after the party and trip to Japan, President Ikeda was invited to Los Angeles by the Mayor and aforementioned Councilman for the purpose of being designated an honorary citizen of Los Angeles.

A more common but less dramatic application of celebrity ingratiation is evidenced whenever NSA conducts a public parade. During such occasions NSA invites several politicians and other celebrities to lead the parade and then join movement leaders on the viewing platform at the end of the parade route.   In addition to this fact, the President and General Director spend considerable time conducting brief meetings with national and international dignitaries. And while the movement's leaders go about the work of soliciting the favor and endorsement of public figures, rank-and-file members invoke the names of these very celebrities as they go about the business of recruitment, presumably to lend an air of importance and respectability to the strange-sounding mantra they are attempting to promote.

Conducting Oneself with Propriety and Deferential Regard

The final tactical way in which NSA has gone about the business of courting the favor and respect of outsiders is by instructing members to conduct themselves with propriety and deferential regard when engaged in focused interaction or just rubbing shoulders with outsiders. This presentational tactic, which also constitutes a form of Shakubuku by example, is nicely illustrated by the following titular reminders and directives appearing in the *World Tribune*:

True Faith Implies Responsibility in Citizenship
Be a Responsible Citizen for Society's Welfare
Respecting Senior Citizens Should be a Daily Attitude
Every Action is a Reflection of Nichiren Shoshu
Use Common Sense to Put Forth a Good Image of NSA
Consideration of Neighbors Leads to Understanding of NSA
Good Conduct Creates a Favorable Impression

In addition to such general directives, members are also provided with instructions elaborating just what it means in practical terms to conduct and present oneself with propriety and deferential regard in various and sundry situations. They are told, for example, that in whatever restaurants or coffee shops they frequent, they "should always be mannerly and courteous to the waitresses, because they will judge NSA by our actions." Or "when stopping on the street to talk with someone about NSA," they are reminded "to be very polite and humble" and not to "act like a fanatic." To do so otherwise, as one member emphasized at a meeting, "can result in people misunderstanding the purpose of NSA." It is therefore important, he continued "to always keep in mind that our conduct must appear respectable in the eyes of the public."

Members are also reminded to attend to their personal appearance. In one guidance session, for example, the leader indicated that "members who are sloppy and negligent in their appearance are not true disciples of Nichiren Daishonin." And one guidance article even advised the young female members that their success is partially contingent on whether they keep up their appearance and conduct themselves with "an air of charm."[26] The major underlying reasons for appearing neat and well-groomed is, of course, Shakubuku. As one editorial, titled "Each Individual's Daily Life is an Act of Shakubuku," explained:

> When a young man who was once lazy and untidy becomes a well-dressed and responsible youth, he is carrying out the practice of Shakubuku. His parents, classmates and neighbors - those who have known him for any length of time, will without further explanation realize the greatness of the Gohonzon.[27]

When it comes to chanting at home or holding discussion meetings, members are again reminded to consider the rights and feelings of non-members, to "be responsible and aware enough not to disturb others." When practicing at home, "... this means to do Gongyo and chant Daimoku at a reasonable volume."[28] And when conducting discussion meetings, this means that "the person living next door or around the corner is to be respected."[29] To be sure, "a lively and open meeting" is expected, but, at the same time, members are repeatedly reminded of the importance of conducting themselves with deferential regard toward their neighbors. Consider, for example, the following instructions appearing in an April 1974 guidance article:

> Meeting places are where we should be the most careful not to trouble neighbors. When arriving at the meeting we should take utmost care in not parking in front of someone's driveway or walking across their lawns. After 10:00 p.m. there should be no loud singing or chanting and we should be especially careful not to talk loudly or slam car doors when leaving the meeting place.

And as another article added, even such "small things as not gunning the car to take off to a screeching start after the meeting should also be kept in mind." While "all of these points are very simple and are nothing but an exercise in common sense," it is important to remember, the article continued, that "such actions play a vital role for Kosen-rufu."[30]

How so? From both a theoretical and practical standpoint, what difference does it make, insofar as NSA's propagation efforts and the content of its message are concerned, whether members gun their cars, walk across neighbors' lawns, or conduct their meetings in an unusually loud and boisterous manner? The difference such actions or gestures make resides in the fact that when interactants or performers monitor and read each other, their respective assessments and reactions are not based merely on what is verbally communicated, but also on what is communicated non-verbally. That is, as students of microsocial interaction have emphasized, communication consists of two separate types of language or sign activity: the verbal or what we say by way of mouth; and the nonverbal or what we say by way of facial and body gestures, and by way of appearance and conduct.[31]

It thus follows that failure to control the nonverbal aspect of communication can mean the difference between having one's verbal message accepted or rejected, between a favorable and unfavorable response. Or, in the language of Erving Goffman, an actor or performer, whether an individual or team, will be more effective in fostering and maintaining the kind of audience reaction desired if both levels of communication are under control and symmetrical; whereas the audience is likely to be lost or respond unfavorably when there is a lack of consistency between what is communicated verbally and nonverbally.

That NSA has intuitively grasped this principle, and that it has a good common-sense understanding of its practical implications is not only suggested by the foregoing discussion, but is illustrated even more graphically by such statements as the following:

> No matter how much or how well we expound the greatness of Nichiren Daishonin's life philosophy, if we are obnoxious and irresponsible in our actions around others, our words will seem false and empty.[32]

The reason, then, that members should not gun their cars, walk across neighbors' lawns, appear sloppy and unkempt, and conduct themselves in a disrespectful manner is, as the movement's leadership repeatedly emphasizes, because "such actions" can "play a vital role" in the way in which NSA is perceived and defined by the larger public and, therefore, in the success of its promotion and recruitment efforts.

Since this discussion of the importance NSA places on having members conduct themselves with propriety and deferential regard has drawn heavily on the directives and instructions provided by the movement's leadership and appearing in its newspaper, the question arises as to the extent to which members actually conduct and present themselves and their activities in accordance with these directives and instructions. In general, it is clear that these directives do not fall on deaf ears. That is, a good many, if not all, members are aware of such directives and their underlying rationale, and they adjust their lines of action accordingly. That this is so was dramatically driven home one evening during a discussion meeting when a non-member, who lived in the apartment unit above the one in which the meeting was being held, burst into the meeting and complained about the noise. The nature of the intrusion and the corresponding complaint, and the group's response were described in my field notes as follows:

> After the chanting session, which was followed by the vigorous singing of a new convention song, an uninvited outsider shoved open the front door of the apartment unit in which the meeting was being held, and blurted out: 'Sam (the member whose apartment we were in), I can take the

chanting but I can't take the singing and yelling any longer. I'm trying to study for some exams at UCLA and I can't concentrate with all this yelling and screaming going on. So will you please keep it down!'

There was an instant pregnant pause during which everyone was looking at each other in disbelief. Sam had a look on his face as if to say - 'Oh no, what are we going to do now?' The intrusion was obviously disruptive and seemed to throw the group into a momentary state of flux.

After about two minutes of stunned silence, the district chief quietly announced that we would continue the meeting in a subdued manner. The next item on the agenda was the testimony session. So four members took their turn quietly explaining the benefits that have resulting from chanting. Although each testimony is normally interrupted by applause and yells of approval, and is always followed by even louder and more enthusiastic applause, such was not the case this evening. Rather, members just smiled, nodded their approval, and went through the motion of applauding without actually doing so.

After the testimonies were completed, the district chief apologized to members and guests for the 'unfortunate incident' and the subdued manner in which the meeting was conducted. Looking at the three guests, he stated: 'The meeting tonight was not reflective of the true NSA spirit - a spirit which makes you want to yell out that life is great, a spirit that stimulates great vigor and happiness.'

'But,' he added, 'we must also be respectful towards our neighbors and try not to disturb them. You know we don't want to give them the wrong impression. Such an attitude is also part of the NSA spirit.' He then indicated that he would talk to the chapter chief about tonight's incident, and discuss the possibility of finding a new meeting place. He also pointed out that this had never happened before and that maybe it was the environment telling us to find a new meeting place. The meeting then broke up and everyone left in a very quiet and restrained manner.

Thus, rather than scoffing at and ignoring the neighbor's request by continuing the meeting as usual, the group took into account the neighbor's complaint and adjusted its lines of action accordingly. Moreover, the following evening the group met at another location. In fact, we never met again at that particular apartment, not because the landlord or some tenant suggested that we meet elsewhere, but because such incidents are to be avoided because "they give the wrong impression."

To recapitulate for a moment, we have examined in the preceding pages NSA's efforts to render itself respectable and legitimate within the public eye through Shakubuku by means of dramatic ingratiation - a type of accommodative strategy aimed at securing the favor and respect of outsiders by actively attempting to foster the impression that the movement's values, aims, and conduct are supportive of and in conformity with certain values, traditions, and normative standards within the larger society. As illustrative of this accommodative strategy, I noted that in addition to constantly instructing members to conduct themselves with propriety and deferential regard and to become "winners" in whatever they do, the leadership also solicits the endorsement of public figures and attempts to link the movement's goals and values with those of America's founding fathers.

All of this suggests that NSA is a highly, and perhaps unusually, flexible and accommodative movement. Yet, this strategic response seems strikingly incongruent with the movement's value orientation and ritual practices. Does it not seem ironic that a culturally transplanted religious movement, with an underlying philosophy and set of ritual practices that are drastically offbeat in comparison to conventional religious beliefs and practices in this country, would encourage its members - in a manner similar to Calvinist strands of Christianity - to become "winners," to become the "best and not merely content with whatever one does?" Is it not also seem ironic that a movement which, on the one hand, sees the world in a state of decay and all major philosophies but its own as being "incapable of bringing happiness to mankind," would, on the other hand, articulate a value linkage with some philosophical tradition in that world. And is it not paradoxical that a movement that seeks to change the world by changing individuals would compulsively encourage external conventionality and conformity? In short, does not NSA's almost compulsive concern with its public image and its highly accommodative orientation seem somewhat inconsistent with its diagnosis of the world's woes, its proposed remedy, and its goal of Kosen-rufu.

How might these ironies be explained? How might we account for NSA's almost compulsive concern with its public image and the nature of its corresponding efforts to render itself respectable and legitimate in the public eye?

Toward a Theoretical Understanding of NSA's Accommodative Behavior

Accommodation as a Means to Securing a Group's Existence and Operation as a Collective Entity. In attempting to make theoretic sense of NSA's accommodative behavior and the above ironies, the principle of interactive rather than immanent determination provides a useful point of departure. According to this principle, the course and character of a movement are neither fixed nor determined solely by its ideology and goals, but are in large part the product of the dynamic interplay between the way in which the movement is defined and reacted to by the community or society in which it exists and by movement adaptation to this response.

Drawing on this principle in their classification of movements on the basis of the way in which they are defined, Turner and Killian have argued that "every movement is engaged in a continuous two-way exchange with the communities and society in which it operates," such that movement actions provoke a community reaction which can affect the movement's recruitment patterns and opportunities, the means or tactics the movement is able to use to further its ends, and the strategies which the movement evolves.[33]

Thus, regardless of a movement's goals and stance with respect to the society in which it exists, it must, if it is to avoid being driven underground, take into account and adapt itself in part to some of the normative traditions and institutional patterns of that social order.[34] And frequently, such adaptation means accommodation; for, as noted earlier, the need for resources contained within the social environment and on which the movement's collective existence is often dependent frequently necessitates that some attention be directed to fostering an accommodative relationship with the larger society or at least some influential group within.

If a movement is to remain viable and be allowed to operate above ground, then it must do what the historical Christ reportedly instructed his early followers to do: "Render unto Caesar that which is Caesar's, and to God that which is God's." Or, as similarly expressed in the parallel Buddhist principle of "Zuiho Bini," a principle which NSA regularly invokes: one is to follow the customs and traditions of their society as long as they do not conflict with the spirit and aims of True Buddhism.

This process of adaptation and accommodation is, of course, an ongoing problem that confronts any movement, just as any social system or organization, and is therefore intimately tied to a movement's course and character. But why do some movements, such as NSA, seem to render unto Caesar more than is necessary for their survival and operation as a collective entity? Or, more specifically, why does NSA seem to encourage its members "to follow the customs and traditions of their society" more rigorously than most other members of that society? Why, in other words, does NSA encourage behavior that borders on over-compliance or over-conformity with both culturally defined aspirations or goals[35] and institutional norms?[36]

Towards Building "Idiosyncrasy Credit?" An answer to these questions and an understanding of NSA's highly accommodative behavior is suggested by E.P. Hollander's concept of idiosyncrasy credit.[37] This concept, which is based on the proposition that conformity can be exchanged for the acceptance and support of others, suggests that behavior which fosters the impression of conformity and competence can result in the accumulation of favorable impressions or credits that have relevance with respect to subsequent interaction. Specifically, these credits have the property of allowing a certain amount of idiosyncratic behavior or nonconformity, or at least secure the tolerance of others with respect to the idiosyncratic action in question. As Hollander wrote it in his initial discussion of the concept, idiosyncrasy credit

> ... represents an accumulation of positively-disposed impressions residing in the perceptions of relevant others; it is defined operationally in terms of the degree to which an individual may deviate from the common expectancies of the group. In this view, each individual within a group ... may

be thought of as having a degree of group-awarded credits such as to permit idiosyncratic behavior in certain dimensions before group sanctions are applied. By definition, affiliation with the group - as perceived by the group - ceases when the individual's credit balance reaches zero ... Affixed to this concept of 'credit' is the further consideration that 'debits' of varying magnitudes may be charged against the credit balance, syncrasy manifested, and the credit level which the individual holds.[38]

Or as explained in another work borrowing on this concept:

... Each participant in a social system is thought to have a sort of 'bank account' of goodwill from his fellow members ... which he builds up by his contributions to the system. An increment of goodwill is called a unit of idiosyncrasy credit because it gives the person license to behave in idiosyncratic ways to a certain extent. A person is able to 'buy' license to engage in deviant behavior by maintaining a favorable balance of idiosyncrasy credit, because of his potential or previous contributions to the group. Were he to continue deviating from group standards without making positive contributions, an individual would deplete his bank account and be expelled from the group in a state of bankruptcy.[39]

Accordingly, the larger one's credit balance or bank account of favorable impressions in the eyes of relevant others, the greater the latitude for a certain amount of nonconformity or idiosyncratic behavior.

Although this proposition has been examined and supported by studies focusing primarily on individuals, and particularly leaders, in small group situations, it seems equally applicable to certain group and intergroup processes at a more macro-level. More specifically, it would seem analytically fruitful to conceptualize NSA's almost compulsive emphasis on having its members conform to both culturally defined goals and institutional norms as an attempt to build idiosyncrasy credit.

As a culturally transplanted movement engaged in the business of propagating a set of beliefs and ritual practices that are unquestionably idiosyncratic from the standpoint of conventional religious beliefs and practices in America, not only has NSA been confronted with being defined as strange and suspect in the public eye, but, as a consequence, it has also run the risk of having its recruitment efforts and operation encumbered. It has thus been confronted with the problem of reducing or neutralizing the stigma often attached to such idiosyncratic groups in order to gain some elbow room to pursue its promotion and recruitment efforts. Hence, the strategic practice of attempting to build idiosyncrasy credit by attempting to render itself respectable and legitimate in the public eye through the various tactical manifestations of dramatic ingratiation described earlier. In other words, by emphasizing that it is carrying out the unfinished work of America's founding fathers and early pioneers, by respectfully deferring to various American traditions and customs, and by actively encouraging members to become "winners" on the job and "model citizens" who are "respected and loved by everyone," NSA has tried to build up its credit or balance of favorable impressions so that outsiders will tolerate or overlook the more idiosyncratic aspects of its philosophy and ritual practices and perhaps grant it a certain amount of respectability and legitimacy.

Viewed in this way, NSA's almost compulsive concern with having its members conform to culturally defined goals and institutional norms, while simultaneously seeking to alter the world by spreading its own philosophy and practices, does not seem quite so ironic and paradoxical. Rather, this highly accommodative emphasis represents a strategic attempt to secure for the movement some latitude for not only engaging in its idiosyncratic practices behind closed doors, but for also nurturing and extracting from the environment those resources it needs in order to sustain its collective existence and advance towards its larger objective of Kosen-rufu, that is, the attainment of worldwide peace and happiness by incorporating an ever-increasing number of people within its ranks and transforming them into converts.

EXPANDING THE RANKS: THE PROBLEM OF
SECURING RECRUITS AND NOMINAL CONVERSION

In the preceding pages in this chapter, we have seen how NSA has dealt with the problem of outreach and information dissemination and the problem of building and maintaining a balance of respectability and legitimacy so as to guarantee its survival and operation as a collective entity. But two related questions still require examination in order to round out our understanding of NSA's propagation and recruitment efforts. First, once an outsider has been engaged in a face-to-face encounter, how do members go about the business of luring this potential convert back to the fold? That is, what kinds of interpersonal tactics and appeals, besides those already mentioned, do members typically employ in their attempts to coax an outsider into attending a discussion meeting? And second, once back at the discussion meeting, how do members collectively go about the business of getting potential converts to become nominal converts? That is, how do they go about the work of selling recruits on the idea that they should give chanting a try?

Face-to-Face Proselytizing on the Streets: Luring Strangers Back to the Fold[40]

As noted earlier, members seem to devote more time and energy to recruiting on the streets than to any other single promotion and information dissemination activity. This is hardly surprising, considering the premium that is placed on expanding the ranks and the fact that discussion meetings, which are held at least four nights a week, do not "go on" unless a new face or recruit is in attendance.

My understanding of how members go about this work is based primarily on what I observed during the numerous occasions I accompanied other members on these recruiting forays. The customary mode of operation was to work in teams of two or three, with one member functioning as the initiator of interaction and as the main purveyor of information, while the others would gather around the recruitee and stand by in a supportive manner. Although the leader and initiator of interaction was usually a senior member or junior leader, the other members of the team often took their turn at establishing contact. While this turn-taking occasionally happened spontaneously, it was normally encouraged by the team leader. On several occasions, for example, the senior member or leader of the team I was with would turn to me and say, "All right Dave, it's your turn."[41]

As for the style of presentation, members were reminded to appear neat and radiant, with a smile on their face, and to conduct themselves in a cordial, courteous, and controlled manner - that is, they should try not to appear overly enthusiastic and aggressive or fanatical.

Although most members seemed to adhere to these instructions, some undoubtedly found it difficult to control their enthusiasm. For example, one member, with whom I spent a good deal of time combing the streets in search of recruits, was so enthusiastic about chanting and the practice of Shakubuku that she would get a special glow on her face and become visibly excited even before arriving at the target area. And once there, she would jump out of the car and scurry up to the nearest person in sight. Moreover, she was reluctant to take "no" for an answer, as evidenced by the fact that she would frequently walk, step-for-step, with a potential recruit for a hundred feet or so before giving up. Because of her persistence and determination, I often found myself drifting away out of embarrassment or occasionally tugging on her arm and whispering that perhaps we should Shakubuku some other passer-by.

Her enthusiasm for and almost total involvement in this work was also reflected by the fact that she would often become oblivious to the time. If, for example, the district leader had reminded us to be back at the meeting house by a certain time, she would seem to forget and I would have to remind her. Even then, she would insist on one more try or as she frequently put it, on "making one more cause" or "planting one more seed." The zealotry displayed by this member seemed to be somewhat unusual. That is not to say that other members were not just as enthusiastic about chanting and promoting the movement. Rather, it is merely to point out that most members seemed to go about this work in a more controlled and less persistent manner.

Turning to the content of the appeals, members were often told that they "shouldn't tell the prospects too much, but just enough to stimulate their curiosity." Furthermore, they were reminded "not to hold meetings on the street, because then the prospects wouldn't feel it's necessary to come to the meeting." The interpersonal task, then, was to whet the prospect's appetite, to get the prospect interested enough that he would agree to return to the district house with the team who had contacted him.

Toward this end, members employed the same interpersonal techniques we all employ to a greater or lesser degree when attempting to realize our intentions in interactional encounters, when we attempt, that is, to get others to do, think, or feel what we want them to. The interpersonal techniques I refer to include the perceptual and interpretive role-taking process and the interpersonal tactics of impression management and altercasting. The way in which these were employed, combined, and alternated will become clear as we proceed.

In establishing contact and getting the ball rolling, the initiator of interaction would usually attempt to gain the attention of a passer-by with an opening spiel that typically contained the following lines:

Hi! How are you? Have you heard of Nichiren Shoshu
or Nam-Myoho-Renge-Kyo?

What transpired was then dependent on the initial response of the person to whom these opening lines had been directed. Here there seemed to be three general types of initial response. Some people would just mutter "not interested" and keep on walking without so much as even hesitating or missing a step. Some would slow their pace or stop for a few seconds and quickly indicate that they had heard of Nichiren Shoshu or that they had been approached before, but that they were just not interested. And oftentimes they would grin and chuckle, as if to say, "Not these people again!" And then there was the third category of respondents who would stop, listen, and talk for a few minutes - some out of curiosity perhaps and some out of deference to the fact that someone had said hello in a personable manner.

Aside from the overly persistent and zealous members, most members would let the blatantly negative respondents continue on their way. As for those whose initial response was positive, as indicated by their willingness to stop and talk for a few minutes, the content of information conveyed seemed to depend largely on the flow of interaction and how the initiator read and sized up the prospect. That is, members would adjust their lines of action according to the responses or cues provided by the prospect.

The initial tactic, in addition to presenting oneself in a cordial, courteous and happy manner, was to cast the prospect into the role of the inquisitor - by asking, for example, if he or she had ever heard of Nam-Myoho-Renge-Kyo - in hopes of getting the prospect to provide the member with an opportunity to say a few words and discover what might be of interest or importance to the prospect. One member was particularly adept at employing this technique. If the prospect simply responded to the opening spiel or initial question by indicating that he or she had never heard of Nam-Myoho-Renge-Kyo, without asking for further information, then this member would often try again by rephrasing the question and recasting the prospect:

> You mean you haven't heard of Nam-Myoho-Renge-Kyo? Gee, I figured that somebody like you would certainly know about Nam-Myoho-Renge-Kyo. After all, just about everybody knows about Nam-Myoho-Renge-Kyo.

In this way, then, the prospect was being cast into the role of someone who would or should know about such things in hopes of compelling him or her to ask what Nam-Myoho-Renge-Kyo is all about. And frequently it worked.

Once the prospect indicated interest in learning more, whether in response to the opening spiel or question or to subsequent prodding, members would then offer a statement that typically included the following lines:

> Nam-Myoho-Renge-Kyo is a chant. Here is a card with the chant on it. By chanting these words you can get whatever you want, whether it be material, physical, or spiritual. It really works.

And oftentimes, so as to lend an air of importance and respectability to the muttering of these strange-sounding words, members would invoke the name of some public figure who allegedly chanted or point out that "twenty-some million people around the world are practicing it, and it works for them."

The prospect would then be asked if he or she would like to attend a meeting in order to learn more about the practice. If the response was negative or one of disinterest, then members would frequently begin to probe and feel out the prospect with a barrage of questions and appeals until the prospect decided to leave or provided a hint of further interest and curiosity. This additional probing would usually begin with such questions as: "Don't you want to attain true happiness?" Or, "Aren't you interested in world peace?" But since the point of all of this is not to sell the movement's goals or provide a detailed explanation of the practice and philosophy, but to lure outsiders back to a meeting, members would usually cast these last resort questions and appeals in terms of something other than the movement's primary goals. Simply put, they would try to discover by asking, suggesting, or inferring, something of interest to the prospect, and then emphasize that this interest could be realized by chanting or attending the meeting.

Sometimes the thrust of these final appeals was in terms of some lateral or auxiliary NSA activity, such as playing a musical instrument, belonging to a band or a dance or song group, or going to Hawaii or wherever the next convention was being held. And sometimes the appeal was in terms of getting good grades, acquiring some material object, such as a new car, or even in terms of pretty girls and sex. As one male member related:

> I didn't want to go to a meeting when first asked. But then (the person who recruited me) started telling me about the many pretty girls that would be there. So I said, 'Well, it can't be that bad if they have all those pretty girls in this religion.' So I agreed to go to a meeting that night and take a look at all those girls ...

Such sex-based appeals seemed fairly common to male members as it was not unusual to hear them indicate during their testimonies that the reason they attended their first meeting was because they thought they might be "attending an orgy" or that they might "find some action." Along this same line, it is not surprising that female members were often more successful in bringing in recruits off the streets, and that those they lured back were typically male.

That members would attempt to make appeals and stimulate interest in terms of something other than the movement's manifest goals is hardly surprising given the movement's concern with expanding its ranks, the fact that next to chanting, Shakubuku is the most important thing a member can do, the fact that Shakubuku, like chanting, is seen as a source of benefit, and the fact that success in one's Shakubuku efforts, as measured most directly by the number of members one has actually recruited, is a means to gaining favor and esteem in the eyes of movement leaders and peers. In light of all of these considerations, it stands to reason that members would attempt to lure outsiders to meetings by couching their appeals in terms of just about anything under the sun.[42] And, in turn, it stands to reason that the initial but not always stated motives for attending a meeting and perhaps joining are likely to be just as varied and numerous as the appeals or motives provided by members during these recruiting forays.

Discussion Meetings: Promoting and Securing Nominal Conversion

All that has been discussed in this chapter thus far is directly or indirectly related to the recruitment of potential converts, to, metaphorically speaking, bringing in the sheep. But what happens once recruits have been secured, once the sheep have been corralled?

To answer this question we have to step into the world of an NSA discussion meeting, which constitutes the last major step in the recruitment process and the first major step in the conversion process; for it is to these meetings that newly secured recruits are brought in hopes of getting them agree to give chanting a try. As stated in one of the many *World Tribune* articles dealing with these meetings:

> The purpose of a discussion meeting is to give new-comers the best possible reasons for receiving their own Gohonzon and to begin chanting.[43]

Before examining the character and organization of these meetings from a sociological standpoint, let us first take a look at them in the sequential manner in which they unfold in the eyes of a new recruit or "guest."

Setting. Discussion meetings, which are also referred to as Shakubuku meetings, are normally held four nights a week in the home or apartment of a district chief or some other senior member of the district. Before entering the house or room in which the meeting is being conducted, members and guests remove their shoes - allegedly in keeping with the Japanese tradition and in deference to the situation and particularly to the Gohonzon. Once inside, members and guests situate themselves on the floor of what would normally function as a living room but which has been converted into a shrine-like meeting room.

This room is usually carpeted but sparsely furnished, with what little furniture there is being pushed against the walls, and it is usually well-lit, with several florescent lights scattered about. The walls are customarily laden with pictures of the Master (President Ikeda), the Sho Hondo or Grand Main Temple in Japan, and with various posters and progress charts pertaining to current and coming recruitment and *World Tribune* promotion campaigns. And situated against the wall at one end of the room is the focal point - the altar or Butsudan, with its doors open to reveal the "splendor and power" of the Gohonzon. In deference to and veneration for this sacred object, a vase of fresh water, a vase of evergreen twigs, a bowl of fresh fruit, two candles, and an incense tray are neatly arranged on the part of the altar directly in front of the Gohonzon.

Since the chanting session is usually in progress by the time all of the guests arrive, they are greeted by the smell of sweet incense wafting through the air and the sounds and sight of the strange language and rituals of another time and place.

Sequence of Events. The first item on the agenda is the chanting session, which normally begins at 7:00 p.m. and runs from thirty to forty-five minutes. The session commences wtih the sounding of a bell-like gong, which is struck by the district chief kneeling, with his buttocks resting on his heels, directly in front of the altar. Situated in a like position directly to his right is the assistant district chief, who was always female; and on his left is the emcee, who was always male. The rest of the members are huddled together in a kneeling position directly behind these three central figures. As soon as the gong is sounded, the chanting of Nam-Myoho-Renge-Kyo begins. In order to get the guests involved, they are given cards on which the chant is printed and they are encouraged to chant along.

After around ten minutes of Daimoku (chanting Nam-Myoho-Renge-Kyo), members begin to recite, in a chanting-like manner, what is called Gongyo. It is a liturgical prayer service consisting of parts of several chapters of the *Lotus Sutra* and contained within "a little blue book" titled *The Liturgy of Nichiren Shoshu*. Although all members have a copy of this "little blue book," most seldom refer to it when chanting for the simple reason that most have memorized its contents.

Here members with guests also try to get them involved by holding the book in front of them and helping them along. It is, however, a fruitless task, not only because Gongyo is recited in Japanese, but also because it is recited at such a rapid pace. Following Gongyo, which usually takes about twenty minutes, there is another five to ten minutes of Daimoku.

Accompanying the chanting is the dry rustle of beads being rubbed together. Each member has a string or rosary of a hundred and some beads which are constantly rubbed together throughout the entire chanting session. Sometimes the beads are rubbed together in a fashion analogous to the way in which one rubs their hands together when cold; and sometimes the hands and beads are brought up in front of the face in a prayer-like fashion. Regardless, the rhythmical chanting, accompanied by the constant rustle of beads and the scent of incense hanging in the air, produces a most unusual and soothing atmosphere, an atmosphere that is exotic, pleasant and relaxing all at the same time.

The chanting session comes to a close with the ringing of the bell-like gong, during which time the members offer the following silent prayer:

> I pray for my ancestors and for those of all Nichiren Shoshu members and for the deceased.
> I sincerely pray for the earliest realization of world peace and happiness, through the Gohonzon's bestowal of equal benefits upon the entire universe and the whole world.[44]

This prayer is then followed by another ring of the gong and the chanting of three Daimoku, after which there is a pregnant pause.

Then, all of a sudden, this exotic and soothing sound and atmosphere of another world is immediately and dramtically transformed into the atmosphere of a 20th century, American high school pep rally and sales meeting combined into one. The silence is dramatically cut by vigorous applauding and yelling of "A-A-O" (the Sokagakkai-Nichiren Shoshu equivalent of Hip-Hip-Hurrah), while two male members rush a coffee-like table before the district chief, who turns around to face the gathering. At the same time, the emcee springs to his feet and yells out: "Welcome to a vigorous and happy meeting of the _____ District of NSA." And then, without pausing to catch his breath, he calls upon members of the YWD (Young

Women's Division) to lead the gathering in a rousing rendition of a Gakkai song. Just as quickly as a cat bouncing on a canary, they bound to their feet and begin the singing. And once done, the YMD (Young Men's Division) members are usually called upon to follow suit.

Both the YWD and the YMD members lead the singing in a vigorous, animated, and cheerleader-like fashion: standing with legs spread apart, the upper torso bent slightly forward, and one hand resting on the hip while the other arm is jerked back and forth in keeping with the rhythm of the song. And their faces - aside from the movement of their lips - take on the fixed form of Lewis Carroll's Cheshire Cat.

All of this - the yelling, applauding, singing, and excessive animation and exuberance - happens so suddenly and dramatically, and is so out of character with the chanting that preceded it, that it is almost stupefying and unbelievable. Indeed, one is inclined either towards laughter or just sitting there in stunned silence with a dumbfounded look, as if to say, "You've gotta be kidding? What is this anyway?" Whatever the immediate reaction, whether it is a state of laughter or a state of suspended sensibility, the effect is the same: one is, figuratively speaking, swept off his or her feet.

Following this enthusiastic song-fest and this dramatic bridging of two seemingly incompatible worlds, the emcee leaps back to his feet and asks for an introduction of guests. Members who have brought guests then proceed to yell out their names, after which the emcee calls upon a member to give a brief explanation of what NSA is all about. The explanations that are given, regardless of who gives them, are usually quite consistent and typically sound much like the following one:

> What you are attending tonight is a meeting of NSA, which stands for Nichiren Shoshu Academy or Nichiren Shoshu of America. It is a worldwide organization and not just the few people in here. What we are practicing is a really groovy life philosophy. And what that philosophy consists of is not just a book we read or something we believe in, but something we can do and get benefits from. And what we do is chant Nam-Myoho-Renge-Kyo to the scroll in the altar which is called the Gohonzon. And we

also recite a little sutra every morning and evening to establish a rhythm in our life and become the happiest people around.

The next item on the agenda is the rendering of testimonies, or what members commonly refer to as "giving experiences." So with the completion of the brief explanation of what NSA is all about, the emcee calls for experiences by asking: "Who would like to give an experience?" In response, most members thrust their hands into the air, wave them back and forth, and bounce up and down with exuberance and anticipation. The emcee then looks over the gathering and calls upon one of the members, who bounds to his or her feet, scurries to the front of the room amidst much applause and yelling, and then proceeds to relate, while smiling from ear-to-ear, how chanting has changed the course of his or her life and resulted in the realization of one or more material, spiritual, or interpersonal benefits. As soon as the first member is finished, another is called upon, and then another and another.

Normally this scenario is repeated four times during this part of the meeting. Each testimony is always interrupted by applause and yelling whenever a benefit is alluded to, and at the end of each there is thunderous applause accompanied by the shoulting of "A-A-O." Although there is some variance in the content of each testimony, their nature and structure is much the same.

Following the testimonial session, the emcee introduces the district leader, who then proceeds to answer guests' questions or, if there are no questions, relates how chanting has changed his life and discusses in more detail what the philosophy and practice and the discussion meeting are all about. Regarding the purpose of the meeting, there is seldom any beating-around-the-bush. Rather, guests are customarily told the following:

These meetings are to get you to experiment with the practice, not to believe in it. The reason for having you come to this meeting is to get you to try and test the practice. We don't expect you to believe in it right away, but we do want you to give it a try.

What this meeting is actually for and what all of this
comes down to is to get you guests to experiment with this
practice and philosophy ... No matter what you believe, the
most important thing is that you get a Gohonzon and try
chanting. We're not asking you to believe in it; we're just
asking you to try it and see if it works. And that's what this
meeting is all about - to encourage you to try it.

It is during this question and answer session, then, that guests are
directly asked for the first time to give chanting a try. If the smiling
faces, the happy, cordial, and exuberant atmosphere, and particularly
the testimonies, have not provided the guests with sufficient reason to
give chanting a try, then the district leader begins to shift gears a bit by
employing a number of uncodified interpersonal tactics (which will be
discussed in a few pages) aimed at getting the unimpressed or
unconvinced to change their minds.

Following the question and answer session, which normally runs
for around thirty minutes, there is a series of announcements, given by
the Assistant District Chief, regarding up-and-coming meetings and
campaigns. The formal part of the meeting is then brought to a close
by chanting Nam-Myoho-Renge-Kyo three times, after which members
immediately begin to engage in what is referred to as informal
Shakubuku. That is, armed with smiles, unrelenting determination, and
pencils and application forms for membership and the Gohonzon, the
members "rush" the guests further by gathering around them in groups
of three or more.

Those guests who have expressed an interest in chanting are
congratulated and coaxed into signing up; whereas those who are still
unimpressed are worked on further as members relate additional
experiences and benefits and bring added pressure to bear in a final
effort to convince these unconvinced that they should give chanting a
try. Throughout all of this, the District Chief and his assistant circulate
about, congratulating the newly-secured nominal converts (those who
agreed to give chanting a try by filling out the application form to
receive the Gohonzon) and assisting the other members engaged in the
business of breaking down the more resilient and resistant guests.[45]

All of this draws to a close around 9:30 p.m., as the members and
the newly secured nominal converts leave for a nearby NSA
Community Center in order to receive guidance from higher-level

leaders, to add the names of the new converts to the Chapter tally sheet, to chant some more, and to fraternize with members from other districts. And the unimpressed, the guests who did not succumb to the members' efforts to secure their nominal conversion, just leave: some shaking their heads in amazement, some shaking their heads in disgust, and some scratching their heads out of curiosity.

It is at these discussion meetings, then, that NSA gets on with the real work of promoting and securing nominal conversion, of attempting to get recruits to take the first major step toward conversion by agreeing to receive a Gohonzon and to give chanting a try. And since gaining converts is, in large part, what this movement is all about, "nothing is more basic to the activities of NSA," as noted in the Winter edition of the 1975 *NSA Quarterly*, "than the discussion meeting." Or, as one district leader emphasized when discussing the importance of these meetings: "Discussion meetings are indispensable to the spread of the practice and the attainment of Kosen-rufu."

The Character and Organization of These Meetings from a Sociological Standpoint

Given the purpose and importance of these discussion meetings, the question arises as to how they are organized and brought off in a strategic manner. In other words, what is the underlying strategy guiding this work of securing nominal conversion, and what are the kinds of tactical adjustments made at the line of scrimmage when the plan of attack does not appear to be advancing the group towards its goal of getting guests to agree to give chanting a try. In order to answer these question in a sociological manner, let us step out of the shoes of a guest and into those of a sociological with insiders' knowledge.

The Strategy of Theatrical Persuasion. Although members and the movement's literature like to characterize these meetings as being forums for free and open discussion and the spontaneous expression and flow of happiness and excitement, they are a far cry from gatherings characterized by spontaneity and unstructured discussion and interaction. Rather, they are meticulously planned and highly orchestrated meetings that can be best conceptualized, from a dramaturgical perspective, as theatrical-like presentations staged and conducted by a set of individuals (NSA members) who not only work together as a team but whose intimate cooperation is expected and required in order to foster and sustain a convincing impression or definition of the situation in the eyes of the audience (the recruits or guests).[46]

Although the staged character of these meetings is seldom readily discernible to the unsuspecting guest, the appropriateness of conceptualizing these meetings in this way is suggested by the following considerations. First, the purpose of the meeting, as already indicated, is to sell guests on the idea of chanting, to so impress them that they feel compelled to give this practice call chanting a try.

Secondly, there is a division of labor such that all members have one or more roles to play. These various roles include the leadership role, the role of emcee, a general, overarching supportive role, and several more specific supportive roles, such as the role of giving an explanation of what NSA is all about, the role of a song leader, and the role of giving testimony. And even more significantly, members are provided with fairly detailed instructions, or, in the language of the theater, with scripts indicating what each role involves and how best to perform or play it.

The main leadership role, assumed by the district chief or, in his absence, the assistant district chief, includes, for example, the tasks of leading the chanting in a vigorous manner, conducting the question-and-answer session, meeting with each of the guests, and providing an inspirational role model for the other members. In performing these tasks, the leader is reminded that rather than putting on the air of a great sage, he should make a point of displaying great vitality, warmth, and compassion.[47] Furthermore, he is expected "to be able to give clear explanations of the philosophy and practice," and is instructed to "always tailor his answers and encouragement to the audience."

> Answers should always be tailored to the audience. If the guests are young, then the answers should include examples they can relate to. If the questions are too mystical or one-sided, the leader must have the wisdom to change the subject or break off the question-and-answer period diplomatically.[48]

The emcee role is also regarded as particularly important, so much so that "the success of the meeting" is said to be contingent on how well it is performed. In fact, "so much depends on the emcee" that the discussion meeting is described for him as "a battleground in which he must struggle to bring victory to the members."[49] Specific responsibilities include setting "the gears of the meeting in motion"[50] and keeping the meeting going in a rhythmical and orderly manner.

> The emcee must develop the ability to keep the rhythm of the meeting going by making sure that there are no pauses or interruptions. If someone is causing a disorder, he should quiet the person in a polite manner. If a baby starts crying, he should see to it that either the mother or one of the young women at the meeting takes the child to another room to calm it down.[51]

The emcee is also charged with being "the eyes and ears of the person leading the meeting."

> Before and during the meeting, he should watch guests, be on the lookout for disruptions, and in general, be aware of everything that's happening. He should inform the person leading the meeting how many guests are present and whether they are young or old, so the leader can set the rhythm of the meeting accordingly.[52]

In addition, the emcee is expected to talk, act, and appear in a manner that displays or exudes strength, confidence, vitality and neatness.

> The emcee must speak in a vigorous, strong and clear voice, but not screaming. The way he sits, stands up and moves the table must display confidence. In fact, he should stand up smartly whenever he is talking. As for appearance, he should reflect the image of NSA - clean and neat clothes and personal grooming.[53]

And finally, the emcee is instructed to have the details of the meeting worked out and the setting in order before the meeting begins.

The emcee must have a plan for the meeting. He should
write up a schedule showing who will give the explanation,
what songs will be sung, who will give experiences and so
on, and present it to the leader at least two days prior to the
meeting. The emcee must prepare for the meeting. He
should check to see if the meeting place is clean and neat,
that all lights work and there is an appropriate meeting table.
Most of all, he should do Shakubuku for the success of the
meeting.[54]

Turning to the supporting cast, members are constantly reminded
that the success of the meeting is dependent on everyone uniting and
working together. As one guidance article put it, since "the purpose
of any meeting is to Shakubuku the guests, this requires a joint effort
of all ..."[55] Accordingly, members are instructed to have a "seeking
mind" - to seek out the guidance of their leaders in order to discover
what is expected of them and how to do it, to be in constant
communication with the leaders and with each other before, during, and
after the meeting. Moreover, they are instructed to "enthusiastically
support all aspects of the meeting by," in the words of one district
chief, "playing whatever role (they) are assigned to the hilt."

This means giving an experience, leading a powerful
song or just sitting with a broad smile and your attention
focused on the leader, or whoever else is talking at that point
of the program.[56]

And it also means "blending in with and following the leader." As one
district chief explained during a planning meeting for senior and junior
leaders within the district and which I was invited to by one of my key
informants:

Make sure to tell your members to chant in rhythm with
the leaders. There shouldn't be any more than one rhythm.
Everyone should be together so that there is unity. And
remember to have them support the leader in whatever he
says; the guests won't know whether he is right or wrong.
So even if you don't agree with what is being said, act as if

you do. this way there is unity at the meeting and the guests will be more impressed.

In addition to the general supportive role, members are provided with instructions regarding the more specific role activity. That is, they are coached as to how to give explanations of what NSA is all about, to lead songs, and to give testimonies. Regarding the latter, for example, members are reminded to respond to the emcee's request for experiences with great alacrity and enthusiasm by thrusting their hands in the air in a vigorous manner and yelling out "hi." And if called upon, they are reminded to attend to the five major points or the "five S's" of giving a good experience.

The first point is *Shakubuku*. Remember, the guests have absolutely no understanding of this practice or any NSA terminology. Always talk to the guests and not to the members. The sole purpose of an experience is to make the guests curious enough to join ... Don't use Buddhist terms and names the guests won't understand...

Point number two is *story*. Make sure an experience is just that - something which happened to you and which you either changed into a benefit or changed an aspect of your life-condition through chanting. Basically, an experience should be structured as (a) before chanting I had a problem or I was satisfied with my life and (b) then I chanted, solved the problem or changed that aspect of my life which I wasn't satisfied with... Make sure that you stress that chanting was the ingredient which changed those aspects of your life. Otherwise, the guests won't be able to connect just how chanting and a person's problems relate.

The third point to keep in mind is *simplicity*. Make each point of the story simple and to the point. Don't clutter the issue with unnecessary details. Try to be as brief as possible.

The fourth point is that of a *seeking mind*. What this means is that the person giving an experience should try to find out what type of experience the leader wants to have conveyed to the guests that will most benefit them. We're not saying that there is a "one" type of experience that is sought, but experiences have to be geared to the guests at the meeting. A middle-aged person is definitely going to have hard time relating to the change in values of a college student... The point is, make sure you are perceptive enough to give the type of experience which the guests at the meeting can relate to best.

The final point is one of the most important - *sincerity* ... Even if your experience isn't that spectacular or full of content, the guests can relate to a person' sincere way of giving the experience...[57]

These five pointers on how to construct and give a "good" experience are mentioned repeatedly in the movement's literature and by its leaders. Furthermore, members can learn how to construct testimonies in accordance with these instructions by simply watching and listening to other members, and especially core converts, when giving their respective experiences. Indeed, rank-and-file members and new converts are often told to watch and listen to how so-and-so gives an experience.

It should thus come as no surprise that the testimonies given at these meetings, or wherever, are usually structured in accordance with the above pointers or instructions. And when they are not, the violators are usually pulled aside after the meeting and provided with corrective suggestions. At the end of several meetings, for example, I overheard the district chief reprimanding and re-instructing members regarding the unsuitable testimonies they had given earlier in the evening. This sanctioning and corrective work occurs not only when unsatisfactory testimonies are given but whenever meeting or movement-related roles are performed in an unsatisfactory manner and whenever members visibly engage in conduct that is inappropriate from the standpoint of NSA. During the San Diego Convention weekend, for example, I observed on several occasions members who were being brought back into line for engaging in unbecoming conduct, such as smoking grass on the bus while en route to the convention. That members who conduct themselves and perform their roles in an unsuitable and unconvincing manner are frequently pulled aside and provided with corrective guidance thus suggests a third consideration pointing to the highly orchestrated and theatrical character of discussion meetings in particular and of NSA in general.

A fourth indication of the staged character of discussion meetings is provided by the fact that planning meetings are held at both the district and chapter level for the purpose of discussing how to improve discussion meetings and make them more successful. Although rank-and-file members (those who have not attained that status of a junior or senior leader) are not normally invited to these planning meetings, I was able to attend several of them at the invitation of both my district chief and a junior leader who was one of my key informants. It was during these planning meetings that I became deeply sensitized to the highly orchestrated and dramaturgical character of not only the discussion meetings but of NSA's overall operation.

A fifth consideration suggesting that staged character of discussion meetings is the fact that much of what members do and say, both verbally and nonverbally, during the course of a meeting is to appear natural and spontaneous rather than artificial and contrived. In other words, these meetings are not to appear as staged performances or as the product of dramaturgical cooperation. This concern is evidenced by the emphasis placed on exuding sincerity and responding to calls from the emcee and to what the leader says and does with alacrity and enthusiasm. It is also suggested by some of the rituals engaged in by the emcee, as when he scans the gathering after he has called for an experience so as to foster the impression that whom he calls is a spontaneous decision rather than one that has been pre-arranged, as indicated by the fact that those called on are already listed on his meeting agenda and by the fact that members frequently know beforehand whether they will be giving an experience.

But none of this is evident to the guest. Rather, what transpires - who gives the explanation, who gives testimonies, and so on - is staged in such a way that it all appears as if it is spontaneous and independent of prior planning, negotiation, and decision-making among the members. As a consequence, it seems reasonable to suggest that NSA in general and the district members in particular have something of the character of a secret society.[58] This is not particularly surprising, however, when considering the nature of theatrical-like teamwork. As Erving Goffman noted in his seminal discussion of this kind of work:

> ... if a performance is to be effective it will be likely that
> the extent of cooperation that makes this possible will be
> concealed and kept secret... The audience may appreciate,
> of course, that all members of the team are held together by
> a bond that no member of the audience shares ... But (the
> members of the team) form a secret society ... insofar as a
> secret is kept as to how they are cooperating together to
> maintain a particular definition of the situation.[59]

The sixth and final consideration suggesting the appropriateness
of viewing these meetings from a dramaturgical perspective is the fact
that they do not "go on" unless there is an audience, that is unless
guests are in attendance. When I first discovered this I was somewhat
startled, for I had assumed that these meetings were conducted in their
entirety regardless of the presence or absence of a new face. But as I
learned one evening, this is not the case. Following the chanting
session on this particular evening, the leader emphasized that since
these meetings were for guests and none were present, we would have
to go out and round up one or two. So the members in attendance
were divided into Shakubuku teams and sent out in search of prospects.
Although three of the four teams returned empty-handed, one had
managed to corral a single guest. But one is all that is needed; and so
the formal meeting began as usual. During my tenure as a member I
saw this particular scenario re-enacted on four different occasions, and
on one occasion we were sent back into the streets three times in
succession. Around 8:30 p.m., after the third try and with one guest
in hand, the show finally got on the road.

Perhaps even more illustrative of the theatrical character of these
meetings and the fact that they are staged for guests is the following
course of events that transpired one evening during a meeting I
attended:

> Although no guests were present when the chanting
> began, a young couple came in toward the end of the
> chanting session and situated themselves on the floor at the
> back of the room. But apparently the emcee didn't notice
> them; for upon completion of the chanting session he didn't
> jump up and yell out: 'Welcome to a vigorous and happy
> meeting of the _____ District of NSA!' But the district

leader, who had apparently seen this couple come in, punched the emcee in the ribs and whispered that some guests were present. And so this member immediately assumed his role of the emcee and proceeded as usual by springing to his feet, putting on a big smile, and blurting out: 'Welcome to a vigorous and happy meeting of the __ District of NSA!'

In light of the foregoing considerations and observations, there seems to be little question about the appropriateness of conceptualizing NSA discussion meetings as "shows" or presentations staged by the members, who constitute a performance team, before an audience composed of recruits or "guests."[60]

Tactical Maneuvering in the Face of Unimpressed Guests. Since there are usually different responses to a performance among those constituting the audience, the question arises as to what additional lines of action are employed in the face of an unfavorable response. In other words, since not all recruits are so impressed by the show that they agree to give chanting a try when asked by the district chief during the question-and-answer session, what do members do in an attempt to get the unimpressed and unconvinced to change their minds?

It was noted earlier that the district leader and the supporting cast begin to shift gears a bit in the face of an unfavorable response. This shift, which begins during the question-and-answer period and is usually continued and intensified during the informal Shakubuku period, is characterized by a move from the relatively soft-sell theatrical approach to a more hard-sell and high-pressured approach normally consisting of several uncodified lines of action that can be conceptualized in sociological terms as high-pressured altercasting and bargaining.

By altercasting, I refer to the interpersonal tactic of creating an identity for another that is congruent with one's goals by casting the other into a particular identity or role type that compels him or her into the desired line of action.[61] And by bargaining I refer to the interpersonal tactic of inducing others to do what you want by offering to add some new advantage or culturally salient and exchangeable value to their situation.

Since NSA does not directly possess the remunerative or status-granting wherewithal to enable it to appeal initially to outsiders or recruits on the basis of salary, wages, prestige, and the like, it is not in an enviable bargaining position. Yet, it does possess what it considers to be a prize value: the value-creating practice of chanting to the Gohonzon, a practice that can allegedly add new physical, spiritual, material and interpersonal benefits and advantages to the life situation of those who will pursue it. But before this prize value can function as a viable inducement, recruits must first be moderately sold on the efficacy of the practice and on its relevance to their own life situations, or at least be convinced that they have nothing to lose by trying it. Hence, the necessity of the meetings and the strategic work of theatrical persuasion.

As noted above, however, this strategy is not always effective. That is, many recruits remain unimpressed or unconvinced following the testimonies and so on, as evidenced by their negative response when asked for the first time by the district chief if they would like to give chanting a try. So what normally transpires after this first negative reply is that the district chief attempts to strike a bargain by casting the recruit into the role of a challenger or debunker with a seeking mind and then suggesting that he or she try to prove the practice wrong or false. Illustrative of this tactical line are the following statements and excerpts from my field notes:

> We're just asking you to try it and see; to prove it right or wrong to yourself. If you have a seeking mind, you'll try to see if it's a bunch of hogwash or if it really works. It doesn't make any difference if you try to prove it wrong; that's fine, as long as you try it. So if you 're really an inquisitive and curious person, which I think you are, then you'll test it to see if it really works. And besides, you have nothing to lose, but only something to gain - you will either gain the satisfaction of proving it wrong or you will gain benefits.

> The leader turned to a guest and asked her if she would give chanting a try. She indicated that she wasn't interested in chanting, that she didn't think she needed it, and that she felt that most of the benefits members talked about could

have been realized without chanting. The leader said he felt
the same way when he joined eight years ago. He said he
thought all the members were a bunch of emotional cripples,
and that he joined partly as a joke and partly to prove them
wrong. He then said to the unimpressed guest: If you're
convinced that this is all a lark and that it won't help you in
any way, then why don't you test it for three months and
come back and tell us that chanting is useless? And if this
is what you discover, if you prove it wrong at the end of
three months, then I'll quit myself. Doesn't that sound like
a fair deal?

Even if you're not convinced, you should give it a try.
You've got nothing to lose. You should at least have the
curiosity and courage to try it and see. Test it for a hundred
days and see if it works. You might prove it right and you
might prove it wrong, but either way, you have nothing to
lose.

In addition to attempting to bargain with resistant recruits by
casting them into the role of a challenger or debunker, they are also
frequently cast into the identity of a fad jumper, of a person with low
impulse control who will try just about anything that comes along.
Consider the comments of my district chief directed at unyielding
guests:

How many foolish things have you done in your life?
Lots, probably? Well, why don't you try one more
seemingly foolish thing? You'll never regret it. You owe
it to yourself to try one more crazy thing. And unlike many
of the crazy things you've done, this one won't hurt you.
So why don't you try it? You've got nothing to lose but a
few minutes a day, and everything to gain.

If you're like most everyone else, you've tried so many
stupid and crazy things to get happy that you might as well
try one more thing. Besides, chanting isn't going to damage
you or cost you anything. You don't have to take a pill
internally or anything as crazy as that. So you should really

try it for at least three months. You have nothing to lose.
It won't hurt you. And if you really give a sincere effort,
I can assure you that it will help you get more of the things
you want out of life. So I really encourage you to try what
might seem to you as one more stupid thing.

When such altercasting and bargaining lines as the above fail to
move the resistant and still unconvinced recruits, then the pressure is
frequently escalated and the altercasting lines become more pungent and
pointed. Simply put, the unimpressed recruits are frequently cast into
the role or identity of a person who is alienated, unhappy, unfulfilled,
and the like. The following exchange nicely illustrates this tactical line:

Leader:	Won't you give it a try?
Recruit:	No. It may be beautiful for the members since they're smiling and seemingly happy. But it's not for me.
Leader:	Why not? Are you afraid?
Recruit:	No, I'm not afraid. But I just don't think I need you or chanting. And I'm happy anyway.
Leader:	Well, you don't seem happy. And you may not need me, but you need to find yourself.
Recruit:	I've got myself. I know who I am.
Leader:	Well, it seems to me that your true self is hidden. All I can say is that the very essence of your self hasn't surfaced yet. And it won't unless you start chanting.

And sometimes, after all of the above has failed in advancing the
group towards securing nominal conversion, members make one final
try by resorting to sheer pressure. That is, they keep at the guest until
they break or just get up and leave. On several occasions, for
example, I observed guests becoming exceedingly impatient and
nervous, and then suddenly get up and leave. And when asked why,
while heading for the door, they simply indicated that they could not

stand the pressure. Although such occurrences were rare, and although members do not seem to consciously employ this last resort technique, it did surface from time to time, nonetheless, and is graphically illustrated by the following exchange.

Leader:	Are you going to receive your Gohonzon this Sunday?
Recruit:	(a fellow who had already come to several meetings but who had not yet agreed to get a Gohonzon) I'm thinking about it, but I'm not ready to receive it on Sunday.
Leader:	Why not?
Recruit:	Because I don't have any room for it where I'm living.
Leader:	If you really wanted it, you could find room.
Recruit:	I'm not putting you on. It's not my place and I don't want to nail something into the wall.
Leader:	If you don't make the cause, you'll always find an excuse. It's like learning to swim. You have to plunge in and try it.
Recruit:	I'll receive the Gohonzon when I'm ready. Right now I'm not ready.
Leader:	What do you mean, you're not ready?
Recruit:	Well, I'm not sure about it. And besides, so many of the members seem so materially oriented. All a lot of them ever talk about are material benefits. I'm looking for something more spiritual.
Leader:	Members chant for what they need. If you need or are looking for spiritual benefits, then you can get them if you chant for them.

Recruit:	Well, that's not the only thing I'm not sure about. I also don't like the pressure you put on everyone - like the way you're pressuring me right now.
Leader:	I'm not pressuring you. I'm just trying to explain that if you're going to find out about this practice and give it a fair chance, you have to get a Gohonzon and chant to it.
Recruit:	Well, let me think about it some more.
Leader:	You can think about it forever. But what you have to do is just make a decision to get the Gohonzon. I'll talk with you a bit later.

Although the recruit referred to in this exchange never did consent to receiving a Gohonzon, there is little question but that a good many guests do respond favorably to NSA's efforts to secure their nominal conversion by means of theatrical persuasion and the variety of altercasting and bargaining lines discussed above. As we learned in Chapter 3, NSA claims to have expanded its ranks from less than five hundred in 1960 to around a quarter of a million by the mid-1970s. Or, stated differently, it managed to secure, if not maintain, the nominal conversion of around 200,000 Americans within a ten-year span. In light of this rather phenomenal growth, the intriguing question arises again as to who has expanded its ranks, and why? It is to an examination of this question that we turn in the following chapter.

NOTES

1. See, for example, Neil Smelser's dichotomous classification of movements according to whether they are norm-oriented or value-oriented, in the *Theory of Collective Behavior* (New York: The Free Press, 1963); and David Aberle's cross-classification of movements according to the locus and amount of change sought, in *The Peyote Religion among the Navaho* (Chicago: Aldine, 1966).

2. Ralph H. Turner and Lewis M. Killian, *Collective Behavior*, Second Edition (Englewood Cliffs, New Jersey: Prentice-Hall, 1972), p. 289.

3. For a discussion of these aggressive tactics, see Noah S. Brannen, *Sokagakkai: Japan's Militant Buddhists* (Richmond: John Knox Press, 1968); Kiyoaki Murata, *Japan's New Buddhism* (New York: Weatherhill, 1969); and Hirotatsu Fujiwara, *I Denounce Sokagakkai* (Tokyo: Nisshin Hodo Co., 1970).

4. For a more detailed discussion of this perspective, see: William A. Gamson, *Power and Discontent* (Homewood, Ill.: Dorsey Press, 1968) and *The Strategy of Social Protest* (Homewood, Ill.: Dorsey Press, 1975); John McCarthy and Mayer Zald, *The Trend of Social Movements in America: Professionalization and Resource Mobilization* (Morristown, NJ: General Learning Press, 1973); Anthony Oberschall, *Social Conflict and Social Movements* (Englewood Cliffs, New Jersey: Prentice Hall, 1973); and Mancur Olson, Jr., *The Logic of Collective Action* (Cambridge: Harvard University Press, 1965), the seminal source of many of the ideas incorporated into this perspective.

5. For a discussion of this distinction and related behavioral implications, see Erving Goffman, *Behavior in Public Places* (New York: The Free Press, 1963); and Stanford M. Lyman and Marvin B. Scott, "Territoriality: A Neglected Sociological Dimension," *Social Problems*, Vol. 15 (1967), pp. 236-248.

6. For a discussion of this distinction, see Erving Goffman, *op. cit.* (1963), especially p. 14. Also, see John Lofland's *Doomsday Cult* (Englewood Cliffs, New Jersey, 1966) pp. 65-119, in which this distinction was employed in examining the cult's promotion efforts.

7. *NSA Seminar Report, 1968-1971* (Santa Monica: World Tribune Press, 1972), pp. i-ii.

8. See, for example, Daniel J. Boorstin, *The Image: A Guide to Pseudo-Events in America* (New York: Harper and Row, 1964).

9. *World Tribune* (April 7, 1975).

10. *San Diego Union* (April 7, 1974), p. B-1.

11. *World Tribune* (April 7, 1975).

12. *World Tribune* (April 7, 1975).

13. Here it is important to bear in mind that since all non-members are outsiders but not all outsiders are actual strangers, there is a qualitative difference between door-to-door canvassing and promotion along interpersonal networks. In the case of the former, not only will a greater number of outsiders be contacted, but most, if not all, will be actual strangers; whereas if the latter possibility is followed, only those outsiders who are tied to members by virtue of acquaintanceship, friendship, or kinship run the risk of good fortune of being contacted.

14. See, for example: "Buddhists Celebrate Happiness," *San Diego Union* (April 7, 1974), "Growing Buddhist Sect in Southland Thrives on Hopeful Image of Man," *Los Angeles Times* (December 9, 1974).

15. See, for example: "The Power of Positive Chanting," *Time* (January 17, 1969), p. 51; "The Super Missionary," *Time* (January 13, 1975), p. 26; and "Happy Talk," *Newsweek* (June 5, 1972).

16. Although the reasons for this are not clear, I would guess that they are lodged in several basic considerations: first, the expense of advertising via radio and TV, and even in newspapers if the ad is going to catch the eye of a large number of readers, is much too great in relation to the dividends such advertising might yield. And this is especially true when the group in question can afford only a limited number of such ads and when there is no guarantee that a sizable number of people will be tuned in when the ad is being run. Secondly, information appropriation or promotion via telephone and mail, which can also be costly, is not usually as effective as when conducted by face-to-face means. And finally, unsolicited promotion via phone or mail also constitutes a form of territorial invasion that is not often appreciated by those on the receiving end.

17. *World Tribune* (September 21, 1974).

18. The classic sociological statement regarding the nature of dramatic face-work or impression management is provided by Erving Goffman, *The Presentation of Self In Everyday Life* (New York: Doubleday Anchor Books, 1959); and *Interaction Ritual* (New York: Doubleday Anchor Books, 1967), pp. 5-95. Regarding the conceptualization of "ingratiation" as an interpersonal tactic or strategy, see Edward E. Jones, *Ingratiation* (New York: Appleton, Century, Crofts, 1964); and "Conformity as a Tactic of Ingratiation," *Science* (1965), pp. 144-150.

19. Here it is important to bear in mind that while accommodation is often dramaturgical in character, it need not be simultaneously ingratiating. Similarly, while all ingratiating work has something of the character of dramaturgy, not all face-work or impression management is of the ingratiating variety.

20. *World Tribune* (May 29, 1974).

21. *World Tribune* (May 2, 1973).

22. *World Tribune* (May 5, 1974).

23. Who knows? Maybe she's right when she attributes the fellowship to chanting, for I was chanting at that point in time. But the connection could also be completely accidental and spurious; for like a good Calvinist, just as like a good NSA member, I had also been working hard. But I had also been imbued with the spirit of the Protestant ethic long before I had evern heard of Nam-Myoho-Renge-Kyo. But then again, who knows? Other students work hard also. So maybe she was right. Maybe the difference was that I chanted whereas they did not. Such is the nature of religious claims and the attribution of causality to some supernatural or magical power; who knows for sure?

24. *World Tribune* (August 26, 1974).

25. *World Tribune* (July 31, 1974).

26. *World Tribune* (February 13, 1970).

27. *World Tribune* (August 25, 1969).

28. *World Tribune* (August 26, 1974).

29. *World Tribune* (May 24, 1968).

30. *World Tribune* (September 30, 1974).

31. See, for example: Ray L. Birdwhistell, *Kinesics and Context* (New York: Ballantine Books, 1972); Erving Goffman, *The Presentation of Self in Everyday Life*, op. cit.; Edward T. Hall, *The Silent Language* (New York: Doubleday 1959); Albert Mehrabian, *Silent Messages* (Belmont, Ca.: Wadsworth Publishing Company, 1971).

32. *World Tribune* (April 17, 1974).

33. Ralph H. Turner and Lewis M. Killian, *op. cit.* (1972), pp. 257-259. Also, see Mayer N. Zald and Roberta Ash, "Social Movement Organizations: Growth, Decay and Change," *Social Forces*, Vol. 44 (1966), pp. 327-341.

34. For further discussion and empirical documentation of this dynamic interplay, see, for example: Benjamin R. Epstein and Arnold Forster, *Report on the John Birch Society* (1966); Joseph R. Gusfield, *Symbolic Crusade* (Urbana, Ill.): University of Illinois Press, 1963); and Sheldon L. Messinger, "Organizational Transformation: A Case Study of A Declining Social Movement," *American Sociological Review*, Vol. 20 (1955), pp. 3-10.

35. As a further illustration of the extent to which NSA encourages behavior in accordance with culturally- defined goals, such as winning and material success, consider the following statement provided by a district leader in response to an inquiry from a guest regarding the emphasis that is given to material benefits: "If success and winning in one's society is defined partly on the basis of material possessions, then to chant to improve one's material condition is not wrong or immoral, but is only natural."

36. The language here should call to mind Merton's discussion of "ritualism' as a mode of deviant adaptation, a mode which is defined as "a pattern of response in which culturally defined aspirations are abandoned while one continues to abide almost compulsively by institutional norms." See Robert K. Merton, *Social Theory and Social Structure* (New York: The Free Press, 1968), p. 238. Since NSA encourages - almost compulsively - behavior that rigidly conforms to both cultural aspirations and institutional norms, then it is not ritualistic in the Mertonian sense. But, it seems conceptually interesting to ask, nonetheless, if such compulsive conformity to both goals and norms might not constitute a mode of adaptation not included within Merton's scheme, a mode of adaptation we might refer to as "hyper-ritualism."

37. E. P. Hollander, "Conformity, Status and Idiosyncrasy Credit," *Psychological Review*, Vol. 65 (1958), pp. 117-127. Also, see Hollander's "Competence and Conformity in the Acceptance of Influence," *Journal of Abnormal and Social Psychology*, Vol. 61 (1960), pp. 365-369.

38. E. P. Hollander, *op. cit.* (1958), pp. 120-121.

39. Rodolfo Alvarez, "Informal Reactions to Deviance in Simulated Work Organizations: A Laboratory Experiment," *American Sociological Review*, Vol. 33 (1969), p. 896.

40. Although members attempt to lure outsiders into attending movement meetings by also working their respective interpersonal networks, I was seldom able to observe their work along these lines. Therefore, my discussion of face-to-face proselytizing aimed directly at bringing in recruits is confined solely to how members went about this work on the streets.

41. This was always a most difficult role for me to be cast into. Although it was experientially interesting and illuminating, it presented certain ethical problems. Since my primary commitment was to observe how members went about this work and not to NSA in general or securing potential converts in particular, I felt somewhat uneasy about doing this work and especially about the possibility of being personally responsible for luring some stranger back to a meeting. I thus made it a practice of attempting to talk myself out of this lead role; and when not successful, I would try to sound as unconvincing as possible and would defer all questions to other members of the team.

42. And why not; for "you can get just about whatever you want by chanting," unless it is, as I heard emphasized on several occasions, something that is "inappropriate or harmful to you and others in the eyes of the Gohonzon."

43. *World Tribune* (September 9, 1974).

44. From *The Liturgy of Nichiren Shoshu* (Nichiren Shoshu Academy, 1973), p. 47. There are four other silent prayers which are also recited during Gongyo.

45. It is interesting to note that these discussion meetings are remarkably similar to the meetings conducted by The Oxford Group Movement that existed in the 1920s and 30s. This movement was also known as Buchmanism and Moral Rearmament (MRA). See, for example, Allen W. Eister, *Drawing Room Conversion: A Sociological*

Account of the Oxford Group Movement (Durham, N.C.: Duke University Press, 1950).

46. For a detailed discussion of dramaturgical teamwork, see Erving Goffman, *The Presentation of Self in Everyday Life* (1959), pp. 77-105.

47. *World Tribune* (June 3, 1974).

48. *NSA Quarterly* (Winter, 1975), pp. 8-9.

49. Ibid., p. 10.

50. *World Tribune* (June 3, 1974).

51. *NSA Quarterly* (Winter, 1975), p. 10.

52. *NSA Quarterly* (Winter, 1975), p. 11.

53. Ibid., p. 10.

54. Ibid., p. 11.

55. *NSA Quarterly* (Winter, 1975), p. 14.

56. Ibid.

57. "The Five S's of Giving a Good Experience," *World Tribune* (September 11, 1974). Also, see the *NSA Quarterly* (Winter, 1975), p. 13; and the *World Tribune* (October 25, 1974).

58. See Georg Simmel, "The Secret Society," in Kurt H. Wolff, ed., *The Sociology of Georg Simmel* (New York: The Free Press, 1964).

59. Erving Goffman, *op. cit.* (1959), pp. 104-105. Here it is interesting to note that since such teamwork involves some idealization and concealment, each member is a potential danger to the team's presentation in that he or she might give away the team's secrets. Since not all NSA members are total converts or fully committed to the

movement, there is the very real problem that some may betray certain backstage information. Hence, the necessity of not inviting all members to all of the planning meetings and of not making all information available to all members.

60. Here I want to emphasize that in describing and analyzing NSA discussion meetings from a dramaturgical standpoint, the intent has not been to "debunk" NSA in general or these meetings in particular. Rather, the aim has been to render these meetings sociologically understandable. But as often the case with sociological examination, "debunking" is one of the consequences, whether intended or unintended.

Furthermore, it is also important to emphasize that there is nothing particularly unique or surprising about the fact that these meetings are dramaturgical in character; for just about any collective enterprise involving the promotion of a particular product or message has something of the character of a dramatistic enterprise. As Goffman has noted (op. cit., 1959, p. 105): "Since we all participate on teams, we must all carry within ourselves something of the sweet guilt of conspirators. And since each team is engaged in maintaining the stability of some definitions of the situation, concealing or playing down certain facts in order to do this, we can expect the performer to live out his conspiratorial career in some furtiveness."

61. See E.A. Weinstein and P. Deutschberger, "Some Dimensions of Altercasting," *Sociometry*, Vol. 26 (December 1963), pp. 454-466.

5
THE PARTICIPANTS:
WHO JOINED AND WHY

In order to round out and complete our examination of the growth of NSA, we now turn to a consideration of the convert side of the recruitment equation and to the issue of differential recruitment. More explicitly, we will examine in this chapter the question of who has joined or agreed to give chanting a try, and why some people rather than others?

Our examination of this general problem will be organized in terms of four distinct but interrelated questions, each of which must be considered if we are to gain a comprehensive understanding of who it is that has swelled the movement's ranks and why. First, from a social demographic level of analysis, the question of who joins or who has the movement appealed to calls for information pertaining to the social demographic categories from which the movement has drawn the majority of its adherents. Second, given the fact that NSA, just as most movements, has drawn the majority of its adherents from certain, specifiable social categories rather than at random throughout the social structure, the question arises as to the macrostructural and organizational determinants of the movement's recruitment base. Why some social categories rather than others?

The third question focuses attention on the sociospatial and social relational or network determinants of differential recruitment. In other words, are members typically drawn off the streets or from among existing members' extra-movement acquaintances, friends, and kin? In addressing this question, we move from a macrostructural to a more microstructural and interactional level of analysis by attempting to ascertain whether the movement's network attributes and recruitment patterns and outsiders' interpersonal ties and associations make any significant difference in determining who is most likely to be recruited. Simply put, we are interested here in discovering the microstructural determinants of the movement's spread.

And fourth, there is the question of why do people join and participate from a motivational standpoint. In examining this question, we shift our attention from a structural to a social psychological level of analysis, which typically involves an attempt to isolate the cognitive and attitudinal factors that hypothetically render some people more susceptible to participation than others.

A DEMOGRAPHIC PROFILE OF NSA'S MEMBERSHIP COMPOSITION OVER TIME

To whom has Nichiren Shoshu appealed during its fifteen years of operation in this country? From what social demographic categories has the movement drawn the majority of its adherents? To answer this question, two sets of data are inspected and compared: (1) NSA's own demographic information presented primarily in its *Seminar Report*,[1] and secondarily in various movement newspapers; and (2) the demographic data I compiled from an examination of 504 randomly selected members' testimonies appearing in the *World Tribune* from 1966 through 1974, excluding the years 1972 and 1973.

An important difference in the two data sets should be kept in mind as we proceed: NSA's demographic information pertains to the entire membership, whereas the data derived from my sample pertains more directly to the core or more highly committed and active members. This is suggested by the fact that the average length of membership at the time of each experience or testimony was twenty months, with the mode being one year and the median around fourteen months. Also, when it is considered that the *World Tribune* is, in part, a promotion vehicle, it stands to reason that the less active, less committed, and more peripheral members, who are included in the movement's demographic reports, would not be included in my sample. Other differences between the two data sources will be discussed when appropriate.

Ethnic Composition

In Chapter 3 we noted that NSA has drawn its membership from two general demographic categories or constituencies over time. During the early part of its career in this country - from 1960 to 1965, when it functioned mainly as a Sokagakkai outpost - the movement appealed primarily to culturally transplanted Japanese females and their families. And then, in the middle of the decade, it began to change its orientation, spread its wings, and expand its membership beyond this initial constituency. This change in both orientation and ethnic composition of NSA's membership is clearly reflected in the following table based on NSA's own demographic reports.

TABLE 2
Cumulative Ethnic Composition of Membership over Time*
1960 to 1974

	1960	1965	1970	1974
Oriental	96%	77%	30%	10%
non-Oriental	4%	23%	70%	90%
Total Membership	500	20,000	200,000	220,000

*The figures in the first three columns are derived from the *NSA Seminar Report*. The figures in the last column are reported in the *Mainichi Daily News*, April 6, 1974.

Although this drastic turnover in the ethnic composition of the membership after 1965 appears startling at first glance, it is not so surprising when it is noted that NSA's ranks were allegedly expanded by 180,000 between 1965 and 1971, with the greatest increase occurring after 1967. This rather remarkable change is also indicated in the following table based on the information derived from my sample of members giving testimony in the *World Tribune*.

The correspondence between the figures presented in the two tables is not perfect.[2] Yet, both tables document the same trend: that as NSA began to expand its operation and ranks, there was a corresponding increase in the number and proportion of non-Oriental participants, so much so, in fact, that we can conclusively state that it was non-Oriental Americans who swelled the movement's ranks.[3]

TABLE 3
Ethnicity of Sample of Members Giving Testimony over Time
1966 to 1974

	Before 1968 (1966/1967)	1968	After 1968 (69/70/71/74)	Totals
Oriental	35%	14%	4%	14%
non-Oriental	65%	86%	96%	86%
Totals	144	72	288	504

Gender Composition

The demographic data presented in NSA's *Seminar Report* indicates that as of 1970, 59 percent of the membership was female and 41 percent male. Although the gender composition of my sample of 504 members through 1974 shows the opposite, with 53 percent male and 47 percent female, I do not find the disparity between these two estimates particularly troublesome for the following reasons.

First, when we recall that NSA appealed primarily to Japanese females living in this country during the first five years of its operation,[4] it stands to reason that the movement's overall gender composition might be skewed in the direction of females as of 1970. And second, it is reasonable to suggest that my newspaper sample is probably a bit overrepresented with males for much the same reason offered for the underrepresentation of Oriental experiences in the *World Tribune*. That is, since the movement was attempting to appeal to non-Orientals, and since the majority of Oriental members were female, it follows that the majority of non-Oriental experiences might be male.

Where do these considerations leave us in terms of the overall gender composition of the movement's membership? With a gender profile that changed over time: until 1968-1969 the typical member was female; since then the gender composition balanced out, with the typical core member just as likely to be male as female.

Age Composition

Just as there has been a significant change over time in the ethnic and gender composition of the membership, so there has also been a significant reversal in the age composition of the movement, with the membership becoming considerably younger beginning around 1968. As indicated in the following table based on the data I compiled, only 41 percent of the membership was under thirty prior to 1968, whereas this figure averaged 76 percent after 1968. Accordingly, it seems reasonable to suggest that prior to 1968, not only was the typical member Oriental and female, but she was also over 30; whereas after 1968, the typical member was non-Oriental, of either gender, and under 30.[5]

TABLE 4

Age Composition of Membership over Time

1966 to 1974

	Before 1968 (1966/1967)	1968	After 1968 (69/70/71/74)	Totals
Under 30	41%	54%	76%	63%
Over 30	59%	46%	24%	37%
31 to 40	37%	25%	15%	23%
41 plus	22%	21%	9%	14%
Totals	144	72	288	504

Marital Status

To these two emerging modal membership profiles, we can also add that prior to 1968, the typical core member was married; whereas after 1968, the typical member was single. As indicated in the following table, based on my sample of 504 members, not only has there been a significant increase in the proportion of single members since around 1968, but more than two-thirds of at least the core members are unmarried - a finding that is in keeping with the previous observation regarding the age composition of the membership.

TABLE 5
Marital Status of the Membership over Time
1966 to 1974

	Before 1968 (1966/1967)	1968	After 1968 (69/70/71/74)	Totals
Married	51%	46%	18%	31%
Divorced or Widowed	8%	4%	13%	10%
	41%	50%	69%	59%
Totals	144	72	288	504

Socioeconomic Composition of the Membership

In order to round out the demographic profile of NSA's membership and thereby move closer to a more precise understanding of who has joined the movement, one further question calls for examination: from what social classes or socioeconomic categories within the larger social struture has the movement drawn the majority of its adherents? Although I was not able to secure data pertaining directly to members' income characteristics, both of the data sources on which this demographic profile has been based contained information regarding the occupational composition of the membership. Accordingly, I will attempt to shed some light on the above question by inferring the movement's socioeconomic base from its occupational profile, which is provided in the following table. The figures in the

TABLE 6
Occupational Profile of NSA's Membership
And Correspondent Median Earnings

	Occupational Profile Through 1970 (N: Not Reported)	Occupational Profile Through 1974 (N: 553)	Median Earnings of Male Civilians As of 1969
Professional & Technical	18%	16%	$10,516.
Managers and Administrators	4%	6%	$10,300.
Clerical and Sales Workers	10%	15%	$6,812.
Blue Collar	15%	7%	$7,096.
Service Workers	---	5%	$3,684.
Military	---	10%	---
Housewives	27%	16%	---
Students	19%	25%	---
Other	7%	---	---

first column are derived from NSA's *Seminar Report*; those in the second column are based on my sample of members in the *World Tribune*; and the figures in the last column, which refer to the median earnings of male civilians by occupation as of 1969, were included so as to provide a basis for gauging the approximate economic status of the movement's membership.[6]

Given the fact that both profiles indicate that only 22 percent of the membership is employed in the typically higher income and more prestigious professional and managerial lines of work, and given the fact that at least half of NSA's membership is female and the corresponding fact that the median earnings for females have been considerably less than for males, it seems fair to conclude that NSA has drawn the majority of its adherents from the lower half of the socio-economic structure.

That this seems to be a reasonable conclusion is also suggested by the following considerations. First, a more detailed look at members' lines of work categorized as professional or technical indicates that the vast majority are not the incumbents of the higher salaried professional positions. For example, of the fifty-three members whose jobs fall into this category in my sample, 30 percent are employed as teachers, nurses, and the like, and 57 percent point to the field of entertainment as their main line of work, most of whom indicated that they are actors or actresses. Most of this group reside in southern California, and like the majority of individuals associated with the world of Hollywood, most engage in entertainment work on a part-time basis.

A second consideration supporting the above contention is the previously discussed finding that most of the movement's earlier members were culturally transplanted Japanese females and their American husbands or male friends associated with the military. From the personal accounts of many of these earlier members and the fact that few of those associated with the military were officers, it is reasonable to conclude that the majority were in modest financial circumstances.

Also supporting the contention that few of NSA's members have been drawn from the upper-half of the socioeconomic structure are my own ethnographic observations. Nearly all of the discussion meetings I attended were held in homes or apartments that were moderately priced and which were situated in middle-to-working-class residential areas or in neighborhoods characterized by mixed land use and transition. This characterization also applies to most of the members' homes or apartments I visited during promotion activities.

Furthermore, of the ten or so members whom I came to know quite well, most seemed to have fairly checkered occupational careers characterized by movement from one job to another or by working part-time at several different lines of work. One member aspired to be a novelist; so he spent most of his working hours writing and the remainder selling pots and pans and other houseware. Four others pursued their acting careers whenever they could secure a role. Two others combined the student role with various odd jobs, such as working as a short-order cook at a local hot dog stand. Another worked as a teacher's aide whenever called upon, and one jumped from one sales job to another.

In light of the above occupational profile and supportive observations, it seems reasonable to conclude that NSA has appealed primarily to those in the lower-half of the socioeconomic structure, and particularly to those in the lower-middle class. Although this finding is descriptively interesting, it is not surprising from a theoretical standpoint; for it is in keeping with much of the literature exploring the the basis of social support for offbeat religious movements, cults, and sects.[7]

In addition to suggesting the general socioeconomic strata from which the movement has drawn the majority of its adherents, the occupational profile of NSA's membership presented in the preceding table points to some change and variation in the occupational composition of the membership over time. This change is reflected most clearly in the lack of correspondence between the clerical and sales, blue-collar, and student categories in columns one and two, and is illustrated even more clearly in the following table based on the occupational data derived from my sample.[8]

Upon comparing the figures in the three columns, several interesting and seemingly significant trends emerge. First, while there is a fairly sharp increase in the proportion of members employed in white-collar jobs, and particularly in sales and clerical work - from 2 percent prior to 1969 to 22 percent after 1968 - the proportion employed in blue-collar and service work remains constant over time. Second, there is a fairly radical decrease in the proportion of military personnel and particularly military dependents (housewives) over time. And third, there is almost a doubling in the proportion of students.[9]

TABLE 7
Change in the Occupational Composition
of NSA's Membership over Time

	Before 1968 (1966/1967)	1968	After 1968 (69/70/71/74)	Totals
White Collar	14%	30%	49%	38%
Blue Collar and Service Workers	12%	11%	12%	12%
Military (including Housewives)	58%	41%	9%	26%
Students	16%	18%	30%	25%
Totals	84	44	203	331

When the first two trends are considered together, there seems to be some basis for suggesting that the movement's occupational composition and profile became increasingly more white-collar over time. When we consider the trend pointing to a decrease in the proportion of military personnel and housewives, along with the earlier findings pointing to a decrease in the proportion of married and Oriental members, we have additional support for the previous contention that the movement has had essentially two constituencies over time. And this is supported even further by the final trend indicating a sizeable increase in the proportion of students and by the previously mentioned correspondent finding that the movement has been supported primarily by those under thirty since around 1966.

All told, we can now conclusively state what has been suggested in passing: that the question of who the movement appealed to, or who joined from a demographic standpoint, calls for two different answers, each of which points to a different modal membership profile that corresponds with a different time period in the movement's career.

Prior to around 1967, the typical core member was female, Japanese, married, over thirty, most probably a housewife, and of upper-lower to lower-middle class; whereas after 1967-68, the typical core member was non-Oriental, single, under thirty, probably of either gender, a student, lower-level white collar worker, or marginally employed, and lower-middle class in terms of socioeconomic standing.

Although the demographic data derived from my sample of members giving testimonies in the *World Tribune* suggests that the tipping point was around 1968, the exact year marking this transition is not as important as the fact that there was such a change in the movement's membership composition and that this change occurred sometime between 1965 and 1970, the period in which the movement allegedly expanded its ranks by 180,000. Accordingly, the initial question of who has swelled the movement's ranks can now be answered in a definitive manner: its ranks were expanded primarily by non-Orientals and particularly Caucasians, of either sex, who were single, under thirty, and students, lower level white-collar workers or marginally employed during the period between 1965 and 1970.

THE MACROSTRUCTURAL AND ORGANIZATIONAL DETERMINANTS OF NSA'S GROWTH AMONG ITS SECOND GENERAL CONSTITUENCY

In the final pages of James Dator's pre-1965 examination of the Japanese and American members of Sokagakkai, he writes that it would be unlikely that the Gakkai would spread beyond its initial American constitutency.

> We discovered that almost all of the Americans were lower-class, poorly educated, alienated American servicemen who - most importantly - were married to Japanese female members of the Sokagakkai who were much older than their husbands. We doubt that the Sokagakkai will spread much beyond people like these ... because of its Japanese culture-bound forms, language, and administration.[10]

Since the foregoing examination of NSA's demographic composition indicates that NSA has, in fact, spread widely beyond this initial constituency, the intriguing question arises as to what factors accounted for or at least facilitated this diffusion, not only beyond this initial constituency but particuarly among that large category of Americans who, during the second half of the sixties and the early seventies, were under thirty, single, students and/or in a state of role transition, and situated primarily in the middle third of the socioeconomic structure.

The Emergence of a General Social Climate Conducive to the Movement's Spread

In attempting to provide a reasoned answer to the above question, we begin by noting several general underlying social conditions and trends that produced a climate conducive to NSA's flowering and diffusion.

In looking back over the kaleidoscopic American cultural scenario in the decade and a half between 1960 and 1975, one of the more intriguing events was the emergence and diffusion of a complex of collecive phenomena which were, in comparison to much of the political activism and protest that marked the sixties, decidedly more spiritual and inward-looking in terms of orientation and more religious or psychiatric in terms of problem-solving perspective. That is, rather than locating both the origin and solution to various problems and discontents in the socioeconomic political structure, they were located in the psyche or supernatural.

Whereas a good portion of the 1960s, for example, was filled with political demonstrations, sit-ins, and slogans and chants such as "strike, strike, shut it down," "power to the people," and "we shall overcome," the early 1970s witnessed an ascendance of sidewalk proselytizing, various fundamentalistic "Jesus" groups and the Reverand Sun Myung Moon exhorting us to repent, the chanting of various Eastern mantras, and the spread of various meditative and consciousness-expanding techniques. Even John Lennon's 1966 pronouncement that the Beatles were more popular than Christ gave way to George Harrison singing "My Sweet Lord," and Rennie Davis' cry for revolution gave way to his devotion to the Guru Maharaj Ji.

Whether or not the emergence and spread of such phenomena as Transcendental Meditation, Yoga, chanting, and EST (Erhard Seminars

Training), and the apparent shift in the problem-solving orientation of many Americans were in fact manifestations of what Sorokin[11] might have called a swing toward the opposite cultural pole, or, instead, merely forms of faddism and cultism that were episodic and ephemeral, is difficult to say with confidence. One thing is certain, however, and that is that many Americans began in the latter half of the sixties to discover and experiment with various Eastern philosophies and religious and meditative practices in response to what has been variously referred to in the academic literature as collective search for identity, a search for greater meaning, and a search for the real self or at least a more satisfactory locus or base for reconstituting the self.[12]

The connection between this emerging climate of collective exploration or search for greater meaning and the inner or real self and NSA's growth is suggested by the following findings derived from my *World Tribune* sample of members: the fact that nearly twenty-five percent indicated that they had explored other off-beat religious, psychiatric, and non-political phenomena prior to joining NSA; that around another twenty percent indicated that they were "hippies" or wanderers in search of a more meaningful existence, and that fifteen percent experimented with drugs. This searching behavior is suggested even more graphically by the following statements extracted from members' testimomies appearing in the *World Tribune* or given during discussion meetings that I attended.

Male, non-Oriental, Single, under 30: I was searching for a true religion that could fill my basic needs and console my searching mind.

Female, non-Oriental, Married, under 30: I have been a member of several religions, and try as I did to live by them, somehow I fell away. I didn't realize then, but my reason for leaving was always the same. They all lacked something I was searching for. I read many books about different religions. But every way I tried I failed to reach the fulfillment I was seeking.

Male, non-Oriental, Single, under 30: Prior to joining NSA, I had spent a year-and-a-half just roaming around the country looking for something that would bring me a greater happiness. Having grown up in an environment where all emphasis was placed on the material side of life, I saw that this did not prove to be the way to happiness. I therefore rejected everything around me in a search for something of lasting value. I could not work. I wasn't able to see any benefit in any way from working. I dropped out of college because I did not believe this would bring me happiness. I had taken a lot of drugs in an attempt to find myself. I felt as if I was a tiny piece of driftwood afloat in a great current without any power to change the direction in which I was headed.

Male, non-Oriental, Single, under 30: I think I was typical of many young Americans before I was introduced to the life philosophy of Nichiren Shoshu. I felt alienated from my entire environment ... I began searching for something to give meaning and happiness to my life ... So this past summer I encouraged a friend of mine to accompany me to that magical land of California I had heard so much about. I arrived in the Golden State searching for happiness in those things which I realize now would never bring happiness and contentment to my life.

Female, non-Oriental, Single, over 30. Up until I was 34, I did nothing but indulge myself... By that time I had become mixed-up, unhappy, lonely, and withdrawn... Then, at 34, in California, my search began. First it was Science of the Mind. I received their monthly magazine, trying to follow the guidance on how to live. Then I followed Unity, listening to their radio programs and hearing answers for specific problems... . Next I looked at Christian Science, attending the church with a friend... . Then I was into metaphysics, and my involvement deepended at this point. I was guided by the Ouiji Board. It said that three of us were going to the Salton Sea shortly. Sure enough, we left that weekend, driving through the night towards the desert. In the back seat with a flashlight, a friend of mine was reading "I Rode a Flying Saucer" by George Von Tassle.

Von Tassle had a large camp where hundreds of people met in the desert ... to watch for flying saucers.

For the next two or three years I was there each weekend sitting in the darkness ... At these gatherings I met some people who believed in the living dead. I experienced astro-projections. As I left my physical body behind, I didn't know where I could want to travel to. Then, when Von Tassle announced that he wanted to run for President, I quit ... I then went to Subid meetings, tried Yoga exercises, and finally ended up in psychotherapy. The next three years were in Freudian therapy, then two more years in Reichian analysis. I then stopped and tried to apply this to my life ... Transcendental meditation involved my attention for the next few months...

In presenting these few accounts, the last of which is probably somewhat exceptional, I do not mean to imply that all individuals who joined NSA were necessarily seekers or searchers. Rather, these accounts are presented merely to illustrate further that beginning in the second half of the sixties, a growing number of Americans were intrigued by and actively experimenting with a variety of off-beat and purportedly therapeutic philosphies and practices in hopes of finding greater meaning in their lives, that a virtual smorgasbord of such philosophies and practices was beginning to emerge, and that the language of alienation, meaninglessness, and spiritual search was becoming part of our everyday vernacular. And, as a consequence, a climate began to emerge that was more favorable for the propagation and diffusion of culturally imported philosophies and practices such as chanting Nam-Myoho-Renge-Kyo. Indeed, by the mid-1970s, it seemed as though active experimentation with many forms of chanting, meditation, and self-discovery had become an accepted and even respectable pursuit in many social circles.

These observations suggest, then, that NSA flowered and spread beyond its initial constituency during a period in which a growing number of Americans were becoming more receptive to such off-beat practices as chanting, and in a climate that was therefore more conducive to the expansion of its ranks.

The Emergence of a General Movement Constituency

Another interesting aspect of the sixties was the emergence of what I think can be referred to as a propitious, general movement constituency, a constituency from which not only NSA drew the majority of its members but from which many contemporary movements have drawn their active adherents. Here I refer to part of that large demographic cohort of individuals who were born shortly after World II and who were unmarried, under thirty, situated primarily in the middle third of the socioeconomic structure, and either students, marginally employed, or in a state of occupational flux and role transition during the 1960s and early 1970s.

Although one might question the assertion that many contemporary movements have drawn the majority of their active adherents from this general demographic cohort, earlier examination of the demographic composition of NSA's membership, as well as a close look at the demographic characteristics of the active participants in such collective phenomena as the Krishna movement, the Jesus movement, the Moon Movement, and even in the anti-war movement and the civil rights movement, suggests that this assertion is, in fact, empirically grounded. The question thus arises as to how we might account for the fact that a disproportionate number of the active particpants in many contemporary movements, including NSA, have been drawn from the same general demographic cohort.

Most attempts to account for both the origins and basis of social support for movements typically take the form of a structural strain explanation, an explanation that posits a linkage between movement emergence and participation and the actual or perceived existence of conflicts, inequities, ambiguities, and deprivations in the social order at large or among particular groupings within the society.[13]

Since this approach focuses attention on the fact that movements do not arise in a social vacuum but have their origins in social conditions perceived to be problematic, we might hypothesize that the reason for active support of many contemporary movements by members of the demographic cohort in question is because many members of this category have defined certain social events, discrepancies, and trends to be more problematic than have members of other social demographic categories. While there may well be some merit to this proposition, I find it unsatisfactory and question-begging for a number of reasons. First, since we have yet to develop an objective measure or set of indicators of strain that consistently correlate with and predict movement activity, most structural strain explanations tend to be tautological in that movement activity and participation is taken as evidence for the existence of underlying strains that are assumed to be experienced most acutely by those who participate. And second, not all individuals who share the same demographic attributes and who are similarly situated in the social structure participate in or verbally support movements that are directed at alleviating problems or strains that purportedly affect them.

Although this can be explained in part by differences in individual ideological orientation and problem perception, such that some individuals define some societal conditions as problematic whereas other similarly situated individuals do not, the fact remains that not all individuals who perceive or feel certain ambiguities, tensions, conflicts, or deprivations act upon these perceptions or feelings by participating in movements, protest activities, cults or fads. In other words, not all individuals who were strongly opposed to the Vietnam War actively participated in anti-war protests, not all ghetto Blacks took part in the ghetto riots, and not all individuals who find their daily lives and routines devoid of meaning and positive feedback experiment with chanting, encounter groups, and other meditative and self-discovery techniques.

Taken together, these observations suggest that while the existence of perceived societal conditions, trends, and ambiguities that are defined as troublesome and in need of alteration may be a necessary condition for movement activity, it clearly is not sufficient for explaining who participates and who does not. Hence, the question posed earlier remains problematic. That is, why has NSA, just as many contemporary movements, drawn the majority of its active adherents primarily from among those individuals who are single, under thirty, and either students, marginally employed, or in a state of occupational flux and role transition?

One way of getting at the nub of this is by considering several neglected overlapping structural-demographic factors that operate independently of the structural strain idea and that tend to render some individuals more available for both participation in and active support of social movements. First, those individuals who share the demographic characteristics in question generally lack the number of extraneous commitments and countervailing ties that tend to keep most people from active participation in movements.[14]   Being young, unmarried, in a transitional role such as that of a student or in a state of occupational flux and marginality, and in the process of developing issue and political alignments, such that each new issue or cause can lead to renewed interest and involvement,[15] tends to allow one to follow their ideological fancies and act upon many of their feelings and interests to a greater extent than those individuals who are bound to certain lines of action by virtue of having developed extraneous commitments or countervailing ties such as spouse, children, monetary bills, job, and occupational career and reputation.

Second, and related to the above, is the fact that those in basic transitional roles, such as adolescents and students, those in a state of occupational flux or marginality, such as the unemployed or periodically employed, and those who are the incumbents of occupational positions that enable them to adjust their schedules according to their interests and priorities, such as professors, many social workers and lawyers, and actors and actresses, tend to be more available for active participation in movements for the reason that they have a greater amount of discretionary time that can be allocated to movement activities.

Third, and regarding the active participation of students in particular, it is important to note that the growth and massification of higher education has created, by virtue of lengthening the student generation and expanding the size of student cohorts, a large pool of people who are more readily available to participate in movements because they possess a greater amount of discretionary time and generally lack the pressing extraneous commitments that can tend to inhibit participation among others.[16]

Returning to the earlier question of how we might account for the fact that NSA, just as many contemporary movements, drew the majority of its active adherents from among those individuals who were unmarried, under thirty, and so on at the time of joining, it does not seem unreasonable to suggest that one important factor at play was that members of this demographic cohort tended to be more available for participation in and active support of contemporary movements for the reasons outlined above. Furthermore, it might even be argued that had it not been for the post-World War II baby boom, increasing economic prosperity, and the lengthening of the student generation and the expansion of the size of student cohorts, that this propitious, general movement constituency would not have emerged and that the volume of movement activity that surfaced during the 1960s and early 1970s would have been considerably less. I do not mean to suggest that the actual or perceived existence of underlying conflicts, ambiguities, and inequities are of little importance in the generation of social movements. Nor am I contending that the availability of discretionary time and the lack of pressing extraneous commitments are the only important factors in the determination of who joins and participates. Rather, I am merely arguing that without these two factors the probability of active movement participation diminishes considerably.

The Import of the Nature and Channelling of NSA's Recruitment Efforts

A third factor facilitating NSA's flowering and spread beyond its initial constituency during the second half of the sixties was its own accommodative flexibility and recruitment efforts during this period. Since we have already discussed its recruitment efforts, it will suffice to emphasize that not only did the movement organization direct much of its attention and appeals to students and the young via such outreach mechanisms as the NSA college seminar program and such slogans as "hippy to happy," but it also made various accommodative adjustments, such as proscribing the use of Japanese at meetings and ceasing to publish articles in Japanese in the *World Tribune*, so as to facilitate participation.

In the past few pages I have attempted to account for NSA's flowering and spread beyond its initial constituency to those who were single and under thirty during the second half of the sixties by considering three general factors operating simultaneously: (1) the emergence of a social climate conducive to the propagation of and experimentation with such practices as chanting Nam-Myoho-Renge-Kyo; (2) the emergence of a propitious, general movement constituency consisting of a cohort of individuals who were structurally more available for active movement participation than were members of most other demographic categories and from which NSA drew the vast majority of its active adherents; and (3) NSA's own propagation and recruitment efforts.

While these three factors, in conjunction with the earlier examination of the demographic composition of NSA's membership, provide a fair understanding of who has expanded the movement's ranks and why from a structural-demographic level of analysis, two questions pertaining to the issue of differential recruitment still beg for further examination and analysis: why do some people join already existing movements, whereas other people who are equally available for participation, do not? And, given the number of competing cults and movements that frequently are on the market at the same time, how and why is it that people end up in one rather than another? In other words, why NSA rather than some other, if any other, movement or cult?

THE MICROSTRUCTURAL DETERMINANTS OF NSA'S SPREAD OR WHO JOINS

Although questions such as the above are typically approached from a social psychological level of analysis, it is an obvious but frequently overlooked fact that whatever the reasons or motivations verbalized by movement members or imputed by social scientists for movement participation, such participation cannot occur without prior contact with some catalytic agent. In some way or another, the potential member has to be informed about and introduced into the movement. Thus, even if we assume that some individuals are more inclined towards movement participation than others, the following question still remains: what determines which outsiders or potential participants are most likely to be informed about and brought into contact with one movement rather than another, if any movement at all?

Aside from the work of a handful of social scientists,[17] this bridging process, its determinants, and its relation to the spread of collective behavior and particularly to the question of who joins, has received relatively little attention in the collective behavior literature. In fact, one could assert that a theoretical gap exists between the various hypothesized conditions leading to individual susceptibility to movement participation and actual recruitment to and particpation in one movement or another.

This gap is evident in much of the literature. Toch, for example, contends that the transaction between individual susceptibility and movement appeals is central to understanding who joins and why, but he fails to provide us with an explanation of the way in which this transaction occurs.[18] Similarly, Blumer fails to describe the processes linking social unrest and movement participation.[19] And the various works emphasizing such cognitive states as alienation and relative deprivation as the key determinants of movement participation also fail to consider the mechanisms and processes by means of which these hypothesized susceptibilities and movement appeals and ideology are bridged.

In getting at the crux of this bridging process, what we want to know, then, is what determines the likelihood or probability that outsider A will be contacted rather than outsider B? And, what determines the probability that the contact will be made by one movement rather than another?

In thinking about these questions, it seems logical to begin by considering the ways in which contact between member and outsider or any two individuals might occur. In general, there are only two possibilities. Contact can either occur randomly, in which case every outsider has an equal chance of being contacted by a movement member; or it can be structured, in which case the range of possibilities is narrowed, such that there is a greater probability that only some outsiders will be contacted and recruited. This structuring can occur in two general ways. It can be predicated on spatial factors and patterns, such that the probability for contact increases with a decrease in spatial distance and separation. Or it can be predicated on social factors and patterns, such that the probability for contact between outsider and movement varies with such factors as the movement's structure, strategies, and recruitment opportunities, and the number and intensity of an outsider's secondary and primary relationships.

Since it is a basic sociological tenet that social phenomena (i.e., crime, suicide, life chances, status) are not distributed randomly but are structured or patterned according to aggregate and group membership, role incumbency, and so on, it is reasonable to assume that movement recruitment and information dissemination, rather than being random, will also be structured by certain spatial and social factors and patterns. Hence, the following general orienting proposition:

> The probability of contact between movement members and outsiders will be structured, such that some outsiders,

however, available for or inclined towards participation, will
not be reached, whereas others will have a greater
probability of being contacted and subjected to members'
recruitment efforts.

While this general proposition directs our attention to the probable
importance of structural variables that exist independent of individual
social-psychological attributes, the question still remains as to the type
of structural variables that are hypothetically most influential in the
determination of who is most likely to be informed about, brought into
contact with, and actually join the movement. Since we have already
considered the macrostructural and demographic factors related to the
movement's growth and spread, we are interested here in ascertaining
the microstructural determinants of this problem.

During the course of our earlier examination of the organization
and channelling of NSA's recruitment or Shakubuku efforts, we learned
that its recruitment efforts are concentrated among strangers in public
places and along the lines of members' extra-movement social networks
or interpersonal ties. Accordingly, we can shed some empirical light
on the above proposition and the question pertaining to the
microstructural variables at play by taking a close look at where the
members came from. Were both recruits and members typically drawn
at random off the streets, or from among existing members' extra-
movement acquaintances, friends, and kin? By examining this question,
we will be able to ascertain whether the movement's network attributes
and recruitment patterns and outsiders' interpersonal ties and
associations has made any significant difference in determining who has
been most likely to be recruited into the movement's span of influence.

The data on which this examination is based are derived from two
sources: (1) my own ethnographic observations and the information I
was able to gather from guests and members pertaining to mode of
recruitment; and (2) my sample of 504 members giving testimony in
the *World Tribune*, 330 of whom indicated mode of recruitment.

Regarding my own observations and experiences, I began to
notice, after accompanying members on numerous recruiting
expeditions in public places, that these recruiting forays were not
terribly successful. The recruitment teams in my district seemed to
return empty-handed more often than not. While I ventured into the

streets with other members on over forty different occasions, only twice did we return with recruits. Yet, guests were usually present for most of the meetings. Since they were not being recruited directly off the streets, I began to inquire as to how they had learned about NSA. Invariably, they indicated that they had come with members who were friends or acquaintances. This pattern also surfaced upon investigating the manner in which the fifteen most active members in my district were recruited: two were recruited by spouse, one by another relative, ten by friends or acquaintances, and only two by strangers. All but two of the fifteen members were thus drawn into contact with the movement by virtue of being linked to a member through a preexisting, extra-movement interpersonal tie.

That this pattern of recruitment was not unique to the district or chanting cell in which I was a member, but characterizes the way in which the vast majority of NSA members were brought into sustained contact with the movement, is strongly suggested by the findings pertaining to the mode of recruitment of my sample of members giving testimony in the *World Tribune*. As indicated in the following table, 82 percent revealed that they were recruited by members with whom they had preexisting, extra-movement interpersonal ties, whereas only 18 percent were recruited directly off the streets by strangers.

TABLE 8
Channels and Patterns of Recruitment
1966 to 1974

	Before 1968	1968	1969-71	1974	Totals
Recruited through:					
Social Networks	89%	78%	77%	85%	82%
By Friends or Acquaintances	66%	46%	52%	68%	58%
By Relatives	23%	32%	25%	17%	24%
Recruited Outside of					
Networks (by Strangers)	11%	22%	23%	15%	18%
Number	89	50	137	54	330

In light of these data and my own observations and experiences, and assuming that my sample is representative of the movement's core membership, we can now suggest some provisional answers and propositions with respect to the questions raised earlier. First, regarding the question pertaining to the kinds of microstructural and organizational variables that are hypothetically most influential in determining a movement's recruitment patterns, the above findings point to the role of a movement's network attributes or, more specifically, to the import of members' extra-movement interpersonal networks and ties. Accordingly, it seems reasonable to suggest the following proposition:

> For those movements that have not been driven underground and that are not structurally isolated, in the sense that members are required to sever their extra-movement ties, members' extra-movement social networks and interpersonal ties will function as the most important microstructural determinant of the movement's recruitment patterns and spread.

Second, and regarding the question of what determines the probability that outsider A rather than outsider B will be recruited, the above findings suggest the following corresponding hypothesis:

> Those outsiders who are linked to movement members through preexisting, extra-movement networks will have a greater probability of being contacted and recruited into that particular movement than will those individuals who are outside of members' extra-movement networks.

Since social networks constitute microstructures, what is being emphasized is the primacy of structure in the determination of movement recruitment patterns in general and differential recruitment in particular. In other words, the above findings and propositions suggest that perhaps the network attributes of movements and their participants may be just as, if not more, important in the recruitment process than the social psychological attributes and susceptibilities of outsiders or potential participants.

Whatever the case, the foregoing findings indicate that at least for NSA, the interconnection between its network attributes and outsiders' interpersonal ties and associations has been a most important factor in the determination of its recruitment patterns and diffusion. And what is more, NSA seems to be well aware of all of this. As one informant indicated when we were disscussing this matter of recruitment:

> It has been my experience that the best results come from Shakubukuing friends. I was Shakubukued by a friend, and nearly all the members I'm responsible for were friends or at least people I knew.

And as noted in an October 1974 edition of the *World Tribune*:

> Many people feel that a certain area is good or bad by judging the type of people they see walking the streets at any given time. But a district that depends on people pulled off the street for its Shakubuku is in a weak condition. The wisest and most meaningful Shakubuku is done with a heart-to-heart communication between friends. Of course, occasional guests will come in from the streets, but it is more of an exception than a rule.

Discussion of Related Questions and Theoretical Implications

The Street Recruits: Who Are They? Although there seems to be little question but that the vast majority of members are recruited by friends, acquaintances, or relatives, and although the likelihood of being recruited into NSA seems to be largely dependent on whether one is linked to one or more members via an extra-movement interpersonal tie, the fact that a good many guests and members are actual strangers should not be glossed over. As indicated earlier, 18 percent of the members in my sample were recruited off the street, and as suggested above, guests occasionally come from the streets, even though "it is more of an exception than a rule." The question thus arises as to who are these street recruits? In other words, who, out of the large pool of individuals contacted on the street, agrees to attend a meeting, and of those that do so, who are the few that assume nominal membership by agreeing to give chanting a try?

Regarding those individuals who consent to attend a meeting, but who neither join nor return to another meeting, most shared the following characteristcs: they usually resided in the general area in which they were recruited; they usually attended the meeting in the company of another non-member friend or two; they were not doing anything in particular at the time of contact - that is, they had unscheduled time; they usually indicated that they attended out of curiosity or some counter-missionary interest; and they were not structural or social isolates in that they had ongoing, proximal ties and extraneous commitments that tend to function as countervailing influences.

In contrast to these street recruits who attended a meeting but failed to join, those few who did both all had one critical feature of their life-situation in common at the time of recruitment: social isolation in the sense of not having any strong, proximal ties or countervailing commitments. More explicitly, most seemed to have been recent arrivals to the particular area in which they were recruited; most seemed to have few, if any, close friends or relatives within this area; and all had a great amount of unscheduled and discretionary time. As illustrative of these observations, consider the following account, extracted from a testimony given during a chapter discussion meeting, of how and why one twenty-five year old male came to join NSA:

> I found myself here in L.A., with nothing but the clothes I was wearing. I didn't know anybody. I didn't have any money. It was really a strange situation.
>
> I had just flown into the L.A. Airport, and all my baggage came up missing. This was on Saturday night. Since I didn't know anybody and didn't have any place to go, I went to the airport police station and was told to go to Travelers' Aid. But I learned that they wouldn't be open until Tuesday, since this was Labor Day weekend. So I waited around the airport until Tuesday and then went down to Travelers' Aid. They sent me to the Welfare Department. After spending four days waiting and filling out forms, I was told I couldn't qualify for welfare because I wasn't a California resident.

At this point I didn't know what to do. So I spent a few nights at the Midnight Mission, and then decided to go to the Santa Monica Beach. That evening, while I was walking around downtown Santa Monica, this guy came up to me and started talking about Nam-Myoho-Renge-Kyo, and asked if I would like to go to a meeting. Since I didn't have anything to do, I went along.

And all of a sudden I find myself at this meeting where everybody was chanting. I didn't have the faintest idea about what was going on. I had never heard of the chant before, and didn't know there was such a group as NSA. But since everybody was telling me to give chanting a try, I figured why not? I literally didn't have anything to lose. So I joined, and I've been chanting ever since - which is about four months.

Since this account typifies the life-situation, at the time of contact, of most members recruited directly off the street, it seems reasonable to suggest that in the absence of preexisting, extra-movement ties to one or more members, differential recruitment (i.e,. why one movement rather than another, or why any movement at all) is largely a function of: (1) time, space, and chance - that is, being in the right place at the right time; (2) the possession of unscheduled time; and (3) the lack of strong, proximal interpersonal ties and extraneous commitments. It thus follows that few people are recruited off the streets for two basic reasons: first, most people walking the streets are engaged in the business of completing a particular line of action - such as shopping, going to a movie, and the like - and, therefore, have little if any unscheduled or free time when confronted by movement recruiters. And second, most individuals walking the streets in most urban areas have a number of fairly strong, proximal ties and extraneous commitments that function as countervailing influences, at least when confronted by a proselytizing stranger.

The Relationship between Movement Network Attributes, Recruitment Patterns, and Growth. In the preceding chapter, I hypothesized that a movement that constitutes a relatively closed, insulated, and interlocking network of social relations is structurally compelled to concentrate its promotion and recruitment efforts in public places; whereas a movement that constitutes a structurally more open and inclusive network of social relations, such as NSA, can channel its recruitment efforts along the lines of members' extra-movement social networks as well as in public places. I then asked whether such differences in movement network attributes and corresponding recruitment patterns make any significant difference in the success of a movement's recruitment efforts and growth.

Since the aforementioned findings and observations suggest that recruitment among extra-movement acquaintances, friends, and kin yields a greater return in terms of actual recruits than does recruitment in public places, it follows that a movement's network attributes and corresponding recruitment patterns do, in fact, make a significant difference in a movement's recruitment efforts and growth. Hence, the following corresponding propositions:

> The success of movement recruitment efforts, measured by the number of outsiders actually recruited, will vary with the extent to which movements are linked to other groups and networks via members' extra-movement interpersonal ties; such that:

> Movements that are linked to other groups and networks will normally grow at a more rapid rate and normally attain a larger membership than will movements that are structurally more isolated and closed.[20]

Most social network analyses and studies of social isolation have focused on the individual and the extent and strength of his or her interpersonal ties, with a paucity of social ties taken as a reflection of structural social isolation. This focus may be useful for understanding some individual behavioral patterns and propensities, such as voting and movement joining. However, it tends to obscure the fact that social isolation can also occur at the group or movement level, as when a movement has few, if any, direct links with other groups and therefore constitutes a closed network or insulated system of social relations. When this occurs, the above findings and propositions suggest that such movements will differ markedly from structurally less isolated groups in terms of recruitment possibilities and patterns and overall growth. The foregoing analysis thus posits an additional but frequently neglected and hypothetically significant determinant of the movement recruitment process: the extent to which a movement is linked to or isolated from other groups and networks within the larger society of operation.

Additional Empirical Support and Theoretical Implications: An Examination of the Literature. As indicated earlier, the relationship between movement network attributes, outsiders' interpersonal ties and associations, and movement recruitment patterns and growth has received relatively little theoretical or empirical attention in the literature pertaining to movement recruitment in general and differential recruitment in particular. Yet, there are a few works that not only shed additional empirical light on this neglected problem but whose findings are in keeping with and supportive of the above findings and propositions.

Aside from the tangentially related work of Kerckhoff and Back,[21] which points to the role of social networks in the spread and channelling of an epidemic of hysterical contagion, Gerlach and Hine, in their study of a number of Pentecostal groups, found that new members' first contact with the movement usually followed pre-existing social network lines. In most cases, new members were introduced to the movement by a relative, a close friend, a neighbor, or an associate of some sort with whom the new convert had meaningful contact prior to recruitment.[22] Similarly, Harrison's examination of recruitment to Catholic Pentecostalism revealed that "over half (59 percent, $N = 169$) of all members who received the Baptism after encountering the movement first heard about it from close friends.[23] Lofland's study of recruitment and conversion to a small millenarian cult also suggests the importance of pre-existing friendship ties and networks.[24] And several of the works pertaining to the growth and spread of the Sokagakkai in Japan indicate that the vast majority of its adherents were recruited by membrs who were pre-existing friends, acquaintances or kin.[25]

Although the works cited above all pertain to religious cults and movements, there are also a number of studies that allude to the importance of overlapping networks and interpersonal ties in recruitment to political and nonreligious, reformist-like movements.[26] And one study that set out to examine the social psychological orientation hypothetically predisposing individuals to participation in the peace movement even reached the tentative conclusion that:

... recruitment into peace groups is less often the result of
self-selection of the group by the recruit than of being
recruited through belonging to social networks, some of
whose members already belong to the peace group.[27]

In light of these corroborating findings, there seems to be little question
but that the aforementioned propositions rest on firm empirical ground.

Additionally, my findings regarding recruitment to NSA, along
with those presented above, provide us with an empirical basis for
assessing two prominent, contrasting theoretical perspectives in the
social movement literature: the mass society perspective, as presented
most clearly by Kornhauser;[28] and the so-called power-conflict
perspective articulated in the works of Gamson[29] and Oberschall.[30]
While both perspectives attempt to account for the emergence and
sources of support for a variety of movements that are radical or
reformist in character, each offers a contrasting explanation.

The mass society approach argues that vulnerability to movement
participation is largely a function of being weakly attached and
peripheral to existing social networks and solidary groups. Movement
participants are thus seen as those individuals who lack a series of
institutional affiliations and group loyalties that presumably bind people
to the larger socio-political system; whereas those who are connected
to and embedded in various intermediate associations are hypothetically
less available for participation in emergent collective phenomena and,
therefore, less susceptible to the appeals of proffered social movements.
In short, readiness to participate comes from an absence of those
conditions that integrate others into the system and constrain them from
involvement.

In contrast, the power-conflict perspective contends that movement
participants are recruited primarily from among those who are attached
to and embedded in various social networks and intermediate
groupings. From this vantage point, it is not the socially isolated,
atomized, and uprooted who are most available for recruitment to and
participation in social movements.

Since this latter perspective suggests that overlapping networks
and membership in secondary and primary groups can facilitate
movement recruitment, and since this is in keeping with the above
findings and grounded propositions, we might conclude that the power-

conflict approach is empirically more on target than is the mass society perspective insofar as the issue of movement recruitment is concerned.

Yet, I think we must be careful not to dismiss the mass society perspective in toto. While there is a lack of convincing empirical support for its central thesis, it is not totally unfounded. As indicated in the preceding table (Table 8), 18 percent of the members of my sample were not only drawn off the streets, but this figure hovered close to 25 percent in the years between 1966-67 and 1972, a period in which there was a seemingly inordinate number of young people wandering the streets. Furthermore, the mass society perspective implicitly or explicitly underscores several factors suggested earlier as being of major importance in the determination of who is most available for, if not susceptible to, movement participation. Here I am referring to such situational and microstructural factors as the possession of unscheduled and discretionary time and the lack of strong extraneous commitments and countervailing ties. And finally, it is difficult to take exception with its contention that the confluence of various large-scale structural trends and events frequently gives rise to the emergence of propitious, general movement constituencies that are characterized in part by cultural estrangement and social isolation.[31]

What these considerations suggest, then, is that while mass society theory overemphasizes the import of social isolation at the level of individuals and while it fails to explain how it is that the weakly attached and social isolated get involved in the movements that they hypothetically join, there are, nonetheless, certain components of this approach that are worthy of retention and perhaps incorporation into a general theory of movement recruitment.

A Reconsideration of the Function of Sidewalk Promotion and Recruitment. In the previous chapter we saw that NSA members spend a great deal of time and energy promoting the *World Tribune* in public places and combing the streets in search of recruits. But we also learned that relatively few people contacted on the street buy the *World Tribune*, much less take out a subscription, and that relatively few guests and members are actually drawn off the streets. The question thus arises as to why core members devote so much time and energy to street-side promotion and recruitment when it does not seem to be a terribly productive enterprise in terms of what it actually yields.

Additionally, it is important to bear in mind that confronting strangers on the street is a rather difficult interpersonal task that would seem to require a considerable amount of courage and conviction. I know I was terribly reluctant about doing this sort of thing, both for ethical reasons, and because I lacked the requisite courage and conviction. I also sensed that other members were equally reluctant from time to time. In fact, the difficulty of doing this sidewalk promotion was openly discussed on occasion. As one district leader explained while discussing Shakubuku during a new members meeting:

> When I was a brand new member like you, I didn't want
> to do Shakubuku in the streets at all. I had already chanted,
> and knew that chanting to the Gohonzon worked. But for
> me to go out in the street and walk up to a stranger and ask
> if he'd ever heard of Nam-Myoho-Renge-Kyo was too much.
> I couldn't do it at first. I'd muster up some courage, walk
> up to someone, and then excuse myself and walk away.

Given the difficult nature of this work, why are members encouraged to take to the streets? And why do they do so? What, then, are the functions of sidewalk promotion and recruitment, and what or where is the reinforcement? In attempting to shed some light on this issue, I begin by examining the major organizational and goal-related functions of this work, and then turn to a consideration of its functions at the level of the individual member and the corresponding problem of reinforcement.

From the standpoint of the movement organization and its goals, recall that sidewalk promotion and recruitment constitutes one of several outward-reaching goal attainment activities engaged in for the purpose of enhancing outsiders' awareness of the movement, spreading the word, and bringing in recruits. Although it may not be the most productive Shakubuku activity insofar as some of these interests are concerned, the fact remains that strangers will occasionally purchase an edition of the *World Tribune* and that guests and members are occasionally recruited off the streets. As a consequence, deployment of members in sidewalk promotion is not a total waste of time, energy, and people. And this is especially true when we consider that the actual doing of this work can function as an important commitment-building mechanism.

Since the movement places a great deal of emphasis on the doing of Shakubuku in general and street-side Shakubuku in particular, and since this work involves a considerable amount of time, energy, and courage, members are expected to forego other extraneous activities and the comfort or security of standing on the sidelines and watching. Through this double-edged process of making personal sacrifices for the sake of the movement, on the one hand, while committing one's time and energy to this rather difficult task, on the other hand, one's linkage to and investment in the movement increases over time. As Kanter discovered in her examination of the factors accounting for the differential durability of thirty nineteenth-century communes, the more successful ones - those lasting thirty-three years or more - were those with a greater number and variety of commitment building strategies and mechanisms, one of which was the requirement that members devote their time and energy to communal activities. As she writes in her discussion of investment mechanisms:

> ... Investment can be a simple economic process involving tangible resources, or it can involve intangibles like time and energy. If a group desires a set of committed members, it should require them to devote their time and energy to the system ... Through investment, individuals are integrated with the system, since their time and resources have become part of its economy. They have, in effect, purchased a share in the proceeds of the community, and now hold a stake in its continued good operation.[32]

But not only does street-side promotion and recruitment function to foster and sustain commitment to the movement by requiring members to devote a considerable amount of time and energy; it also, and perhaps more importantly, forces members to lodge or anchor their self-conceptions and identities in the movement. Each time a member confronts an outsider for the purpose of Shakubuku, for example, he or she is publicly announcing association with the movement and thereby forcing others - including members - to respond in terms of that association or identity, all of which functions to establish and strengthen the linkage between self and movement. As Turner and Killian have noted in this regard:

> When the individual goes on record in public in support of a movement, he becomes committed because persons around him are inclined to treat him as an adherent and to expect continued adherence from him.[33]

In addition to building commitment to the movement in the ways suggested above, the doing of Shakubuku, rather among extra-movement associates or strangers on the street, can also function to strengthen a member's belief with respect to the movement's interpretive system and ideology. Since the primary purpose of Shakubuku is to persuade others to attend a meeting and give chanting a try, members can unwittingly convince themselves while trying to convince others. In other words, the mere act of Shakubuku can deepen a member's belief in the message being pushed and the lines employed. That NSA sees the practice of Shakubuku as partly functioning in this way is nicely illustrated by the following statement recorded one evening during a guidance session:

> Every night NSA members are busy in their chapters or districts doing Shakubuku or promoting the *World Tribune*. And because of such a hectic schedule, other people looking at NSA may wonder just what the purpose is behind all of this Shakubuku. Is it to become professional *World Tribune* promoters or professional Shakubuku-ers? If the answer is yes, then our movement must be a pretty shallow one that will eventually fade away with the passage of time. Nor do we Shakubuku just for the sake of getting new members. No, there is another purpose behind Shakubuku - and that is to build strong members and deepen their faith.

Or as frequently and succinctly put by core members:

> Practice - which includes Shakubuku as well as chanting - is the means to belief and understanding.[34]

While the foregoing suggests why members are encouraged and expected to take to the streets from the standpoint of the movement organization and its leadership and goals, the question of what compels many of the members to actually engage in this work still remains problematic. More explicitly, given the fact that confronting strangers in the street is a rather difficult interpersonal task, the fact that few strangers buy the *World Tribune*, and the fact that few recruits are drawn off the streets, the question arises as to what is in it for the individual member? How is this street-side work justified, and what or where is the reinforcement?

As suggested in several of the preceding chapters, this work is ideologically justified or rationalized in three basic ways. First, it is rationalized from an altruistic and karmic standpoint as the greatest cause one makes for the sake of others. Second, it is rationalized from an egocentric and karmic standpoint as a source of benefit in one's daily life. Here it is important to recall that since Shakubuku is the most important cause a member can make next to chanting, and since the mere act of telling others about Nam-Myoho-Renge-Kyo produces personal benefits, it follows that those who Shakubuku will receive "greater and more divine benefits" than those who just sit on the sidelines and chant. Accordingly, members are told that if they want to receive more and better benefits, they must not only chant, but they must also Shakubuku. And since interpersonal networks can be exhausted in a relatively short period, one may therefore have to turn to the streets in order to maximize his or her benefits.

The third basic ideological justification for engaging in this street-side work is the belief that all of those who are told about Nam-Myoho-Renge-Kyo will eventually chant. This belief is nicely illustrated by the following exchange that occurred one evening as another member and I were returning empty-handed to the district house:

DS: I guess we weren't terribly successful tonight, were we?

Member: What do you mean? We really made a lot of causes tonight. And you know that all of the people we Shakubukued tonight will be chanting some day. Everybody that is told about NSA eventually begins to chant. When did you first hear about NSA?

DS: It was about a year before I joined.

Member: See, it never fails. Everyone we spoke with tonight will end up chanting just like you.

Or as a district leader similarly explained during a new members meeting.

I know it is easy to get frustrated when you try to recruit strangers in the street. But you really shouldn't get upset. Just the other day I went out and Shakubukued forty people, and not one person agreed to come to a meeting. But I didn't get upset; for I felt that I had really done my best in planting seeds of curiosity and interest. Besides, I knew that sometime in the future those people will begin to chant. So don't worry when you do Shakubuku whether the people you contact come to a meeting right away; for they will definitely chant some day - even though it may not be for a year or two.

Thus, rather than seeing street-side Shakubuku as a fruitless enterprise and defining non-responsiveness on behalf of strangers as failure, core members see it otherwise. That is, much like the farmer sowing the field, they operate on the belief that the seeds of curiosity and interest they have planted will eventually blossom and bear them some fruit.

In addition to the above ideological rationalizations and justifications for taking to the streets, there are two other factors that can be equally compelling: peer pressure, and the fact that the doing of Shakubuku is an important means to gaining favor and esteem in the eyes of district peers and movement leaders.

Should all of these factors fail to provide some members with sufficient reason for engaging in street-side Shakubuku, then it is quite likely that they will remain nominal members at best or drop out of the movement at worst. Although it is safe to assume that many members follow one of these two paths, it is also important to keep in mind that it was my experience that a good many members do, in fact, take to the streets, presumably because of one or more of the reasons suggested above or because some of them are full-blown rather than nominal converts.[35]

RATIONALIZING PARTICIPATION: A CRITICAL EXAMINATION OF THE SEARCH FOR SOCIAL PSYCHOLOGICAL/MOTIVATIONAL PREDISPOSITIONS

In the preceding pages in this chapter, I have attempted to answer the question of "who has expanded NSA's ranks and why?" by examining the movement's demographic composition over time, by considering the macrostructural and organizational determinants of its growth, and by examining the situational and microstructural factors that were most influential in determining who was most likely to be subjected to the movement's recruitment efforts, attend a meeting or two, and perhaps join. However important these structural and situational factors in explaining the movement's growth and in furthering our understanding of the recruitment process in general and the issue of differential recruitment in particular, a vexing question still remains: why do some individuals who have been brought directly into the movement's orbit of influence respond negatively, whereas others respond positively by deciding to give chanting a try and to become nominal converts. Why, in other words, do some people decide to join? Pursuit of this question requires that we turn to the social psychological level of analysis and consider the motivational determinants of initial participation.

Underlying most attempts to account for differential recruitment from a social psychological/motivational standpoint is the assumption that movement joiners differ considerably from non-joiners in terms of personality constitution or attitudinal and cognitive orientation. Although there is considerable variation in the theoretical scope and content of the numerous works operating on this assumption - ranging from movement-specific through middle-range to more general and inclusive theories,[36] they generally reflect an attempt to establish a psycho-functional linkage between the social psychological attributes of potential or actual participants (which are usually conceptualized as motivational predispositions or susceptibilities) and the goals and ideologies of movements (which are usually referred to as appeals).

Especially illustrative of this approach is Toch's[37] examination of the relationship between individual predispositions, susceptibility, and types of movement appeal. For Toch, the appeal and growth of movements lie in their offer of favorable prospects for imminent improvement of the life conditions or social psychological strains that characterize a particular constituency or group of individuals. Although Toch does not posit a specific motivational orientation or social psychological attribute as conducive to movement susceptibility, a number of overlapping and hypothetically predisposing motives or orientations are readily discernible in the literature. While these range from a sense of powerlessness and status inconsistency, to a search for greater meaning and a more satisfactory identity, to cultural estrangement and a quest for community, most can be conceptualized as variants of alienation, relative deprivation, or authoritarianism.

Whatever the hypothetical predisposing motives or special psychological strains, though, the central task at this level of analysis is the identification of the personality characteristics or cognitive states that supposedly render some people susceptible to movement appeals and which therefore motivate and sustain movement participation.

A Critical Assessment of the Motivational Approach

Although it seems reasonable to assume that some people are more susceptible than others to movement appeals and participation because of certain preexisting social psychological tensions, cognitive orientations, and personal needs, there are a number of shortcomings with this approach that call into question its analytic and predictive utility. First, much of the literature addressing the hypothetical association between preexisting social psychological strains and participation in movements and various forms of collective protest suggests a relatively indeterminate relationship. For example, not only have alienation and relative deprivation been linked to apathy and non-participation, but such cognitive states have also been associated with participation in such disparate collective phenomena as ghetto riots, cargo cults, religious movements, reform-oriented movements, and political movements on both the right and left. Hence, the relationship between social psychological strains, cognitive orientations, and movement participation in general and the form of activity in which one participates in particular remains empirically and theoretically problematic.[38]

A second and related shortcoming with the social psychological/ motivational mode of explanation is that relatively low correlations have been found between hypothetically predisposing strains and cognitive orientations and participation in movements and collective protest.[39]

A third and more serious shortcoming with this mode of analysis is that it is confronted with an acute methodological problem that is usually side-stepped. If we are interested in ascertaining the reasons or motives for movement participation, how are we to discover these reasons? How are we to assess the various social psychological propositions regarding who joins and why? The only recourse we have is to ask the members themselves or to examine their motivational accounts rendered during movement activities or presented in movement literature. But whichever course is taken, a problem arises in terms of the chronological sequence in which such data are ordinarily gathered and the meaning we give to that data. From both a time-order and variable analysis standpoint, there are normally three basic time-periods involved in the research process:

TIME 1	TIME 2	TIME 3
Independent Variable: Cognitive state or life situation just prior to participation.	Dependent Variable: Participation in movement or protest activity.	Data: Participant's motivational account or response to researcher's inquiry.

The research aim of ascertaining the cognitive states or problem situations that hypothetically precipitated participation at Time 2 is certainly a legitimate and worthwhile problem for investigation. It becomes methodologically questionable, however, when participants are questioned at Time 3 and their retrospective accounts or attitudinal responses are accepted at face value and taken as indicators of their actual cognitive orientation or life situation at Time 1. Participation is thus accounted for in terms of participants' verbalized response to the researchers' motivational inquiry at Time 3.

But unless conducting a before-and-after type of panel study, how can we be sure that the hypothesized independent variables - avowed reasons for joining or elicited attitudes - are not artifacts of the phenomenon we are seeking to explain, that is, participation? Are the avowed preexisting cognitive states or motives alluded to by participants during or after participation the ones that actually led to participation, or does the act of joining and the fact of participation give rise to the avowal of these cognitive states and motives? For example, was participation in many of the civil disturbances of the 1960s a function of some preexisting riot ideology, as many have argued, or was this emergent ideology an epiphenomenon of the disturbance, one that emerged after the fact and provided participants with a post-factum account for their participation?

What is being suggested is that the motivational account extracted at Time 3 may very well be a product of participation or membership itself. Hence, what is frequently conceptualized as the independent or intervening variable may, instead, be a dependent variable or consequence of the participation experience and/or the researcher's motivational challenge or inquiry. And this is especially true when participation occurs in the context of a movement that involves some type of conversion process through which the participant acquires a new primary universe of discourse or informing point of view and its attendant "vocabulary of motives" or set of rationalizations and justifications for acting.[40]

Thus, we are confronted with the following interpretive problem: are we to interpret members' accounts of why they joined NSA as the actual reasons for joining, or are we to interpret them as reflections of the extent to which members have adopted the movement's interpretive schema and its attendant diagnostic view of the world and vocabulary of motives?

The relevance of this problem becomes even more apparent when we consider that conversion to NSA, just as to many movements and alternative world views, entails a total or partial reinterpretation of one's past and the discovery or reconceptualization of various personal needs and problems.[41] That this is so is suggested by the following observations: NSA's diagnostic view of the world, which portrays life without chanting as being laden with problems, unhappiness, and alienation; by the fact that members are instructed to structure their testimonies so as to reflect how chanting resolved one or more pre-participation problems; and by the fact that members do, indeed, reconstitute their past as being troublesome and laden with one or more problems that were not readily identifiable prior to participation. As illustrative of this process, consider the following statements extracted from members' testimonies rendered during discussion meetings or presented in the *World Tribune*:

Female, Caucasian, single, under 30: Approximately a year ago I thought I was really enlightened and completely happy. I was going around screaming and protesting for what I thought was the right cause. Little did I know that I wasn't making the right cause and that I was creating so much anti-value in my life. My ideas were all based on doing exactly what I wanted to do, whether it was good for me or not.

Instead of going around creating anti-value with my old friends, I'm now introducing them to NSA and the Gohonzon. Before, I would have had posters all over the house, now in their place, I have pictures of President Ikeda and photos of the convention. These really have meaning to me.

Female, Black, single, under 30: I am an entirely different person. I never thought I would have much of a future or grow up to enjoy the world. I was against everything. I hated myself the most of all, but I didn't know it until the Gohonzon showed that there was a different kind of world.

Married Couple, Caucasian, over 30: Our relationship with each other improved fantastically after we joined NSA. Where we thought we were happily married before, we found that there were many hidden barriers between us, many illusions hiding our true selves from ourselves, and each other.

Female, Caucasian, single, under 30: Chanting has cleared my mind enough to see that in the years before I chanted I had many misconceptions about life. I saw myself as coming from a happy family and having a good job, but I had many problems that I avoided looking at until chanting brought out the wisdom that could help me see these problems.

Female, Caucasian, divorced, over 30: All the years I lived up until I joined were in a sense a waste of time.

Although I didn't know that until I began chanting, I can now look back and see how things have changed, how much better off I am now than before.

Male, Caucasian, married, over 30: After you've been chanting for a while, you'll look back, just as I have, and see how far you've progressed. After you chant for a while, you'll look back and say, 'Gee, I was sure a rotten, unhappy person.' I know I thought I was a saint before I chanted, but shortly after I discovered what a rotten person I was and how many problems I had. It's really amazing. All the problems you had before chanting will become clear and will be resolved. And you'll look back and say, 'My goodness, I've really changed for the better, I'm a much happier person now.'

The talk, testimonies, and accounts of core members thus suggest that conversion to NSA bifurcates the past and present by driving a wedge between life before chanting and life after chanting. Moreover, old facts or aspects of one's life are given new meaning, encompassing a negative evaluation of former identity and a reconstitution of one's past, or at least some aspect of it, as being problematic and troublesome. Obversely, one's life since chanting is defined as being on the upturn, entailing the resolution of past problems.

All of this, and especially the way in which participation in and conversion to NSA has brought to light personal needs or problems not previously discernible, or at least not defined as troublesome enough to warrant remedial action, strongly suggests that we would be treading on thin ice, both methodologically and analytically, if we were to infer earlier predispositional states from members' accounts gathered after or during participation and then attribute initial participation to these post-factum accounts.

This contention is underscored even further when we consider another core feature of NSA's interpretive schema that is repeatedly reflected in the talk and reasoning of core members or converts. I refer to the attributional component of NSA's interpretive schema that directs members to internalize rather than externalize the blame for "their problems." To externalize blame is to attribute the cause for one's problems and life situation to others or to some structural arrangement. Whichever the case, the cause of one's problems are located outside of the self, and the solution resides in altering the external causal agent or structure. In contrast, the internalization of blame rests on the belief that events in one's life space are contingent upon one's own actions or inactions. Hence, the cause for one's misfortune resides within, and the solution resides in changing oneself or altering one's lines of action.[42]

That the attributional component of NSA's meaning system would reflect the belief that one's life situation and destiny is determined by one's own actions is hardly surprising; for it is in keeping with the ancient Hindu-Buddhist principle of karma. What is particularly interesting, however, are two other related observations. First, as we learned in Chapter 2, NSA not only contends that most people tend to attribute the source of and solution to their problems to some external agent or structure, but it also contends, as reflected in the following statement, that this external attributional orientation is one of the basic problems of modern man.

> The basic problem of modern man is derived from the fact that he fails to recognize that the cause of man's unhappiness exists within his own life. One must accept full responsibility for his destiny ... When man stops complaining that his problems are the 'Will of God' or blaming the establishment, police, or family for his unhappiness, and realize through the practice of true Buddhism that things are his fault, we will find a happy peaceful security.[43]

And second is the fact that the talk and reasoning of core converts indicates that they not only subscribe to the above contention, but that they have undergone a change in terms of attributional orientation since joining, a change from externalization to internalization.[44] Consider the following statements:

> Female, Caucasian, single, under 30: You see, I've come from the revolution, but I've learned that the real revolution is through NSA and its human revolution. It's not the superficial revolution of a culture or a government or an economic system. It's finally gotten down to the

revolution of myself and others through chanting to the Gohonzon.

Male, Caucasian, single, under 30: I discovered that I was running from myself. I came to realize that everything I hated was a part of me. This realization made me a better person, because I am now correcting what was wrong with me instead of blaming it on my parents, the school, and the country.

Female, Caucasian, single, under 30: I now realize that the reason I didn't get along with my roommate wasn't her fault, but my own fault. Chanting and the Gohonzon made me realize that the things I criticized about her were the very faults I possessed. By chanting and changing my character we are now able to get along.

Female, Caucasian, single over 40: When you chant you'll realize that you are the master of your fate, that you are in control of the situation, and that all of your problems and hardships were of your own making.

Thus, core converts reinterpret their past by redefining some aspect of it as more problematic than before, and they redefine or discover the source of blame for these recently acquired or more acutely defined misfortunes. And, in the process, the member also discovers an additional problem that is in need of change: his or her own personal character and demeanor.

In light of these observations, it is reasonable to offer the following tentative conclusions with respect to the question of the motivational determinants of recruitment to NSA in particular and, perhaps, to movements in general. First, without pre-affiliation motivational or attitudinal data it is well-nigh impossible to sort out and identify in a definitive manner the motives or predispositions that hypothetically precipitate initial experimentation with or participation in one or more movements. Certainly a formal questionnaire or an attitudinal survey would not be of much help in this regard; for as suggested above, members' responses and retrospective accounts are more likely to reflect a post-affiliation rather than a pre-participation cognitive orientation.

Second, whatever the motivational reasons that lead to an individual's initial investigation of participation in a movement activity, these may not be crucial, if related at all, to his decision to join and become an active participant. For example, an individual may decide to attend a movement meeting or activity in deference to the request of a friend, or merely out of curiosity, and fortuitously discover during the course of the meeting certain personal needs or problems not previously discernible or at least not previously defined as sufficiently important to warrant some kind of action. If this should occur, and if the movement is presented as a vehicle for the expression and satisfaction of these newly discovered needs, then it is quite probable that the potential member may decide to remain within the movement's orbit of influence. Thus, in contrast to the general social psychological/motivational proposition that posits a direct linkage between preexisting personal needs, problems, and dispositions and movement joining, I am suggesting that the reasons for which some individuals join a movement may oftentimes not be the same as the motivations that brought them to the movement in the first place.

Third, and related to the above, is a frequently neglected consideration regarding the function of movements: that movements function both as vehicles for the expression of prestructured dispositions and strains and as important agitational, problem-defining, need-arousal, and motive-producing agencies. While most motivational analyses typically emphasize the former function, my observations suggest that the latter function may oftentimes have primacy over the former. In other words, if a movement such as NSA is to expand its ranks and remain viable as a collective entity, not only must it attempt to tap and appeal to prestructured dispositions and strains, but it must also create them, intensify them, order them, link them with its value orientation, put them into the service of the movement, and give them more specific forms and means for expression and amelioration. While the data presented in this chapter do not speak directly to the question of how successful NSA has been in tapping and giving expression to prestructured dispositions and needs, there is little question but that it has functioned fairly successfully as a problem-defining, need-arousal, and motive-producing medium. At least this is what the foregoing statements and motivational accounts rendered by core members seem to suggest.

Finally, in light of the above observations and conclusions, it seems reasonable to suggest that rather than attempting to infer motivational predispositions and susceptibilities from data collected during or after participation, that perhaps it would be more methodologically sound to render participants' retrospective accounts and responses problematic. That is, perhaps such data should be treated as dependent phenomena or post-affiliation variables that require explanation.

In following this line of inquiry, we might ask, for example: when a movement or cult participant is confronted with the task of reconstituting some aspect of his or her past as problematic, what will be selected out and defined as problematic, as something that calls for remedial action or change? And what are the factors that determine what is defined as troublesome, and how does this process vary across movements? Or if participants are confronted with the task of rationalizing their involvement, we might seek to investigate the determinants of the accounts rendered and the extent to which they vary across movements and among members of the same movement. For example, do they vary over time, say, from 1965 to 1975? Do they vary with age, gender, marital status, and the like? And do the accounts of relatively new members differ significantly from those of relatively longstanding and core members? Although an examination of such questions may not move us any closer to a precise understanding of the elusive social psychological/motivational determinants of initial participation, it should advance our understanding of the problem-defining, need-arousal, motive-acquisition, and account-construction processes and of the role of movements in relation to these processes.

In suggesting the foregoing tentative conclusions and the above line of inquiry, I do not mean to imply that there are not some personality types who are especially prone to movement participation. Nor am I suggesting that movements do not function as important vehicles for the expression of such preexisting cognitive states as alienation and relative deprivation, or that such prestructured dispositions are not often linked to movement seeking and participation. Rather, I am suggesting the following: first, that neither a certain personality constitution nor a sense of alienation or relative deprivation is a necessary, much less a sufficient, precondition for movement joining and participation. Second, that in the absence of pre-affiliation motivational and attitudinal data, the search for motivational predispositions and susceptibilities should be conducted in a more cautious and tentative manner. And third, regardless of the availability of such pre-affiliation data, we should, when considering the problem of movement joining and differential recruitment, give greater attention to: (a) the character and channelling of movements' recruitment efforts, (b) the microstructural and situational determinants of recruitment, and (c) the manner in which movements function as problem-defining, need-arousal, and motive-producing agencies. The findings and analysis presented in this chapter make it abundantly clear that a consideration of these three factors sheds a great deal of light on the issue of differential recruitment or the question of who joins and why - at least for Nichiren Shoshu, and I suspect for most other movements as well.

NOTES

1. *NSA Seminar Report, 1968-1971* (Santa Monica, Ca.: World Tribune Press, Feb. 1972).

2. If we closely compare the figures in both tables, and use Table 2 as the base, it becomes readily apparent that Table 3 underrepresents the proportion of Orientals in the movement through 1968. I think this apparent over-representation of non-Orientals in Table 3 can be explained by the nature and source of the data: member's testimonies in the *World Tribune*. More specifically, since the *World Tribune* functions, in part, as a promotion tool and recruitment aid, and since the movement began to make a conscious and concerted effort to appeal to non-Oriental Americans around 1966, it stands to reason, from a tactical and, therefore, editorial standpoint, that the movement would attempt to give greater play and publicity to the experiences of its non-Oriental American members. After all, if one wants to promote a specific product or message to a particular social category, is it not tactically wise to emphasize not only how this product can benefit members of the social category in question, but also the fact that some members of that category do, in fact, support or subscribe to the product or message being promoted? Hence, the probable underrepresentation of Oriental members' experiences in the earlier editions of the *World Tribune*.

3. Although I was not able to distinguish the specific ethnicity of non-Oriental members of my sample in a precise manner, NSA's *Seminar Report* provides the following breakdown as of 1970: 41 to 45 percent Caucasian or Anglo; 12 percent Black; and 13 percent Latin American. Although Latin or Mexican Americans seem to be somewhat over-represented in comparison to their proportion of the American population, this is not surprising when it is considered that NSA has flourished most prominently in southern California.

4. This is also substantiated by the fact that 83 percent of the seventy-one Orientals in my sample were female.

5. This is corroborated by NSA's own demographic report, which indicates that no less than 52 percent of the members were under 30 as of 1970.

6. U.S. Bureau of the Census, *Statistical Abstract of the U.S., 1971*, 92nd Edition (Washington, D.C., 1971), Table 360, p. 229.

7. See, for example: H. Richard Niebuhr, *The Social Sources of Denominationalism* (New York: Henry Holt and Co., 1929); Liston Pope, *Millhands and Preachers* (New Haven: Yale University Press, 1942); and Hadley Cantril's discussion of the "Father Divine cult" in *The Psychology of Social Movements* (New York: John Wiley, 1941).

8. Whereas "housewives" are listed as a separate occupational category in the previous table, I added housewives to the military category in this table for the following reasons: first, since housewives are distributed throughout the socioeconomic structure, the housewife category is not one that locates people in the socioeconomic structure insofar as actual class placement is concerned. And secondly, the vast majority of housewives in my sample were wives of military personnel. For example, of the forty-six housewives who joined prior to 1969, 76 percent were married to military personnel.

9. I should note here that had I operated on the reasonable assumption that the family SES (socioeconomic status) of housewives is distributed among the SES or occupational categories in the same proportion as the other members indicating occupation, and therefore omitted housewives from my calculations, several different trends would have emerged. But as indicated earlier, I decided not to proceed on this assumption because of the large percentage of housewives married to military personnel and because only 3 percent of the members indicating occupation after 1968 indicated that they were housewives.

10. James A. Dator, *Soka Gakkai: Builders of the Third Civilization* (Seattle: University of Washington Press, 1969), p. 135.

11. Pitirim A. Sorokin, *Social and Cultural Dynamics* (New York: American Book Company, 1937-41).

12. See, for example, Orrin Klapp, *Collective Search for Identity* (New York: Holt, Rinehart & Winston, 1969).

13. See, for example, Neil Smelser, *Theory of Collective Behavior* (New York: The Free Press, 1963); Daniel Bell, ed., *The Radical Right* (Garden City, N.Y.: Doubleday-Anchor, 1964); Chalmers Johnson, *Revolutionary Change* (Boston: Little, Brown & Co., 1966); and Ted R. Gurr, *Why Men Rebel* (Princeton, N.J.: Princeton University Press, 1970).

14. For a discussion of the concept of extraneous commitments or "side bets," see Howard S. Becker, "Notes on the Concept of Commitment," *American Journal of Sociology*, V. 66 (July 1960).

15. See D. A. Strickland and R. E. Johnston, "Issue Elasticity in Political Systems," *Journal of Political Economy*, V. 78 (1970).

16. This general line of argument, and particularly the link between student involvement in movements and the concept of discretionary time is discussed in John McCarthy and Mayer Zald's *The Trend of Social Movements in America: Professionalization and Resource Mobilization* (Morristown, NJ: General Learning Press, 1973).

17. See, for example, James S. Coleman, et al., *Medical Innovation: A Diffusion Study* (Indianapolis: Bobbs-Merrill, 1966); Alan C. Kerckhoff and Kurt W. Back, *The June Bug: A Study of Hysterical Contagion* (New York: Appleton-Century-Crofts, 1968); Luther P. Gerlach and Virginia H. Hine, *People, Power, Change: Movements of Social Transformation* (Indianapolis: Bobbs-Merrill, 1970).

18. Hans Toch, *The Social Psychology of Social Movements* (Indianapolis: Bobbs-Merrill, 1965).

19. Herbert Blumer, "Collective Behavior," in A. M. Lee, ed., *Principles of Sociology*, 3rd edition (New York: Barnes and Noble, 1969).

20. If this proposition is correct, it suggests that movements which are both structurally isolated and interested in expanding their ranks, such as Hare Krishna, are confronted with a rather significant problem - a problem that is rooted in the lack of correspondence between organizational structure and membership demands and the goal of spreading the word and expanding the ranks.

21. Alan C. Kerckhoff and Kurt W. Back, *op. cit.* (1968).

22. Luther P. Gerlach and Virginia H. Hine, *op. cit.* (1970), p. 80.

23. Michael I. Harrison, "Sources of Recruitment to Catholic Pentecostalism," *Journal of the Scientific Study of Religion*, V. 13 (March 1974), p. 56.

24. John Lofland, *Doomsday Cult* (Englewood Cliffs, New Jersey: Prentice-Hall, 1966), p. 53.

25. Robert Lee, *Stranger in the Land* (London: Lutterworth, 1967), pp. 135-154; Kiyoaki Murata, *Japan's New Buddhism* (New York: John Weatherhill, 1969); and James W. White, *The Sokagakkai and Mass Society* (Stanford, Ca.: Stanford University Press, 1970), p. 84.

26. See, for example: Maurice Pinard, *The Rise of a Third Party: A Study in Crisis Politics* (Englewood Cliffs, N.J.: Prentice-Hall, 1971), pp. 195-219; Jo Freeman, "The Origins of the Women's Liberation Movement," *American Journal of Sociology*, V. 78 (January 1973), pp. 794-95, 803; and Peter J. Leahy, "Mobilization and Recruitment of Leadership to Anti-Abortion Movement," paper presented at the 1976 annual meeting of the Southwestern Sociological Association.

27. Charles D. Bolton, "Alienation and Action: A Study of Peace-Group Members," *American Journal of Sociology*, V. 78 (November 1972), p. 557.

28. William Kornhauser, *The Politics of Mass Society* (New York: Free Press, 1959).

29. William A. Gamson, *Power and Discontent* (Homewood, Ill., Dorsey Press, 1968).

30. Anthony Oberschall, *Social Conflict and Social Movements* (Englewood Cliffs, N.J.: Prentice-Hall, 1973).

31. Regarding this point, see, for example: Norman Cohn, *The Pursuit of the Millennium* (New York: Oxford University Press, 1957); and Peter Worsley, *The Trumpet Shall Sound: A Study of "Cargo" Cults in Melanesia* (New York: Shocken Books, 1968).

32. Rosabeth M. Kanter, *Commitment and Community* (Cambridge: Harvard University Press, 1972), pp. 80-81.

33. Ralph H. Turner and Lewis M. Killian, *Collective Behavior*, 2nd edition (Englewood Cliffs, N.J.: Prentice-Hall, 1972), p. 338.

34. Here it is interesting to note that in the final pages of *The Elementary Forms of Religious Life* (New York: Free Press, 1965), Durkheim reached a similar conclusion regarding the connection between beliefs and ritual practice: that belief, faith, and meaning flow primarily from the performance of religious rites or ritual practices, rather than the other way around. Whether following Durkheim's lead or working independently, others have reached much the same conclusion regarding the relation between belief, meaning, and ritual. See, for example: Anthony F.C. Wallace, *Religion: An Anthropological View* (New York: Random House, 1966); and Orrin Klapp, *op. cit.* (1969).

35. For a discussion of the conversion process and what it means to be a full-blown convert, see the two articles reprinted in the Appendix.

36. Illustrative of movement-specific theories are those advanced by Gabriel A. Almond, *The Appeals of Communism* (Princeton: Princeton University Press, 1954) and Erich Fromm, *Escape from Freedom* (New York: Rinehart, 1941). Examples of middle-range theories pertaining to a general class of movements include Norman Cohn, *op. cit.*, (1957); James C. Davies, "Toward a Theory of Revolution," *American*

Sociological Review, V. 27 (February 1962); Lewis Feuer, *The Conflict of Generations* (New York: Basic Books, 1969); and S. M. Lipset and E. Raab, *The Politics of Unreason* (New York: Harper and Row, 1973). And illustrative of the more general theories are Eric Hoffer, *The True Believer* (New York: Harper and Row, 1951); Hadley Cantril, *The Psychology of Social Movements* (New York: John Wiley, 1941); Orrin Klapp, *op. cit.* (1969); and Hans Toch, *op. cit.* (1965).

37. Hans Toch, *op. cit.* (1965).

38. For further discussion of this issue, see: David Aberle, "A Note on Relative Deprivation Theory as Applied to Millenarian and Other Cult Movements," in W. Lessa and E. Vogt, eds., *Reader in Comparative Religion* (New York: Harper and Row, 1965); Gary Marx and James Wood, "Strands of Theory and Research in Collective Behavior" (1975); and Michael Useem, *Protest Movements in America* (Indianapolis: Bobbs-Merrill, 1975).

39. See, for example: Clark McPhail, "Civil Disorder Participation: A Critical Examination of Recent Research," *American Sociological Review*, V. 36 (December 1971); David Snyder and Charles Tilly, "Hardship and Collective Violence in France, 1830 to 1960," *American Sociological Review*, V. 37 (October 1972); and Seymour Spilerman, "The Causes of Racial Disturbances: A Comparison of Alternative Explanations," *American Sociological Review*, V. 35 (August 1970).

40. For a discussion of the concept of vocabulary of motives and related concepts, see Kenneth Burke, *Permanence and Change* (Indianapolis: Bobbs-Merrill, 1965); C. Wright Mills, "Situated Actions and Vocabularies of Motives," *American Sociological Review*, V. 5 (December, 1940); and Marvin B. Scott and Stanford Lyman, "Accounts," *American Sociological Review*, V. 33 (1968). For elaboration of this conception of conversion, see the reprinted articles in the Appendix, particularly the second one, "The Convert as a Social Type."

41. For a discussion of this feature of conversion, see Peter Berger, *Invitation to Sociology* (Garden City, New York: Doubleday-Anchor, 1963), pp. 54-65; Kenneth Burke, *op. cit.* (1965); and T. Shibutani, *Society and Personality* (Englewood Cliffs, N.J.: Prentice-Hall, 1961), pp. 523-532. For a fuller discussion of this feature of conversion, particularly in reference to Nichiren Shoshu, see the reprinted articles in the Appendix.

42. See Julian B. Rotter, "Generalized Expectancies for Internal vs. External Control of Reinforcements," *Psychological Monographs*, V. 80 (1966), pp. 1-28.

43. *World Tribune* (October 30, 1974).

44. Here it is important to note that since NSA seeks to change the world by changing people, effecting a shift from externalization to internalization would seem to be a critical and necessary step in the conversion process; for chanting has little relevance until this shift is made. It stands to reason that such a shift also is a necessary feature of conversion to most religious movements and probably all psychiatric movements (i.e., the encounter group movement). In the case of political movements, on the other hand, externalization or system blame is the necessary condition, and the shift in blame is the return toward the other structural end of the attributional continuum.

6
SUMMARY, PROJECTIONS, AND IMPLICATIONS

The purpose of this final chapter is to summarize the major descriptive and analytic findings presented in the preceding chapters, to briefly consider the success and future course of Nichiren Shoshu as a social movement, and to link together the previously stated propositions and highlight a number of theoretical implications suggested by the study.

SUMMARY OF MAJOR FINDINGS AND CONCLUSIONS

NSA's Value Orientation or Goals and Ideology

In Chapters 2 and 4 we learned that NSA is a proselytizing movement that seeks to modify the larger social world by incorporating an ever-increasing number of people within its orbit of influence and by remolding them through its ritual practices and in accordance with its ideals. Contending that the condition of humankind and the world in general is one of suffering, alienation, and unhappiness, and contending that one's life situation as well as the state of the world are but a reflection of one's inner state, NSA argues that the only way the condition of humankind can be altered and improved is through human revolution or the personal and spiritual regeneration of all people. Although it is not specified how changes at the individual level will precipitate changes at the structural or global levels, this is not seen as particularly troublesome, for NSA firmly believes that happy, peaceful, spiritually regenerated people will lead to not only a happy, peaceful world but to a world that is totally different from the one in which we now live.

From the standpoint of its goals and the diagnostic and prognostic components of its world view, NSA is thus similar to many other salvationist-like religious movements in that personal transformation is seen as the key to social transformation.   However, unlike most Western salvationist religious sects and movements - such as Pentecostalism, Jehovah's Witnesses, the Children of God, and the Reverend Sun Myung Moon movement - that see Christ or some variant thereof as the answer or "one way," the answer for NSA lies in the repetitive chanting of Nam-Myoho-Renge-Kyo to the Gohonzon, the daily performance of morning and evening Gongyo, and in the unrelenting practice of Shakubuku or the act of spreading the word and bringing others into contact with the Gohonzon and the key to unlocking its power - Nam-Myoho-Renge-Kyo.

NSA's Major Collective Activity

In keeping with its goals and proselytizing orientation, we learned in Chapter 4 that Shakubuku is, next to chanting, not only the most important and time-consuming NSA activity, but that it is also the one activity that arches over and ties together all NSA activities and campaigns.   In whatever members do collectively, whether it be preparing for and attending a convention, participating in a cultural show, marching in a parade, holding a mass rally or discussion meeting, promoting the *World Tribune*, or proselytizing on the street, it is done in part, if not completely, with Shakubuku in mind. Similarly, we discovered that whatever members do individually, whether it be done in the context of family, work, school, or leisure, it is to be done in part, if not completely, with Shakubuku in mind. Shakubuku can thus be done by members acting alone or jointly, and it can be done in a variety of ways and in an extensive array of settings.

Given NSA's preoccupation with Shakubuku and the deployment of members in this work, I suggested that it is the one major activity that renders NSA a true social movement rather than a cult; for it is through the variety of activities and practices that constitute the doing of Shakubuku that NSA acts upon the larger society in order to promote its interests and extend its orbit of influence.

NSA's Propagation and Recruitment Strategies and Tactics

Given NSA's value orientation and the fact that it is a culturally transplanted, proselytizing movement with an underlying philosophy and set of ritual practices that are somewhat offbeat or idiosyncratic by American standards, I argued in Chapter 4 that its success in advancing towards its objectives has been partially contingent on its ability to deal effectively with three overarching problems that hypothetically confront most movements, and particularly proselytizing movements. I then proceeded to delineate, describe, and analyze the variety of strategies, organizational promotion vehicles, and tactics that NSA has developed and employed in order to deal with these three problematic considerations, all of which is summarized in Table 9.

Demographic Composition of NSA's Membership

In examining the demographic composition of NSA's membership over time, we learned that there have been two different modal membership profiles, each of which corresponds with a different time period in the movement's career. Prior to around 1967, the typical core member was female, Japanese, married, over thirty, most often a housewife, and of upper-lower to lower-middle class; after 1967-68 the typical member was non-Oriental, single, under thirty, of either sex, a student, either a lower-level white collar worker or marginally employed, and lower-middle class in terms of socioeconomic standing.

In light of this finding and the fact that the movement expanded its ranks by around 180,000 between 1965 and 1970, it is clear that during this period the movement drew the vast majority of its adherents from among non-Orientals, and particularly Caucasians, of either sex, who were single, under thirty, and students, lower-level white collars workers or marginally employed, and lower-middle class.

TABLE 9
Problems, Strategies, Promotion Vehicles and Tactics
Pertaining to Propagation and Recruitment

Problems	Primary Strategies	Organizational Promotion Vehicles & Tactics
Reaching out and making contact: the problem of bridging the information gap or gaining the attention of outsiders.	Face-to-face promotion in public places coupled with promotion along members' extra-movement interpersonal networks	Streetside proselytizing Promotion of newspaper seminars on campuses Participation in public events Staging events for public consumption
Building idiosyncrasy credit: the problem of gaining respectability and legitimacy in the public eye	Accommodation and dramatic ingratiation	Promoting value congruence Encouraging members to become "winners" Celebrity ingratiation and endorsement seeking Encouraging members to conduct themselves with propriety and deferential regard
Expanding the ranks: the problem of securing recruits and nominal conversion	Couching appeals in terms of interests of prospect; theatrical teamwork and persuasion	Sidewalk proselytizing and promotion along interpersonal networks Discussion meetings Altercasting and bargaining lines

Macrostructural and Organizational Determinants of NSA's Growth

Examination of the structural and organizational factors that facilitated NSA's growth beyond its initial constituency and its flowering in the second half of the 1960s focused on the conjunction of three factors: (1) the emergence of a social climate conducive to the propagation of and experimentation with such offbeat practices as chanting Nam-Myoho-Renge-Kyo; (2) the emergence of a propitious, general movement constituency consisting of a cohort of individuals who were structurally more available for active participation than were members of most other demographic categories because they had fewer pressing extraneous commitments or countervailing ties and because they had a greater amount of discretionary time which could be allocated to movement activities; and (3) NSA's accommodative flexibility and the character of its recruitment efforts during the period in question.

Microstructural and Situational Determinants of NSA's Growth

In examining the microstructural determinants of the movement's spread, we learned that the overlap and interconnection between NSA's network attributes and outsiders' interpersonal ties and associations were especially potent determinants of who was most likely to be informed about, brought into contact with, and actually join the movement. More specifically, the finding that 82 percent of the 330 sampled members indicated that they were drawn into the movement by virtue of being linked to a member through a preexisting, extra-movement interpersonal tie strongly suggests that the movement spread primarily along the lines of members' extra-movement interpersonal networks. I thus proffered the conclusion that those outsiders who were linked to movement members through preexisting, extra-movement networks stood a greater chance of being subjected to the movement's recruitment and conversion efforts than those individuals who were outside members' extra-movement networks. This conclusion was also suggested by the finding that all but two of the fifteen most active members in my district were recruited by friends, acquaintances, or kin.

Since some members are recruited off the street, I also examined the microstructural and situational determinants of recruitment into the movement in the absence of preexisting, extra-movement ties. Here we saw that whether an individual is recruited directly off the street and assumes nominal membership is largely a function of: (a) being in the right place at the right time, (b) the possession of unscheduled time, and (c) the lack of strong, proximal interpersonal ties and extraneous commitments.

Social Psychological/Motivational Determinants of Initial Participation

Although much of the movement literature suggests that movement joiners differ considerably from nonjoiners in terms of personality or attitudinal and cognitive orientation, I was not able to assess the validity of this general proposition for the simple reason that access to pre-affiliation attitudinal and motivational data was limited. Consequently, I made no attempt to sort out and identify in a systematic manner initial motives for participation for the reason that members' accounts of why they joined were retrospective or post-factum rather than preparticipation accounts.

I did note, however, that since members often attempt to lure outsiders to meeting by couching their appeals widely, it stands to reason that the initial motives for attending a meeting and perhaps joining are likely to be emergent and interactional phenomena and just as varied and numerous as the appeals or motives provided by members during their recruiting forays. Along this same line, I noted that whatever the motivational reasons that lead to an individual's initial investigation of and participation in NSA, these may not be crucial, if related at all, to his or her decision to join for the reason that NSA in general and its discussion meetings in particular function, in part, as problem-defining, need-arousal, and motive-producing agencies. As our examination of members' testimonies revealed, participation in and conversion to NSA often brings to light personal needs and problems not previously discernible or at least not defined as troublesome enough to warrant remedial action or movement participation.

Conclusions Regarding the Question of Who Has Joined NSA and Why

On the basis of our examination of the structural-demographic, microstructural and situational determinants of the movement's growth and diffusion, I suggested that the question of "who is most likely to join" can be answered primarily in terms of two factors operating simultaneously:

A) Being structurally situated such that one has a considerable amount of unscheduled and/or discretionary time and few strong extraneous or countervailing commitments; and

B) Being linked to a member via an extra-movement interpersonal
   network or tie.

The first factor suggests who is structurally most available for
participation, while the second factor suggests who is most likely to be
recruited and brought directly into the movement's orbit of influence
and thereby subjected to its problem-defining, need-arousal, motive-
producing efforts.

NSA'S SUCCESS AND FUTURE COURSE
AS A SOCIAL MOVEMENT

How successful has NSA been as a social movement?   More
specifically, how successful has it been in dealing with the three
resource appropriation problems discussed in Chapter 4 and referred to
in the preceding table, and how successful has it been as a problem-
defining, need-arousal, motive-producing, and problem-solving agency?
Clearly, it is a long way from realizing its goals of widespread
individual happiness and peace in America, much less throughout the
world.   Nonetheless, there are a number of reasons for suggesting that
NSA has been reasonably successful as a social movement, at least
through the mid-1970s.

First, it not only was still in existence, but thriving after some
sixteen years of operation in the United States.   Second, it had
developed a viable organization with a sizeable number of ardent
members or core converts who were devoting a good portion, and in
some cases all, of their wakeful hours to the movement.   Third, it had
not been subjected to the barrage of public charges and criticisms
leveled against two other prominent, and contemporary culturally
transplanted movements in America - the Hare Krishna movement and
the Reverend Sun Myung Moon or Unification Church movement.   In
other words, it has managed to deflect or escape the wrath of the anti-
cult movement to a greater extent than most other "new religious
movements."[1] And finally, and perhaps most significantly, it managed
to expand its ranks from less than five hundred in 1960 to - according
to its inflated estimates - around a quarter of a million by the mid-
1970s.   Or, stated more accurately, it managed to secure, if not
maintain, the nominal conversion of around 200,000 Americans in the

ten-year period between 1965 and 1975. Although the criteria for
assessing the success of social movements are not well developed,[2] the
foregoing observations strongly suggest that Nichiren Shoshu has been
quite successful for a proselytizing religious movement, especially a
culturally transplanted one.

Regarding the movement's future course, there is little reason to
forecast any large-scale disintegration in the short run. It is unlikely
that it will grow at the rate it did in the latter third of the 1960s. But
given NSA's continued emphasis on Shakubuku, its accommodative
orientation and concern with its public image, the fact that it has well-
developed organizational infrastructure and a fairly large core of highly
committed adherents, not to mention the enduring success of its parent
organization in Japan, it should remain viable and secure as a
collective, if not expanding, entity for years to come.

THEORETICAL IMPLICATIONS

In discussing the underlying objectives of this study in Chapter 1,
I indicated that I set out from the very beginning to treat my
investigation of NSA as an occasion for not only apprehending and
making available to others the character of NSA as both a social world
and movement, but also for considering and conceptualizing, to
whatever extent possible, various emergent observations and findings
in terms of related issues and questions in the social movement
literature. In other words, I wanted to use NSA as an empirical
referent for examining, extending, and perhaps refining relevant
problematic issues and questions related to the study of social
movements in general. In keeping with this concern, I present in this
final section what I see as the major theoretical implications and
research directives suggested by this study.

Toward a Microstructural Theory of Movement Recruitment?

Throughout the course of our examination of the character and
channelling of NSA's recruitment and outward-reaching goal attainment
efforts, the determinants of its growth, and the issue of differential
recruitment, I have suggested a number of propositions grounded in my
observations and findings pertaining to these concerns. In what

follows, I link together these and some additional propositions in hopes of stimulating further research with respect to the microstructural determinants of the movement recruitment process and differential recruitment.

Propositions Regarding the Structuring and Channelling of Movements' Outreach and Recruitment Opportunities and Patterns.
1) For those movements which have not been driven underground, recruitment and information diffusion, rather than being random, will be structured primarily by each movement's network attributes, such that:

1a) Movements which are structurally more exclusive, closed and isolated, but which can operate above ground - such as the Hare Krishna movement, will have to concentrate their promotion and recruitment efforts in public places to a greater extent than will movements which are linked to outside networks via members' extra-movement interpersonal ties.

1b) Whereas movements which are structurally more open and inclusive - such as NSA - will be able to channel their recruitment efforts along the lines of members' extra-movement networks, as well as in public places.

Propositions Pertaining to the Question of What Determines the Probability that Outsider A Rather than Outsider B Will Be Recruited.
2a) The probability of contact between movement members and outsiders will be structured, such that some outsiders, however available for or inclined towards participation, will not be reached, whereas others will have a greater probability of being contacted and subjected to members' recruitment efforts, such that:

2b) Those outsiders who are linked to movement members through preexisting, extra-movement networks will have a greater probability of being contacted and recruited into that movement than will those individuals who are outside of members' extra-movement networks.

Propositions Regarding the Relationship between Movement Network Attributes, Recruitment Patterns, and the Sociospatial Source of Recruits.
3a) Movements which constitute relatively closed, insulated, and interlocking networks of social relations, and which are therefore

structurally compelled to concentrate their recruitment efforts in public places, will draw their membership primarily off the street.

3b) Whereas those movements which are structurally more open and inclusive will draw their membership primarily from existing members' extra-movement interpersonal networks.

Propositions Regarding the Relationship between Network Attributes, Recruitment Patterns, and Movement Growth.

4a) The success of movement recruitment efforts, measured by the number of outsiders actually recruited, will vary with the extent to which movements are linked to other groups and networks via members' extra-movement interpersonal ties, such that:

4b) Movements that are linked to other groups and networks will normally grow at a more rapid rate and normally attain a larger membership than will movements that are structurally more isolated and closed.

Research Directives Regarding the Motivational Level of Analysis

Our examination of members' accounts of why they joined and our corresponding discussion of the methodological and analytical shortcomings with the social psychological-motivational approach to explaining movement participation suggests the following research directives: (1) that in the absence of pre-affiliation motivational and attitudinal data, the search for motivational predispositions and susceptibilities should be conducted in a most cautious and tentative manner. (2) That we should be especially cautious about treating the reasons for which individuals join movements and the motives that led to their investigation of the movement as one and the same. (3) That greater attention be given to the way in which and the extent to which movements function as problem-defining, need-arousal, and motive-generating agencies. (4) And that perhaps we should treat motives for joining and such cognitive states as alienation and relative deprivation in emergent and interactional terms and not merely as prestructured dispositions or as independent variables.

General Theoretical Implications

Whether one scans the literature pertaining to religious cults and movements, the ghetto revolts of the 1960s, student activism and political protest, or general theoretical discussions of social movements, the issue of differential recruitment - i.e., who participates, why some individuals rather than others, and why one movement rather than another - surfaces again and again as one of the major orienting concerns. Yet, most of the work addressing this issue has focused on the individual participant or convert as the unit of analysis, attempting to explain differential recruitment in terms of various preexisting social psychological strains or cognitive orientations.

Although such a focus is not totally unfounded, this study suggests that it provides a partial and lopsided view of the movement recruitment process. More specifically, the above propositions and research directives and the findings on which they are based strongly suggest that our understanding of the movement recruitment process in general and the issue of differential recruitment in particular would be advanced if we gave greater attention to the following considerations: (1) the character and channelling of movements' recruitment efforts; (2) the microstructural and situational determinants of recruitment; and (3) the manner in which movements function not only as vehicles for the expression of preexisting cognitive states, but as problem-solving, need-arousal, and motive-generating agencies.

NOTES

1. For discussion of the burgeoning anti-cult movement in the second half of the 1970s, see Anson D. Shupe and David G. Bromley, *The New Vigilantes: Deprogrammers, Anti-Cultists and the New Religions* (Beverly Hills, CA: Sage Publications, 1980) and Ted Patrick, *Let Our Children Go* (New York: Ballantine, 1976).

2. But see William A. Gamson's *The Strategy of Social Protest* (Homewood, IL: Dorsey Press, 1975) for an attempt to develop criteria for assessing the outcomes, and thus the relative success, of more politically-oriented movements.

APPENDIX

A REASSESSMENT OF THE
CONVERSION PROCESS*

The most refined and widely cited conversion model within the
sociological literature is the value-added scheme propounded by
Lofland and Stark (1965). This paper is a critical examination
of the Lofland-Stark model. Data derived from an extensive
study of recruitment and conversion to the Nichiren Shoshu
Buddhist movement in America provide little empirical support
for the model in its entirety. Several components of the model
are also theoretically questionable. The analysis suggests that
affective and intensive interaction are not only essential for
conversion to Nichiren Shoshu, but that conversion in general is
highly improbable in the absence of these two factors.

Within sociology, conversion has traditionally been explained as
a sequential "funneling" process, including psychological, situational
and interactional factors (see Gerlach and Hine, 1970; Richardson *et
al.*, 1978; Seggar and Kunz, 1972; Shibutani, 1961; Toch, 1965;
Zablocki, 1971). Of the various works representative of this approach
to conversion, the most prominent is the model propounded by Lofland
and Stark (1965; see also Lofland, 1966). Based on a field study of the
early American devotees of Sun Myung Moon (hereafter referred to as
the Unification Church), the model suggests that "total" conversion,
involving behavioral as well as verbal commitment, is a function of the
accumulation of seven "necessary and constellationally-sufficient
conditions" (Lofland and Stark, 1965: 874).

* Adapted from David A. Snow and Cynthia L. Phillips. "The
Lofland-Conversion Model: A Critical Reassessment." *Social
Problems* 27: 430-447, 1980.

Specifically, a person must (1) experience enduring and acutely-felt "tensions," (2) within a "religious problem-solving perspective," (3) which results in self-designation as a "religious seeker." Additionally, the prospective convert must (4) encounter the movement or cult at a "turning point" in life, (5) form an "affective bond" with one or more believers, (6) "neutralize" or sever "extracult attachments," and (7) be exposed to "intensive interaction" with other converts in order to become an active and dependable adherent. The first three factors are classified as "predisposing." They hypothetically exist prior to contact with the group and function to render the individual susceptible to conversion once contact is established. The remaining four factors are regarded as "situational" contingencies. They hypothetically lead to recruitment to one group rather than another, if any other, and to the adoption of the group's world view. In the absence of these situational factors, total conversion will not occur, no matter how predisposed or susceptible the prospective convert may be. Accordingly, the conversion process is conceptualized as a value-added process in which the addition of each new condition increases the probability that conversion will occur.

The purpose of this paper is to contribute to our understanding of conversion by critically examining the Lofland-Stark model and the extent to which it applies to our findings on conversion to the Nichiren Shoshu Buddhist movement in America. Two issues guide the inquiry. The first has to do with the model's empirical generalizability. Lofland initially suggested that the application of the model was "universal" (1966: 61). Whether this is in fact the case remains an empirical question. Although the Lofland-Stark model is the most widely cited conversion scheme in the sociological literature (see Richardson, 1978; Richardson and Stewart, 1978; Richardson *et al.*, 1978; Robbins and Anthony, 1979; Wilson, 1978), it has rarely been subjected to rigorous empirical examination.[1] Instead, most studies have uncritically used the model as a post factum ordering scheme for classifying data pertaining to the group under investigation (e.g., Judah, 1974; McGee, 1976). Moreover, neither Lofland and Stark nor those scholars drawing on the model have fully considered the extent to which the conversion process may vary across movements - according to differences in value orientations, organizational structure, and the way a movement is publicly defined. Given that communal groups tend to be more demanding than noncommunal groups (Kanter, 1972; 1973), it seems reasonable to assume that such differences in organizational structure might lead to differences in the conversion process. Similarly, we might expect the conversion process to vary according to whether a group is publicly defined as "respectable," "idiosyncratic" or "revolutionary" (see Snow, 1979; Turner and Killian, 1972: 257-59). Consideration of such factors seems especially important given the fact that Nichiren Shoshu is a noncommunal group in contrast to the Unification Church.

Aside from the issue of empirical generalizability, several components of the model strike us as theoretically questionable when viewed from the complementary perspectives of Mead (1932, 1936, 1938), Burke (1965, 1969a,b) and Berger and Luckmann (1967) and the related work on "accounts" or "motive talk" (see Blum and McHugh, 1971; Mills, 1940; Scott and Lyman, 1968). In particular, two aspects of this work inform our approach to conversion and therefore our theoretical critique of the Lofland-Stark model. The first suggests that social conditions and the various elements of one's life situation, including the self, constitute social objects whose meanings are not intrinsic to them but flow from one's "universe of discourse" (Mead, 1962: 89) or "informing point of view" (Burke, 1965: 99) or "meaning system" (Berger, 1963: 61). The second and corollary principle emphasizes that meaning itself is constantly in the process of emergence or evolution; that personal biographies as well as history in general are continuously redefined in the light of new experiences.[2] Since conversion involves the adoption and use of a new or formerly peripheral universe of discourse and its attendant vocabulary of motives, it follows, as Burke (1965) and Berger and Luckmann (1967) have emphasized, that this ongoing process of retrospective interpretation would be heightened and more extensive in conversion than is customary in the course of everyday life.

Drawing on these concepts and on data pertaining to conversion to the Nichiren Shoshu Buddhist movement, we will critically examine the extent to which the Lofland-Stark model is conceptually useful and empirically on target. ...

FINDINGS AND DISCUSSION

Predisposing Conditions

Tension. Lofland and Stark suggest that a state of acutely-felt tension or frustration is a necessary predisposing condition for conversion. This tension, as well as the other predisposing conditions, are viewed as "attributes of persons" that exist "*prior* to their contact with the cult" or group in question (1965: 864; their emphasis). We would thus expect our data to demonstrate that NSA members experienced severe tension and acutely-felt needs prior to joining the movement.

At first glance, it would appear as if our data corroborate this expectation. As indicated in Table 1, like Lofland and Stark's informants, NSA members characterize their preparticipation life situations in terms of various problems and tensions. Sixty-nine percent of the sample, for example, indicated that prior to or at the time of encountering NSA they were experiencing one or more "spiritual" problems, such as meaningless, a lack of direction or purpose, or a sense of powerlessness. Perhaps even more revealing than the specific problems alluded to is the finding that, on the average, core members reported at least three problems per person just prior to conversion (see column three, Table 1).

Looked at uncritically, these findings, and the fact that they are consistent with those of Lofland and Stark (1965) and Richardson et al. (1978), suggest that a state of acutely-felt tension is indeed an important precipitant of conversion. Yet, in the absence of a control group that is representative of the larger population, such a conclusion is methodologically untenable. Until we know whether the problems experienced by preconverts are greater in number or qualitatively different from those experienced by the larger population, it is unreasonable to assume a causal linkage between prestructured tension and susceptibility to conversion.

Acknowledging this issue, Lofland and Stark (1965: 867) suggest that while the problems experienced by preconverts and the larger population "are not qualitatively different," the former experience their problems "rather more acutely and over longer periods of time than most people do." Although they offer no evidence in support of this

TABLE 1
Personal Problems Retrospectively Referred to as
Characterizing Life Situation Prior to Conversion

Problems*	No. of Members Referring to Category (N: 504)		No. of Problems Referred to within Category (N: 1,580)		Average No. of Problems Per Member**
Spiritual[a]	(346)	69%	(526)	33%	1.52
Interpersonal[b]	(244)	48%	(309)	20%	1.26
Character[c]	(262)	52%	(284)	18%	1.08
Material[d]	(214)	43%	(255)	16%	1.19
Physical[e]	(151)	30%	(206)	13%	1.36

* The following problem categories are those used by members when recruiting and giving testimony.

[a] Problems coded as "spiritual" include meaningless, lack of direction and purpose, a sense of powerlessness, poor self-image.

[b] Problems coded as "interpersonal" include marital problems, child rearing problems, parental problems, and other relational problems.

[c] Problems coded as "character" include drugs, alcohol, self-centeredness, and various personality problems such as uncontrollable temper.

[d] Problems coded as "material" include unemployment, job dissatisfaction, finances, and school-related problems.

[e] Problems coded as "physical" include headaches, nervousness, chronic illness, obesity, lack of energy, and so on.

** This column is equal to column two divided by column one. On the average, members reported 3.13 problems.

assertion, a number of studies and polls regarding the worries and problems of American adults suggest that Lofland and Stark are probably right on the first account. A 1957 University of Michigan survey of how American adults viewed their mental health revealed that roughly 41 percent experienced marital problems, 75 percent encountered problems in raising their children, 29 percent had job-related problems, 35 percent avowed various personality shortcomings, and 19 percent felt they were on the verge of a nervous breakdown at one time or another.[3] These and findings of similar surveys (Cantril, 1965; Chase, 1962; Gallup, 1978; Stouffer, 1955) suggest that Americans not only have an overriding concern with themselves and "their immediate environment," but also often "admit" to having "weaknesses and problems" (Gurin *et al.*, 1960: xxiv-xxv).[4] Since the kinds of worries and tensions noted in public opinion polls and surveys are of the same genre as those alluded to by NSA converts and summarized in Table 1, Lofland and Stark appear to be correct in arguing that the worries and problems that plague most Americans are not qualitatively different from those of the preconverts.

However, what about the corollary contention that it is the magnitude and duration of stress, rather than stress per se, that render people differentially susceptible to conversion? This is a difficult question, especially since studies such as those cited above shed little direct light on the matter. However, our data do not indicate a state of acutely-felt and prolonged tension to be a necessary precipitating condition. Although many NSA converts typically characterize their respective preconversion life situations as being laden with several personal problems (Table 1), many others report that they were not aware of having had severe problems prior to conversion to NSA. Consider the following statements extracted from members' testimonies during movement meetings or presented in the movement's newspaper:

> Male, Caucasian, single, under 30: When I joined I didn't think I was burdened by any problems. But as I discovered, I just wasn't aware of them until I joined and they were solved.

> Female, Caucasian, single, under 30: After I attended these meetings and began chanting, I really began to see that my personal life was a mess.

> Male, Caucasian, single, under 30: Now as I look back I feel that I was a total loser. At that time, however, I thought I was pretty cool. But after chanting for a while, I found out that my life before was just a dead thing. The more I chanted, the more clearly I came to see myself and the more I realized just how many problems I had.

> Male, Caucasian, married, over 30: After you've been chanting for a while, you'll look back, just as I have, and

see how far you've progressed. After you chant for a while,
you'll look back and say, 'Gee, I was sure a rotten, unhappy
person.' I know I thought I was a saint before I chanted,
but shortly after I discovered what a rotten person I was and
how many problems I had.

These statements indicate that, for many individuals, conversion
to NSA involves either the redefinition of life before conversion as
being fraught with problems or the discovery of personal problems not
previously discernible or regarded as troublesome enough to warrant
remedial action. In either case, these findings suggest not only that
conversion can occur in the absence of preexisting strains, but also that
the strains or problems alluded to by converts may indeed be a product
of conversion itself - that is, of the internalization of a new interpretive
schema and its attendant vocabulary of motive. Although this
interpretation runs counter to what Lofland and Stark lead us to expect,
it is quite consistent with the Meadian thesis that the past is not a static
entity but is subject to change with new experiences and alterations in
one's universe of discourse. It is also consonant with the corollary
observation that one of the more significant consequences of
conversion, religious or secular, is that it entails a total or partial
reinterpretation of one's biography (Berger, 1963; Berger and
Luckmann, 1967; Burke, 1965; Shibutani, 1961; Travisano, 1970).
We would thus argue on both empirical and theoretical grounds that
while a state of acutely-felt and prolonged tension may be associated
with conversion, it is not necessarily a predisposing condition.[5]

Parallel Problem-Solving Perspectives. Personal problems can be
defined and dealt with in terms of a number of functional alternatives
(Emerson and Messinger, 1971). Lofland and Stark suggest that the
remedy chosen is partly dependent on the correspondence between the
individual's problem-solving perspective and the remedial alternative in
question. If the alternative is political, but the individual views the
world primarily from a religious or psychiatric standpoint, then
conversion to that alternative is not likely. If, on the other hand, the
two are congruent, then the prospect of conversion is heightened.
Accordingly, Lofland and Stark initially hypothesized that conversion
to a religious movement is contingent on the possession of a religious
problem-solving perspective.

While concurring with this hypothetical linkage between problem-solving orientation and susceptibility to conversion, Richardson and Stewart (1978) have sought to extend and refine the linkage by proposing several modifications. First, they suggest, in addition to the religious, political and psychiatric perspectives, a "physiological" perspective (e.g., drugs, alcohol, dieting, exercise). Second, they contend that Lofland and Stark have neglected the role of prior socialization in furnishing individuals with perspectives for defining problems and their solutions and thereby facilitating susceptibility to conversion. Drawing on the hypothesis that some religious traditions make people prone to frustration (Fromm, 1950; Pattison, 1974; Toch, 1965) and on the observation that some converts to the Unification Church and the Jesus movement came from a background of Christian fundamentalism, Richardson and Stewart hypothesize that prior socialization as a fundamentalist not only increases the probability of having a religious problem-solving perspective, but also renders those individuals more susceptible to participation in religious cults and movements.

Although this hypothesis with its emphasis on prior socialization is sociologically appealing, our observations suggest that it may be overstated.[6] In particular, we find no compelling evidence suggesting that converts to NSA were raised in a fundamentalist environment. Moreover, our data provide little support for the corollary proposition that the possession of a religious problem-solving category prior to encountering NSA. In other words, more than three-quarters of the sample saw both the source and solution to problems, whether personal or social, as residing in forces or structures other than mystical, supernatural or occult. As one such member, a twenty-three year old female convert who viewed herself as a "political revolutionary" prior to joining NSA, relates:

> I've come from the revolution, but I've since learned that the real revolution is through NSA and its human revolution. It's not the superficial revolution of a culture or a government or an economic system. It's finally gotten down to the revolution of myself and others through chanting to the Gohonzon.

Similarly, a male convert in his early twenties describes his view of things prior to encountering NSA:

> Right up until I joined NSA I harbored hostility toward my parents, and had a cynical attitude toward society in general. I blamed my parents for my hang-ups and criticized the U.S.'s foreign policy, the President, and so on. I realize now that because I was miserable inside, I perceived the environment as miserable. And I also came to realize that if I wanted things to improve, I had to change myself first.

These statements, which are not exceptional, cast further doubt on the hypothesis that preparticipation ideological congruence is a necessary condition for conversion. They also suggest that conversion to NSA frequently effects a significant change in problem-solving perspective. Not only do converts to NSA reinterpret their past by redefining some aspects of it as more problematic than before, but also they frequently come to redefine or discover the source of blame for their more acutely defined or recently acquired problems.

Some might argue that these observations and findings do not necessarily preclude a causal linkage between prior religious socialization and conversion; the former may still influence which of the many groups, both conventional and offbeat, the potential convert will select or find appealing. With this we have no quarrel, since it seems quite reasonable to expect that those raised in a fundamentalist tradition might find the Unification Church or the Children of God more appealing than NSA or some other Buddhist- or Hindu-inspired movement. In either case, we still maintain that preparticipation ideological congruence is not a necessary condition for conversion in general. To argue otherwise is inconsistent with the logic of the constant comparative method (Glaser and Strauss, 1967). It also ignores the fact that movements function as important agitational, problem-defining, need-arousal and motive-producing agencies. Social movements have traditionally been viewed as vehicles for the expression of prestructured beliefs and dispositions (see Cantril, 1941; Glock, 1964; Hoffer, 1951; Klapp, 1969; Toch, 1965). However, attendance at an NSA meeting demonstrates that movements also function to construct social reality.[7] When this is the case, then ideological congruence, if and when it exists, constitutes a facilitative

TABLE 2
Percentage and Frequency Distribution for Orientation,
Turning Points and Mode of Recruitment

I. Preconversion Problem-Solving Orientation	No.	%
Physiological[a]	117	35
Religious[b]	72	22
Psychiatric[c]	39	12
Political[d]	32	10
Mixed[e]	70	21
Totals*	330	100
II. Possible Preconversion Turning Points	No.	%
Unemployed/Lost Job	52	16
Divorced/Separated	46	14
Military/Draft	38	12
School Dropout	36	11
Institutionalized	34	10
Close Encounter with Death	15	4
Attempted/Contemplated Suicide	17	5
None Mentioned	92	28
Totals*	330	100
III. Mode of Recruitment	No.	%
Recruited through Social Networks	270	82
By Friends	(190)	(58)
By Relatives	(80)	(24)
Recruited Outside of Social Networks	60	18
Totals*	330	100

* Although there were 504 cases in our sample of testimonies, 174 of them did not include information pertaining to orientation, possible turning point or mode of recruitment. Therefore, this table is based on 330 rather than 504 cases.

[a] Physiological orientation includes references to being "into" or resolving personal difficulties through drugs, alcohol, dieting, exercise, sex and the like.

[b] Religious orientation includes self-designation as a religious searcher and/or identification of the supernatural or occult (God, unseen forces) as the key to resolving problems.

[c] Psychiatric orientation includes references to being "into" psychoanalysis, psychotherapy, and groups such as est. Includes statements indicating that manipulation of the self or psyche is seen as key to resolving personal difficulties.

[d] Political orientation includes references to belief that life situation is determined primarily by political and social arrangements. Being "into" peace movement, political activism and civil rights movement.

[e] Mixed orientation includes self-designation as hippie, street person, wanderer or drifter.

rather than a necessary precondition for conversion.

Religious Seekership. The final background factor that Lofland and Stark posited as a necessary precipitant of conversion is religious seekership. The prospect must come "to define himself as a religious seeker," as "a person searching for some satisfactory system of religious meaning to interpret and resolve his discontent" (1965: 868). Recently, Lofland (1978: 12,20) has suggested that perhaps this dimension of the model is not as important as originally assumed, since "people not previously religious at all have joined" movements such as the Unification Church "in noticeable numbers" since the late sixties.

Although Lofland offers no substantial evidence in support of his recent observation, our data suggest that it is well-grounded. Specifically, if we take experimentation with other religious alternatives as an indicator of religious seekership, then, as indicated in the first section of Table 2, the vast majority of our sample were not seekers in the sense of "searching for some satisfactory system of religious meaning" (Lofland and Stark, 1965: 868). We do not suggest, however, that religious seekership was not operative in the case of many preconverts. As one married female convert in her mid-twenties recounts:

> I have been a member of several religions, and try as I did to live by them I somehow fell away. I didn't realize then, but my reason for leaving was always the same. They all lacked something I was searching for. I read many books about different religions. But every way I tried I failed to reach the guidance and fulfillment I was seeking.

Seekership is also suggested by the fact that 22 percent of the sample could be classified as "seekers." Yet, the fact that 78 percent or more were not self-designated religious "experimenters" or "searchers" suggests that the linkage between seekership and conversion is not a necessary one.[8] Moreover, even when people do define themselves as religious seekers, we are again confronted with the problem of interpreting retrospective accounts. Did the avowed state of religious seekership actually exist prior to joining the group in question, or did conversion lead to a reconstruction of personal biographies such that converts came to reevaluate their lives prior to joining as ones seeking some ultimate authority?

Situational Factors

Turning Point. Situational factors refer to those conditions that lead to the successful recruitment and conversion of those individuals who are so inclined on the basis of the foregoing predispositions. One such factor is that prospects encounter the movement shortly after or at the same time as the occurrence of what is perceived as a "turning point" in life. That is, preconverts must come into contact with the movement at or about the same time as being confronted with the necessity or opportunity of doing something different with their lives because of the completion or disruption of old obligations and lines of action. The kinds of personal incidents and situations that Lofland and Stark (1965: 870) allude to as turning points include objective changes such as loss of job; completion, failure or withdrawal from school; divorce; and residential change.

Insofar as such specific events are taken as reliable indicators of turning points, then our data seemingly provide some support for the hypothetical linkage between turning points and conversion. As indicated in the second section of Table 2, 72 percent of the usable cases in our sample report personal experiences that might be construed as turning points. Additionally, if we include as being at a turning point the 21 percent who referred to themselves as "hippies" or "wanderers" at the time of encountering NSA, then roughly 93 percent of the converts in our sample were at a turning point in their lives sometime before or concurrently with their encounter with NSA. While these findings do not unqualifiedly indicate that a turning point is a necessary condition for conversion, they do suggest that it may be an important facilitative condition in that it appears to increase one's susceptibility to conversion.

Yet, looked at more critically, the concept of the turning point and its relation to conversion are, as Lofland (1978: 20) has recently commented, quite "troublesome." The reasons are several. First, the turning point is not a given, but is largely a matter of definition and attitude. There are few, if any, consistently reliable benchmarks for ascertaining when or whether one is at a turning point in one's life. As a consequence, just about any moment could be defined as a turning point. Relatedly, when seeking to establish the occurrence of turning points in the past, we again face the problem of retrospective reporting. Events once seen as routine or inconsequential may emerge as highly significant after one has adopted the world view of NSA. In addition, when NSA converts discuss turning points in their lives, they seldom refer to the kinds of objective major life changes emphasized by Lofland and Stark. As indicated in Table 2, such changes as divorce, unemployment, and completion of school are frequently mentioned, but not as turning points. Instead, this designation seems to be reserved for that point at which members come to align themselves with the movement emotionally, cognitively, and morally - seeing themselves at one with the group. Furthermore, this realization typically occurs during the course of their practice as a member, rather than prior to or at the time of encountering the movement. As one middle-aged convert, employed as a nurse and who was the mother of a seventeen-year old, relates:

> Although I had been a member for some time, things weren't going well. I was beginning to lose my patience and motivation at work, and my son was going through some troublesome phases. I continued to chant, but it wasn't until the Nichiren Shoshu San Diego Convention that I began to develop a real faith in the practice and a sense of mission ... When I got home, things started happening. My whole attitude seemed changed. When I went to work I felt a real sense of confidence that was never there before ... As I look back now, the Convention was the turning point in my life.

Similarly, an unmarried female convert in her early twenties, employed as a retailer in a clothing store, recounts how the turning point in her life came upon seeing President Ikeda, the movement's principal leader, during the movement's 1974 San Diego Convention:

> Prior to the Convention I felt a gap in my life. I loved NSA activities and devoted every spare moment to them, but something was missing in the world outside of NSA. In the month before the Convention I came to realize I needed to

capture the spirit of President Ikeda ... The opportunity
came when the Convention Cultural Festival began and I
found myself sitting five seats away from him. As I
watched he turned and waved in my direction. Astonished,
I waved back. And then he gave me the "V" sign. It was
beyond my greatest dreams. Now I feel that I could follow
him anywhere. At that moment I felt a real connection with
President Ikeda that has opened up a whole new aspect in
my life. ... You stay in your nest until you're ready to fly.
... This is the first time I've been out of the nest. I feel
like I've been born again.

Such accounts, in conjunction with the earlier observations,
suggest that the turning point concept may be related to conversion, but
not necessarily in the way initially hypothesized by Lofland and Stark.
We see two differences. First, rather than assuming that major
objective life changes are necessarily perceived by converts as turning
points (see Lofland and Stark, 1965: 870), we contend that what is
defined as a turning point is largely contingent on the interpretive
schema of the group in question. Thus, a turning point may be
indicated by extramovement status passages or role changes, as Lofland
and Stark assume, or it may be constituted by some illuminating insight
or by heightened or renewed faith. In either case, it is subjectively
determined rather than objectively given. The second difference
follows from the first. Rather than occurring prior to or around the
time in which the movement is encountered, the turning point is more
likely to come after contact with the movement and exposure to its
world view. Inasmuch as conversion involves the acquisition of a new
or more clearly articulated universe of discourse and its attendant
vocabulary of motive, then these observations are neither surprising nor
unreasonable. Accordingly, the turning point might be conceptualized
as an artifact of the conversion process, rather than as a precipitating
condition. Indeed, the turning point may symbolize conversion itself,
for converts are gripped by the realization that they are not the same
as they were moments ago and that their life situation and view of the
world have changed, and for the better.

Cult Affective Bonds. None of the hypothetical precipitants of conversion are regarded as more important than the development of a positive, interpersonal tie between the prospect and one or more movement members. However amenable an individual is to the appeals of a cult or movement, Lofland and Stark (1965: 871) argue that for conversion to occur "an affective bond must develop, if it does not already exist." Such a bond may emerge during the course of movement-specific interaction between two former strangers, or it may be the result of a preexisting, extramovement, interpersonal association. Lofland and Stark found that once the initial bond between the founder and the first convert developed, nearly all subsequent conversions "moved through preexisting friendship pairs or nets."

Our findings tend to agree with those of Lofland and Stark. Examination of the conversion careers of the fifteen most active members of the chanting cell with which the senior author was associated revealed that an affective bond was not only discernible in each case, but that the bond was typically preexisting rather than emergent and movement-specific. Two of the fifteen members were recruited by a spouse, one by another relative, ten by friends or acquaintances, and only two by strangers. All but two of the most active members in the chanting cell were thus drawn into sustained contact with the movement by being linked to a member through a preexisting, extramovement interpersonal tie. Further investigation revealed that the same pattern was evident for the vast majority of NSA members brought into the movement's orbit of influence. As indicated in the third section of Table 2, 82 percent of our sample were recruited by members with whom they had preexisting, extramovement ties. Although the remaining 18 percent were recruited directly from the street by members who were strangers, firsthand association with such recruits suggests that their subsequent conversion was contingent on the development of an affective bond with one or more members of the cell into which they were recruited.

That an affective interpersonal tie between the prospect and one or more members might constitute a necessary condition for conversion is not surprising. Such a bond can function to bridge the information gap between prospect and movement, increase the credibility of the message and cause, and intensify the pressure to consider the message and the corresponding practice. We would thus argue that while conversion involves more than "coming to accept the opinions of one's friends" (Lofland and Stark, 1965: 871), it is rather unlikely in the absence of such an affective bond to one or more members.[9]

Weak Extracult Affective Bonds. The third situational factor Lofland and Stark deem necessary for conversion is the absence or neutralization of extracult attachments. Given the fact that converts to the group they studied had few (if any) strong, proximal, interpersonal ties, and given the corollary finding that "conversion was not consummated" when extracult bonds were not weakened or neutralized (Lofland and Stark, 1965: 873), such a proposition seems well-grounded. Moreover, it is consistent with the argument that extraneous ties and commitments can function as countervailing influences with respect to the interests, demands and ideology of a cult or movement (see Becker, 1960; Kanter, 1972).

However plausible the above hypothesis, both the work of Richardson and his associates and our own findings cast considerable doubt on its generalizability. In their work on conversion to a fundamentalist sect, Richardson et al. (1978: 51) found that while "many members did not have especially rewarding" preexisting "ties" and while "most such ties were generally weakened or broken at least for a time after a person became a member of the group," the "sect members were not isolated from their society to the extent that Lofland and Stark found in their study." Even more significantly, they report finding a number of extragroup significant others, particularly parents, who felt positively toward the group and were even supportive of the convert's participation (Richardson et al., 1978: 51; Richardson and Stewart, 1978: 37).

Our findings similarly provide little support for the hypothesis that either neutralized extramovement ties or social isolation constitutes a necessary condition for conversion. As noted earlier, 82 percent were recruited into the movement via preexisting, extramovement social networks. Moreover, our data suggest that conversion to NSA generally may lead to a strengthening of extramovement bonds, particularly among family, co-workers and classmates. There are two reasons for this. First, because NSA's interpretive beliefs include the karmic principle that one's present life condition is largely contingent on one's own actions, both past and present, converts come to blame themselves for their misfortunes. Consequently, they seek to change themselves rather than others, thereby improving rather than worsening extramovement relations. The account of an unmarried twenty-three year old female convert illustrates our assertion:

> I now realize that the reason I didn't get along with my roommate wasn't her fault, but my fault. Chanting and the Gohonzon made me realize that the things I criticized about her were the very faults I possessed. By chanting and changing my character we are now able to get along.

Or, as an unmarried male convert in his early twenties similarly recounts:

> I discovered that I was running from myself. I came to realize that everything I hated was part of me. This realization made me a better person, because I am now correcting what was wrong with me instead of blaming it on my parents, the school, and the country.

In addition, since NSA is a noncommunal, proselytizing movement that seeks to change the world by expanding its ranks, all nonmembers, and particularly extramovement familiar others, are defined as potential converts: as one informant put it, "like freshly sown seeds, [they] will eventually blossom if only they are tended to." Accordingly, members are constantly reminded to build and nurture extramovement ties in order to facilitate the movement's spread.

These observations suggest that affective ties to both movement members and nonmembers are not necessarily contradictory, and that extramovement affective ties may function to facilitate rather than to counteract conversion. There are at least two reasons why these findings are inconsistent with those by Lofland and Stark. One is that the Unification Church they studied had a communal structure and NSA's is noncommunal. Because communally organized groups are generally more demanding (Kanter, 1972, 1973) or "greedy" (Coser, 1967), the neutralization or severance of extragroup ties and other countervailing influences may well be necessary in order to effect conversion. In contrast, such a break with the outside world hardly seems necessary for conversion to noncommunal movements such as NSA. The other reason is that the relationship between extramovement affective ties and conversion may also be influenced by the public reaction a movement engenders (see Turner and Killian, 1972: 257-59; Snow, 1979). Conversion to movements that are publicly defined as "revolutionary" or "peculiar" or "idiosyncratic" may be contingent on the weakening of extramovement ties - in order to neutralize the stigma frequently associated with participation in such movements. In contrast, participation in movements defined as "respectable" may not be encumbered by resistance from nonmovement significant others. Hence, the maintenance of extramovement ties may not impede conversion to more "respectable" movements. Given the fact that NSA has made a longstanding and concerted effort to render itself respectable and legitimate in the public eye, such an hypothesis seems quite plausible (see Snow, 1979).

Intensive Interaction. While they regard the confluence of the six previous items (three disposing conditions and three situational factors) as sufficient for the production of verbal conversion, Lofland and Stark contend that commitment remains only verbal, and that conversion remains incomplete, in the absence of intensive interaction with group members. Such interaction hypothetically transforms the avowed convert into a "deployable agent" by securing behavioral as well as verbal commitment, and they regard it as the final condition that rounds out the conversion process.

Our observations are not only in line with those of Lofland and Stark but suggest that intensive interaction is perhaps the most important factor in the conversion process once the prospect has been informed about and brought into contact with the movement. In the case of NSA, the interaction begins in earnest once the prospect has been persuaded to attend a cellular (district) discussion meeting. Conducted four evenings per week, these meetings are highly organized affairs staged for the expressed purpose of giving "newcomers the best possible reasons for receiving their own Gohonzon (scroll) and to begin chanting."[10] If the prospect agrees to give chanting a try, he or she is formally initiated into NSA in a conversion ceremony (Gojukai) held at one of its regional temples and conducted by NSA priests. Following this and the enshrinement of the Gohonzon in the newcomer's place of residence, the new member typically becomes the primary responsibility of the member who was the recruiter. Referred to as a Junior Group Leader, this member constitutes the initial primary link between the novitiate and the movement. More than anyone else in the movement, the group leader is expected "to know the situation of the new member, what sort of hopes [he/she] has, and what [his/her] desire is to practice." Moreover, the group leader is to "strive to establish a warm and close relationship with the member [he/she] is taking care of."

The ultimate aim is to get the new member to "stand alone," to be a "self-motivated member," to be, in Lofland and Stark's terms, a "deployable agent." But a new member is only "at level one toward becoming an active, vigorous member of NSA," and has to be "brought along." It is here that the Junior Group Leader comes into play. Alternating between the roles of instructor, informer and confidant, the Junior Leader is charged with maintaining constant contact with the new member - answering questions, advising about movement activities, and nurturing faith. This leader is also responsible for taking new members on recruiting expeditions into public places; coaxing them to attend meetings; introducing them to other group members and movement leaders; and visiting them at home to "help them chant correctly." By performing such duties the Junior Leader is a role model of what it means to be a member, of how members think, talk and act - not only in relation to NSA but with respect to the world in general. It is thus through the Junior Group Leader and through attendance at and participation in movement activities that the new member begins to learn what NSA is all about and begins to become oriented cognitively, emotionally and morally. Members are constantly reminded that "if the link between the new member and the Junior Group Leader is cut off" then "the new member is virtually left out of the rhythm of NSA and is likely to fall away."

In the absence of such constant and intense interaction, conversion to NSA seems unlikely. Since this observation is not only consistent with Lofland and Stark's work, but also is suggested by studies of Hare Krishna (Daner, 1976; Judah, 1974) and Pentecostalism (Gerlach and Hine, 1970; Heirich, 1977), it would appear that the salience of intensive interaction to conversion cannot be overemphasized.

SUMMARY AND CONCLUSIONS

We have sought to extend our understanding of the conversion process by critically examining the Lofland-Stark conversion model. Our data, derived from a study of recruitment and conversion to the Nichiren Shoshu Buddhist movement in America, have not supported the model in its entirety. Our analysis has suggested that several components of the model are theoretically questionable, while others seem more defensible.

Our findings are especially at odds with the contention that personal tension, ideological congruence, and religious seekership are necessary predisposing conditions for conversion. These factors were present in some individual cases, but missing in many others. Moreover, even if they had been uniformly operative, such factors might be best interpreted as consequences rather than precipitants of conversion. Our argument is admittedly inconsistent with the longstanding tendency to approach recruitment and conversion to movements primarily from a social psychological-motivational standpoint which focuses on various prestructured tensions and cognitive orientations as the major explanatory variables (see Cantril, 1941; Glock, 1964; Hoffer, 1951; Klapp, 1969; Peterson and Mauss, 1973). But we believe that this traditional approach is itself empirically questionable and theoretically unfounded. It ignores the fact that motives for behavior are generally emergent and interactional. It also assumes that the explanations given by converts for their conversion were necessarily those that motivated or precipitated it in the first place. We question such an assumption because conversion involves the reconstruction of one's past, frequently including the discovery of personal needs and problems not previously discernible or troublesome enough to warrant remedial action. Hence, the old past and the new past bear slight resemblance to each other.

The findings and analysis here also call into question the necessity of two of the situational factors that were components of the Lofland-Stark model: that of the turning point and that of weak or severed extracult attachments. Their original conceptualization of the connection between the turning point and conversion is at best problematic. Because the identification of something as a turning point is largely a function of the interpretive schema in use, the turning point really cannot be known a priori or without familiarity with the world view in question. Therefore, instead of conceptualizing the turning point as a precipitant of conversion, it might best be thought of as a consequence that can function to symbolize conversion itself.

We found that recruitment and conversion to NSA were typically contingent on the maintenance of extracult affective ties, rather than being associated with weakened or neutralized extramovement affective ties. Data were also reported suggesting that conversion to NSA may even function to strengthen some extramovement ties. These findings ran counter to what the Lofland-Stark model led us to expect, and we suggested that the difference was probably related to: 1) whether the groups involved were organized communally (as was the Unification Church) or noncommunity (true of NSA); and 2) whether the movements involved were considered "respectable" or not by the general public.

Although we have questioned many features of the Lofland-Stark model, our findings indicate that two remaining factors in their model - cult affective bonds and intensive interaction - are essential for conversion to NSA. We would even argue that conversion in general is highly improbable in the absence of affective and intensive interaction. Some critics (Lofland, 1978; Straus, 1976) might object to such a conclusion on the grounds that it views the human actor as a relatively passive agent whose outlook and behavior is unwittingly molded and controlled by various social factors. However, we are not arguing that prospective converts are empty and disinterested vessels into which new ideas and beliefs are poured. To the contrary, we take it for granted that most converts were initially interested in exploring the perspective or group with which they are currently associated. After all, aside from the deprogramming "business" (cf. Patrick, 1976; Shupe et al., 1978), there is little, if any, evidence to suggest that the bulk of contemporary conversions are involuntary or coerced. But to suggest that an individual once had an interest in or taste for something is not explain how that something - whether a philosophy, a lifestyle or a form of music - became a burning preoccupation, in James' (1958: 162) words, "the habitual center of [one's] personal energy." The key to such a transformation, we contend, is in the process of intensive interaction between prospect and converts. Of course, people may facilitate their own conversion, but before they can "go about converting themselves" (Lofland, 1978: 22) they must be privy to a universe of discourse that renders such transformations desirable and possible. Moreover, when a virtual smorgasbord of transformative world views exists, the question arises as to how and why one alternative is selected over another: the answer again seems to lie within the process of affective and intensive interaction.

In summary, our findings and analysis not only question the generalizability of some key elements of the Lofland-Stark model, they also raise questions about related models of conversion that place considerable emphasis on prestructured tensions and cognitive states, and on prior socialization. The analysis also suggests that instead of being the same in all groups, the conversion process may vary, depending, for example, on whether the group in question is communal or noncommunal, and "respectable" or "idiosyncratic." Our analysis, finally, suggests that the interactive process holds the key to understanding conversion. Future research should emphasize understanding this process more fully and pay special attention to the extent to which it varies across groups differing in ideology, organization and public reaction.

NOTES

1. Aside from the work of Richardson et al. (1978), we know of only two studies which might be considered "tests" of the Lofland-Stark model. The first, Seggar and Kunz's (1972) examination of conversion to Mormonism, not only had mixed results, but we question (for reasons that will become clear later in the paper) the extent to which conversion can be adequately studied solely by means of post factum, structured interviews. We also question whether an examination of conversion to an institutionalized religious denomination constitutes a fair test of a conversion model pertaining to "deviant" cults or belief systems. The second study examines the relation between psychological stress, prior socialization and direct social influence (Heirich, 1977). Because its findings bear upon some related components of the Lofland-Stark model but neglect others, it cannot be regarded as a test of the Lofland-Stark model in its entirety.

2. In *The Philosophy of the Present* (1932: 31), Mead notes, for example: "If we had every possible document and every possible monument from the period of J. Caesar, we would unquestionably have a truer picture of the man and of what occurred in his lifetime, but it would be a truth which belongs to the present, and a later present would reconstruct it from the standpoint of its own emergent nature." Similarly, Mead writes in *The Philosophy of the Act* (1936: 616): "...that which arrives that is novel gives a continually new past. A past never was in the form in which it appears as a past. Its reality is in its interpretation of the present."

3. Although the sample consisted of 2,460 American adults over 21, the base for the above figures ranges from 922 for work problems to 2,455 for feelings of impending nervous breakdown. The figures were extrapolated from Gurin et al., 1960: Tables 2.6, 3.4, 4.8, 5.8 and 6.1.

4. A 1976 survey of over 2000 American men and women about their feelings of well-being and distress suggested that Americans still readily avow numerous anxieties and problems. The study revealed that today people tend to be somewhat more anxiety-ridden and "unhappy about

their communities and country, their jobs, and their interpersonal lives" than in 1957 (Institute of Social Research, 1979: 4).

5. That prestructured tension or stress may not be a necessary precondition for conversion is also suggested by Heirich's (1977: 666) finding "that stress, at least as measured here, is insufficient to account" for conversion to Catholic Pentecostalism. Here it is also interesting to note that Heirich's findings suggest that perhaps converts to Catholic Pentecostalism are not as inclined as are converts to Nichiren Shoshu to define their past as problematic and stressful. If this is true, it suggests either that converts to NSA are more "troubled" than converts to Catholic Pentecostalism or that whether converts see their past as stress-ridden is largely dependent on the newly acquired interpretive schema. As argued above, we prefer the latter explanation. This explanation is also consistent with Emerson and Messinger's more general observations (1977: 23) about the natural history of personal difficulties or "troubles." Among other things, they note that troubles initially "appear vague to those concerned. But as steps are taken to remedy or manage that trouble, the trouble itself becomes progressively clarified and specified."

6. Our observations here are also consistent with Heirich's finding (1977: 66) that conversion to Catholic Pentecostalism, as indicated by attending Mass, "does not result from previous conditioning."

7. This is also amply demonstrated by attendance at an Erhard Training Seminar (est) or an evangelistic revival, or by spending an evening at a Krishna commune or with the Moonies, each of which we have done on one or more occasions.

8. Even though Balch and Taylor (1978) and Straus (1976) argue convincingly that many people who participate in contemporary religious groups and mass therapies are "seekers," we find no reason to modify our contention that seekership is not essential for conversion. Based on our observations, we think it is more reasonable to argue that while "there are undoubtedly personality types who are attracted to any movement," only rarely do they ever constitute "more than a small fraction of its members" (Turner and Killian, 1972: 365).

9. In their study of participation in the Bo and Peep UFO cult, Balch and Taylor (1978) report findings apparently questioning the importance of group affective bonds to conversion. They note that "new recruits almost never established close affective ties with members of the cult before they joined," and that "even after a seeker decided to join, he got very little social support from members of the cult." Yet, they also note that "members of the UFO cult were not converts in the true sense of the word." Instead, they were "metaphysical seekers" who defined "their decision to follow the Two" as "a reaffirmation of their seekership ... as a logical extension of their spiritual quest." If the members of the cult had undergone conversion, then it was not to the UFO cult but to the metaphysical world view which came to function for them as a primary authority prior to encountering the Two and their followers. Because the conversion process was not involved in affiliation with the cult, it seems unreasonable to argue that Balch and Taylor's findings contradict either the Lofland-Stark model or our own conclusions about the importance of group affective bonds in relation to conversion.

10. This and the following quoted material are derived from the *World Tribune*, from members' comments during movement meetings, and from informal discussions with the senior author.

THE CONVERT AS A SOCIAL TYPE*

This essay treats the convert as a social type with four specifiable formal properties: biographical reconstruction; adoption of a master attribution scheme; suspension of analogical reasoning; and embracement of the convert role. These properties are derived from the talk and reasoning of converts to a culturally transplanted Buddhist movement and from accounts of other proselytizers and converts. We conclude that it is the convert's rhetoric rather than institutional context or ideological content that denotes the convert as a social type.

The widespread appeal of numerous religious and personal growth movements during the past decade (Lande, 1976; Richardson, 1978; Robbins and Anthony, 1979; Wuthnow, 1976) has stimulated considerable discussion and research about the phenomenon of conversion. Heirich (1977) has suggested that an understanding of conversion requires consideration of both its nature and its causes. To date, however, the bulk of the research has concerned itself with the causes and stages of conversion (Balch, 1980; Bromley and Shupe, 1979b; Lofland, 1978; Lofland and Stark, 1965; Richardson and Stewart, 1978; Snow and Phillips, 1980). Although this research has helped to specify the relative influence of various social, psychological and situational factors in relation to the conversion process, conversion itself is vaguely conceived. Just how one might identify the convert is never clearly explained. Instead, the characteristics of the convert are typically taken for granted. This is a serious oversight, especially since an understanding of the conversion process presupposes the ability to identify the convert.

* Adapted from David A. Snow and Richard Machalek, "The Convert as a Social Type." Pp. 259-289 in Randall Collins, (ed.), *Sociological Theory, 1983*. San Francisco: Jossey-Bass, 1983.

In this chapter, therefore, we propose a more formal and explicit theoretical explanation of the convert. Specifically, we treat the convert as a social type with identifiable formal properties. Following Simmel (Wolff, 1964), we focus on "the typical characteristics of a person when engaging in various sorts of interaction" (Levine, 1965, p. 101) in order to delimit the properties of the convert as a social type. Rather than deriving the properties of the convert from the overt behavior of religious group members and participants in other movements, however, we focus on their talk and reasoning. In keeping with Simmel's formal sociology, we listen not only with an ear for the content of conversion claims but with an ear for the characteristic form of conversion rhetoric. Hence we argue that it is by the form of converts' talk and reasoning that they can be distinguished from other social types.

This line of analysis was suggested during the course of an ethnographic study of the Nichiren Shoshu Buddhist movement in America. As a participant observer of the movement for a year-and-a-half, the senior author had numerous opportunities to observe and informally converse with movement members in various situations. After a period of time it became clear that the talk and reasoning of some members varied considerably from the rhetoric of others. Further investigation revealed discernible patterns in this talk and reasoning. These observations provided the impetus for our study. Our analysis is thus grounded in and illustrated throughout by the talk and reasoning of members of Nichiren Shoshu of America (NSA). These accounts are supplemented with examples drawn from other proselytizing movements and from the biographical accounts of both proselytizers and converts.

We begin by evaluating existing conceptions of conversion. We then propose four formal properties of the convert as a social type. Finally, we discuss the theoretical and methodological implications of the formulation.

COMMON CONCEPTIONS OF CONVERSION

Travisano (1970, p. 600) has suggested that the convert is recognizable by his piety. While this may be true, we are still left with the problem of recognizing piety. There are, however, a number of other characteristics used by laypersons and social scientists as a basis for identifying converts. Since these common conceptions have serious deficiencies, it is necessary to examine them critically.

Physical Aberrations. Some would have us believe that the convert has a characteristic phenotype, a sort of Cain's mark. Delgado (1980, p. 22) cites several adjectives used by psychiatrists, psychologists, and other observers to describe those who convert to cults - autistic-like, zombie-like, programmed, glass-eye stare, fixed facial smile, and stereotyped, robot-like responses. Hargrove (1980, p. 20) reports similar adjectives - a glassy-eyed thousand-mile stare, for example. Many laypersons too believe that converts can be detected by such physical attributes. As an irate parent of a member of the Unification Church was heard to comment at an anticult rally in Dallas in 1976: "You can tell if someone has been brainwashed by looking in their eyes. Haven't you noticed how Moonies seem to look right through you?" However vivid such descriptions, there is little scientific basis for using them as indicators of conversion. Moreover, as Cox (1978) has warned, such beliefs have frequently functioned historically to sanction religious persecution.

Group Membership or Participation. A second line of thinking equates conversion with membership or participation in new or fringe groups. If one is a member of such a group, whatever the criteria of membership, one is thereby regarded as a convert. Probably for purposes of convenience, social scientists often treat membership, especially in "deviant" religious groups, as an indicator of conversion (Enroch, 1977; Harrison, 1974; Heirich, 1977; Lofland and Stark, 1965; Richardson, Stewart, and Simmonds, 1978). To equate membership and conversion, however, strikes us as a questionable assumption. It ignores the sociological axiom that people can be member of the same group or movement in different ways and with varying degrees of commitment (Etzioni, 1975; Kanter, 1972; Turner and Killian, 1972). Evidence also suggests that membership in religious groups is much too heterogeneous to justify its use as a reliable indicator of conversion (Bultena, 1949; Fichter, 1954; Ebaugh, 1977). As Nock (1933) observed some time ago, people often participate in religious rituals and activities without fully adopting the group's value orientation.[1] Balch's (1980) recent study of a millennial UFO cult similarly indicates a tenuous link between participation and conversion. Such observations thus suggest that while membership may be necessary for conversion, it is seldom, if ever, a sufficient condition.

Demonstration Events. A third factor commonly treated as an indicator of conversion is the demonstration event. A demonstration event is essentially a social display of conversion. It may be institutionalized and routinized, as in the case of confirmations and testimonies, or it may be spontaneous and dramatic, as in the case of glossolalia and other ecstatic utterings and trances. Whatever its exact nature it is thought to symbolize what Lang and Lang (1961, p. 157) call the moment of awakening. It is partly for this reason that many religious proselytizers and groups place a premium on demonstration events. Such events ostensibly provide them with a bench mark for distinguishing the novitiate from the convert.[2]

Social scientists also frequently rely on demonstration events to identify converts. Zetterberg (1952, p. 159), in his study of a fundamentalist revival group, identified the convert as one who had openly confessed communion with God or had pursued the same. More recently, Heirich (1977, pp. 660-661) operationally defined the Catholic Pentecostal convert as one who not only avowed membership but who also reported receiving the baptism of the Holy Spirit. On the other hand, some social scientists have urged caution about relying on demonstration events as valid indicators of conversion. Noting that religious groups frequently apply considerable normative pressure, often in emotionally charged situations, for potential converts to demonstrate a conversion experience, Clark (1958, p. 204) has observed that many avowed converts show very little permanent behavioral evidence of personality change. Berger and Luckmann (1967, p. 158) have similarly observed that a conversion is nothing much: "The real thing is to be able to keep on taking it seriously; to retain a sense of its plausibility." Many religious proselytizers also harbor skepticism about taking demonstration events too seriously. Rather than relaxing their vigilance after the prospective convert's spiritual awakening, the more successful proselytizers try to reinforce the demonstration experience with a social infrastructure. John Wesley, the principal founder of Methodism, seemed keenly aware of the fragile relationship between a demonstration event and a sustained conversion. One of Wesley's biographers (Doughty, 1955, p. 57) observed that "from the outset he realized the comparative futility of merely preaching to a miscellaneous crowd of people and leaving the matter there. He realized that individuals needed to be befriended, shepherded, instructed, and encouraged, and hence arose the societies which became the nuclei of the Methodist church."

George Whitefield, an eighteenth-century Calvinist, similarly spent much of his life preaching in England, Scotland, Wales, and the United States. Whitefield was content merely to preach and hope for the best; Wesley, however, declined to preach where it seemed impossible to consolidate his evangelical efforts. When writing from Haverfordwest in August 1763, for example, Wesley noted: "I was more convinced than ever that preaching like an apostle, without joining together those that are awakened and training them up in the ways of God, is only begetting children for the murderer [the devil]" (Doughty, 1955, p. 57). Whitefield ultimately realized the genius of Wesley in this regard. Toward the end of his life Whitefield admitted: "My brother Wesley acted wisely. The souls that were awakened under his ministry he joined in class, and thus preserved the fruit of his labor. This I neglected, and my people are a rope of sand" (p. 57).

Like Wesley, many contemporary religious proselytizers seem suspicious about the connection between demonstration events and sustained conversion. They also seem to have grasped the importance of establishing a plausibility structure (Berger and Luckmann, 1967, p. 158) in order to secure and stabilize conversion experiences. The leaders of the Unification Church, for example, make certain that such experiences are immediately succeeded by a series of workshops during which an intensive study of the theology of the movement is pursued, "thus allowing a firm intellectual faith to support the insight of the first moment" (De Maria, 1978, p. 110); also see Bromely and Shupe, 1979a, and Lofland, 1977, 1978). Nichiren Shoshu leaders are equally skeptical about the value of a demonstration experience in the absence of sustained interaction with authentic converts. As one leader explained:

> It's fairly easy to do Shakubuku [proselytizing] and get a person to attend an NSA discussion meeting. And that person may decide to receive his Gohonzon and start practicing. But the real test comes after he receives the Gohonzon and starts practicing. The important thing is

whether the individual can at least grasp a little of the significance of chanting. That is why attending NSA meetings on a regular basis is so important.

A theological understanding of conversion is not a social scientific understanding. Nevertheless, if the devotees of a religion are reluctant to accept at face value a demonstration event as a valid and reliable indicator of conversion, we think the social scientist may be well served by exercising equal caution.

Conversion as Radical Change. If there is one point about which students of conversion seem virtually unanimous, it is that conversion involves a radical change in a person's experience. James (1958, p. 162), for example, described conversion in terms of new or peripheral ideas that come to "form the habitual center of [one's] energy." Others have referred to it as a "drastic transformation in behavior patterns" (Shibutani, 1961, p. 523), "a complete turnabout in central values" (Lang and Lang, 1961, p. 153), and "a fundamental and wholehearted reversal of former values, attitudes, and beliefs" (Turner and Killian, 1972, pp. 388-389). Some scholars would reserve the term for sudden changes, others would include gradual changes, and still others would include multiple or serial changes (Clark, 1958; Parrucci, 1968; Richardson, 1980; Richardson and Stewart, 1978; Zetterberg, 1952). Nonetheless, the idea of radical change is at the core of all conceptions of conversion.

Taken by itself, the view of conversion as radical change is not particularly helpful. Two problems are immediately apparent. First, to argue that the conversion must be drastic, complete, or dramatic does not specify, either conceptually or operationally, how much change is enough to constitute a conversion. Several students of conversion have implicitly addressed this problem by proposing continua for distinguishing radical and comprehensive changes. Travisano (1970, p. 598) separates conversions from alterations, which he defines as reversible and less drastic: "Complete disruption signals conversion while anything less signals alternation." Similarly, Gordon (1974) distinguishes conversion, "a radical discontinuity in the person's life," from less extreme identity changes.[3] While these conceptual distinctions may be useful in defining what conversion is not, they provide no unambiguous criteria for identifying complete disruptions or radical discontinuities. Hence the refinements proposed by Travisano (1970) and Gordon (1974) are no more satisfactory than the earlier discussions of conversion.

If we were to solve the problem of designating the degree of change required for conversion, we would be left with a logically-prior question: exactly what is it that undergoes radical change? Is it beliefs and values, behavior and identities, or something even more fundamental that changes? A simple declaration of conversion as radical change in belief or behavior does not solve the problem. Questions pertaining to the kinds of belief or behavior that change, the direction of change, and the indicators of change still remain. To raise these questions is not to take issue with the basic conception of conversion as radical change. Rather, it is to insist that the character of that change be specified.

Conversion and the Universe of Discourse. To the extent that conversion is viewed as a radical change, we propose that it is the universe of discourse which changes. As "a system of common or social meanings," a universe of discourse provides a broad interpretive framework in terms of which people live and organize experience (Mead, 1962, pp. 88-90).[4] It constitutes the source of what has been variously referred to as one's sense of ultimate grounding or root reality (Heirich, 1977, pp. 553, 674-676), one's center of energy (James, 1958, p. 162), or one's paradigm (Jones, 1978). To experience a radical and fundamental change in one's universe of discourse is therefore no casual change of attitude, opinion, or belief. It is not merely a matter of rearranging the trivial elements of one's consciousness as one rearranges furniture. Rather, it entails the displacement of one universe of discourse by another and its attendant grammar or rules for putting things together. Perhaps this is why Jones (1978) finds it useful to compare conversion to Kuhn's (1962) idea of paradigm shift.

If it is the universe of discourse that undergoes radical change during conversion, can that change be specified? In short, what can be said to characterize the talk and reasoning of the convert? In the following pages we propose four key properties by which to define the convert: biographical reconstruction, adoption of a master attribution scheme, suspension of analogical reasoning, and embracement of a master role.

PROPERTIES OF CONVERSION

Biographical Reconstruction. In *The Varieties of Religious Experience*, James (1958, p. 177) observed that when one undergoes conversion "a complete division is established in the twinkling of an eye between the old life and the new." While not all conversions occur in the twinkling of an eye, there seems to be little question but that they all involve a division between the old and the new. This division involves the dissolution of the past, on the one hand, and its reconstitution on the other. The dismantling process is clearly illustrated by the Italian writer Ignazio Silone's account of his conversion to communism in the 1930s: "My own internal world, the 'middle ages,' which I had inherited and which were rooted in my soul ... were shaken to their foundations, as though by an earthquake. Everything was thrown into the melting-pot, everything became a problem" (Crossman, 1952, p. 87). But the past is not only shattered; the disjointed pieces are reassembled in accordance with the new universe of discourse and its grammar. Some aspects of the past are jettisoned, others are redefined, and some are put together in ways previously inconceivable. One's biography is, in short, reconstructed. As Silone went on to note, "Life, death, love, good, evil, truth, all changed their meaning or lost it altogether" (p. 87).

James is not the only student of conversion to have alluded to this process of biographical reconstruction. In fact, it is the one property of conversion that is acknowledged with some frequency in the literature (Beckford, 1978; Berger, 1963; Berger and Luckmann, 1967; Burke, 1965; Gordon, 1974; Jones, 1978; Shibutani, 1961; Taylor, 1976, 1978; Travisano, 1970). Perhaps this is because it is such a prominent feature of the talk and reasoning of converts. Converts seldom seem to tire of reminding others of how they have changed, how their life has improved, how they not only see things more clearly now but also differently. Moreover, from the convert's viewpoint such changes are rendered reasonable and understandable by two "facts" about the past. First, the convert's former understanding of self, past events, and others is now regarded as a misunderstanding. Following the formula "then I thought ... now I know" (Berger and Luckmann, 1967, p. 160), previous motives, feelings, and evaluations are regarded as misguided or erroneous. As the following comments of Nichiren

Shoshu converts illustrate, converts talk as if they suffered false consciousness if not actual blindness:

> *Male, white, single, under 30:* At the time I joined I was involved in a hippie-type philosophy, and consequently I felt that I had no need for any material belongings in order to attain happiness. It seems unbelievable now, but because of my erroneous concept of a happy life I was totally blind to my actual condition, which was miserable.

> *Female, white, single, under 30:* Chanting has cleared up my mind enough to see that in the years before I chanted I had many misconceptions about life ... I avoided looking at this until chanting brought out the wisdom that could help me see such problems.

> *Married couple, white, 30-40:* Where we thought we were happily married before, we found that there were many barriers between us, many illusions hiding our true selves from ourselves and each other.

Gripped by the realization that preconversion interpretations were erroneous, the convert comes to redefine that past "correctly." Old facts and aspects of one's biography are thus given new meanings. Not only are former identities evaluated negatively but the course and character of the convert's life history is typically reconstructed as troublesome, misdirected, even loathsome. The talk of Nichiren Shoshu converts abounds with examples of this process:

> *Female, white, single, under 30:* Approximately a year ago [before conversion] ... I was going around screaming and protesting for what I thought was the right cause. Little did I know that I wasn't making the right cause and that I was creating so much antivalue in my life.

> *Female, white single, 16:* Before discovering NSA I almost flunked out of school. All I ever thought about was the weekend, the guy I was going out with, and getting high

with my friends. I was really a bum. ... What I thought was the real cool way to be was really very phony.

Male, white, single, 29: Once I began to chant I came to realize that sometimes behind what seems to be a completely happy person there lie problems and limitations that even the person himself is unaware of. Now, after thirteen months of practice, I can look back and see what the true state of my life was.

That converts can look back and see the "true state" of their lives prior to conversion is understandable considering that the past is viewed from the vantage point of the enlightened present. Since the present functions as the final arbiter of truth about the past, biographical reconstruction may even involve the fabrication and insertion of events "wherever they are needed to harmonize the remembered with the reinterpreted past" (Berger and Luckmann, 1967, p. 160). In this regard, Heirich (1977, p. 658) has suggested that the converts he studied tended to exaggerate their preconversion sinfulness to increase the power and value of their conversions. The senior author's association with a number of Nichiren Shoshu converts revealed that their biographical reconstructions too are frequently laced with exaggerations and fabrications. To point to such observations, however, is not to suggest that exaggerations, fabrications, and denials are intended to deceive. The convert is not perpetuating fraud but aligning the past "with the truth that, necessarily, embraces both present and past" (Berger and Luckmann, 1967, p. 160). Ironically, the convert is not privileged to a nonpartisan knowledge of his or her past. Conversion as biographical reconstruction denies one an undistorted recall of the past. This situation is not restricted, of course, to converts. It is virtually axiomatic in phenomenology and in Mead's (1932, 1938) philosophy of the present that personal biographies and identities are continuously redefined in the light of new experiences. For the convert, however, this everyday phenomenon is greatly amplified and intensified; the fact of conversion represents the dominant feature of the convert's consciousness. It provides the point of view in terms of which both life before and life after conversion are interpreted. Hence the old and the new may bear slight resemblance indeed to each other.

Adoption of a Master Attribution Scheme. The second formal property of conversion involves the adoption of a master attribution scheme. Attribution refers to the cognitive process by which people form causal interpretations of the behavior of self and others and the events in the world around them. Specification of the nature, causes, and consequences of the attribution process has been a major objective of much social psychological research and theorizing during the past several decades (Jones and others, 1972; Shaver, 1975; Wegner and Vallacher, 1977, pp. 39-88). Although there are several distinct models of the attribution process (Heider, 1958; Jones and Davis, 1965; Kelley, 1967, 1971), each rests on a number of common assumptions and observations that are germane to the argument being presented. First, attribution is regarded as an everyday cognitive phenomenon deriving from people's need to make sense of the world around them (Kanouse and Hanson, 1972, p. 47; Shaver, 1975, pp. 4-5, 58). Second, it is assumed that the causes of most behavior are attributed to internal or external factors. To attribute responsibility to internal factors is to assume that there is something about the actor's personal qualities and dispositions that cause the action. To make an external attribution, on the other hand, is to account for the action in terms of the environment, including the actions of other persons. Third, it has been observed that attributions tend to vary with differences in available information, self-interest, and change in role and situation (Jones and Nisbett, 1971; Shaver, 1975; Wegner and Vallacher, 1977). Fourth, attribution theorists assume that people are basically rational problem solvers (Shaver, 1975, p. 58). People are seen as constructive thinkers searching for the causes of the events confronting them in a logical way (Jones and others, 1972, p. x). Kelley (1972) has cautioned, however, that causal attributions are not merely a function of one's perceptual and logical faculties. He argues that they are also circumscribed by causal schemata - the general conceptions people have "about how certain kinds of causes interact to produce a specific kind of effect" (p. 151). Kelley suggests that there are different causal schemata and that people typically draw on a number of these types when searching for causes.

Kelley's argument, in many respects, is consistent with Mills's (1940) contention that causal attributions are largely derived from vocabularies of motive. According to Mills, the motives people avow or impute in response to questioned conduct or events are organized into vocabularies that have currency only in certain social situations or groupings. Hence different vocabularies of motive may come into play in different situations and with different sets of actors.

In sum, then, the foregoing observations suggest that inferring the causes of behavior is an invariant component of the interpretive process, that the direction of causal inferences depends on role and situation, and that attributional analyses are fairly rational but are circumscribed by causal schemes or vocabularies of motive.

If these assumptions are correct, then we would argue that conversion involves the adoption of a master attribution scheme. By this we mean that one causal scheme or vocabulary of motives informs all causal attributions. A single locus of causality is simultaneously sharpened and generalized. Feelings, behavior, and events that were previously inexplicable or accounted for by reference to a number of causal schemes are now interpreted from the standpoint of one pervasive scheme. Interpretive options are thus inhibited. Consequently, causal inferences remain constant despite variation in situations. There is neither equivocation nor negotiation with respect to the cause for the behavior or event under scrutiny. The cause is known beforehand. Hence nothing is ambiguous or fortuitous. A master attribution scheme is thereby substituted for a series of multiple attribution schemes that were used previously. All this is clearly illustrated by Arthur Koestler's discussion of his conversion to communism in 1931. In *The God That Failed* (Crossman, 1952, p. 19), Koestler writes: "By the time I had finished with *Feuerbach* and *State and Revolution*, something had clicked in my brain which shook me like a mental explosion ... The whole universe [fell] into pattern like the stray pieces of a jigsaw puzzle assembled by magic at one stroke. There [was] now an answer to every question, doubts and conflicts [were] a matter of the tortured past."

This process is similarly represented in the talk and reasoning of Nichiren Shoshu converts. Consider, for example, the following statements:

Male, white, married, 28: If you think a woman has no fortune or a certain man has no fortune, who do we blame? We look outside and say it's society's fault, or the woman says it's man's fault. The black man says his condition is the white man's fault. Russia says it is America's fault, and we say it's Russia's fault. Somebody at work told me about a TV program on the correctional system in California. The criminals say that they've been in jail too long and that this system doesn't work. So they blame the system for their problems. In other words, it's always someone else's fault - the system's fault, the country's fault, the environment's fault, the spouse's fault. Actually, the only one or thing at fault is ourself.

Male, black, single, 25: My karma used to be really bad. It was apparent to most everyone but me. I bounced from one job to another and was really irresponsible. Only I didn't know it then. It was always somebody else's fault, or at least I thought so. It is only recently that I have come to realize that I was having these problems because of me. There is no blaming others now.

Apart from illustrating the extent to which conversion involves a sharpening and generalizing of a single causal scheme, these statements suggest that the process is frequently accompanied by a shift in causal locus. Whereas many Nichiren Shoshu converts previously attributed blame for their preconversion problems to other individuals or to some structural arrangement, they now internalize causality and avow personal responsibility. The following testimony of a twenty-year old Nichiren Shoshu convert further illustrates this switch: "Before joining Nichiren Shoshu I blamed any problems I had on other people or on the environment. It was always my parents, or the school, or society. But through chanting I discovered the real source of my difficulties: myself. Chanting has helped me to realize that rather than running around blaming others, I am the one who needs to change."

Inspection of the attributional talk of converts to other movements suggests that a switch in a causal locus is probably a frequent concomitant of conversion in general. As a well known television personality explained when discussing her involvement in est (Erhard Seminar Training): "I took est training and ... it helped me in terms of accepting responsibility. I used to spend a lot of time assigning fault to other people. There is no fault. I'm responsible."

These illustrations have been drawn from the talk of converts to religious and personal growth movements. In each case the shift in causal locus has been in the direction of internalizing blame and responsibility. Since personal transformation constitutes either the primary goal or the major means of changing the world for most religious and personal growth movements, effecting a shift from an external to an internal locus of control seems to be a necessary step in conversion to such groups. Certainly in the case of such groups as Nichiren Shoshu and Transcendental Meditation, chanting makes no sense until such a shift is made. But a shift in the perceived locus of causality is not unique to religious and personal growth movements. It is also frequently a constituent element of conversion to movements that seek change by directly altering sociopolitical structures. In the case of politically-oriented groups, however, the shift involves a change from an internal to an external locus of control - that is , from self-blaming to structural-blaming, from victim-blaming to system-blaming. The importance of this switch in relation to political action is well documented in the annals of movements for sociopolitical change. In discussing the unemployed workers' movement of the 1930s, Piven and Cloward (1979, p. 49) emphasize that people did not begin to demand relief until they realized that "it wasn't they who were to blame, but 'the system.'" Along similar lines, Morrison and Steeve's (1967, p. 427) study of the differences between National Farm Organization (NFO) members and nonparticipating midwestern farmers revealed that fewer NFO members regarded "their difficulties and those of other farmers as due to individual inadequacies of effort, talent, or resources. ... Fewer NFO members blame themselves for their difficulties, and more blame certain features of the farm marketing system ... And just as structural blame rather than self-blame characterizes NFO members, hope in an organizational structure designed to bring changes in the features of the larger system perceived as faulty, rather than self-hope, is their trademark."

Students of the feminist movement have similarly noted that the mobilization of women has been contingent on the realization that their grievances and problems are not personal and idiosyncratic but systemic and thus political (Deckard, 1979, p. 460). Changing the locus of blame is one of the main functions of women's consciousness-raising groups. The primary purpose of such groups, as Bird (1969, p. 216) has noted, is to get women "to recognize the political nature of complaints that are conventionally dismissed as personal."

In emphasizing that mobilization for political action frequently involves a shift in attributional orientation, we do not mean to imply that participants in politically-oriented movements necessarily have undergone conversion. We would, however, argue that when conversion does occur, whether the universe of discourse is religious or secular, it not only involves the adoption of a master attribution scheme but may involve a switch in causal locus as well. Hence converts reinterpret their past by redefining some aspects of it as problematic, but they also come to discover the "correct" source of blame for these recently acquired or more acutely-defined troubles.

Suspension of Analogical Reasoning. To understand the third formal property of conversion, we must first consider the logic of metaphor. A metaphor is a way of describing something in terms of something else. It "involves a transfer (metaphora: carrying over) of one term from one level of meaning to another" (Brown, 1977, p. 80). It is literally an inappropriate application of a concept to a domain. The unfamiliar is made familiar in terms of the already familiar. Since metaphors are fundamental linguistic tools for constructing reality and communicating experience, it is reasonable to expect that metaphor would occupy a prominent position in the talk of converts. Our observations suggest, however, that converts rely only sparingly on metaphorical reasoning. While they may employ iconic metaphors, they typically suspend use of analogical metaphors when talking about their beliefs and practices.

Analogical metaphors demonstrate the ways in which one thing is like another; iconic metaphors portray the uniqueness of a thing. In Brown's words (1977, p. 115), iconic metaphors "picture what things are, rather than how things are alike." Recent Christianity, for example, has embraced as its favorite iconic metaphor "God is love." Similarly, the iconic metaphor "born again" has become a cliche in the evangelical movement. Converts have no aversion to this kind of metaphor. Using iconic metaphors can establish the uniqueness of the group or its world view. Analogical metaphors, on the other hand, are resisted because they violate the convert's position that his or her world view is incomparable to other world views.

If iconic metaphor affirms the authenticity and sacredness of conversion, analogical metaphor threatens to invalidate and profane it.[5] Consider the following example of a Nichiren Shoshu recruit's use of analogical metaphor to understand the movement's recruitment practice referred to as Shakubuku: "Doing Shakubuku as a follower of Nichiren Shoshu is just like witnessing as a follower of Jesus Christ. Shakubuku is just like proselytizing; it's just another word for what the Hare Krishna and Jesus people do in the streets." Upon hearing this, a Nichiren Shoshu convert of several years turned around and exclaimed: "Shakubuku and proselytizing aren't the same! Shakubuku is to tell somebody about Nam-Myoho-Renge-Kyo! It is a great act of mercy and compassion, whereas to proselytize is to put pressure on people and force them to come to meetings. The two aren't the same." By denying the validity of the novice's analogy, the convert laid claim to a certain incomparability regarding Nichiren Shoshu. She asserted the uniqueness of Shakubuku. A social scientist might be quick to point out the functional equivalence between Shakubuku and witnessing. A convert denies precisely this "carrying over" of the term proselytizing from other religious contexts to that of Nichiren Shoshu. It is thus that converts suspend analogical reasoning when describing their world view.

The suspension of analogical reasoning repeatedly manifests itself in the talk of Nichiren Shoshu converts. Just as converts to other contemporary religious movements claim that theirs is the One Way, so Nichiren Shoshu converts insist that only they have The Answer to enlightenment, peace, and happiness. As one member proclaimed, "Nichiren Shoshu is unlike any other group in American society. Only Nichiren Shoshu has the means to change the world." Similarly, Nichiren Shoshu converts assert the incomparability of the movement's leadership. Consider these comments extracted from the senior author's field notes:

> While talking with a middle-level leader following a chanting-conversion meeting, the topic turned to Daisaki Ikeda, the movement's formal president and inspirational leader or "Master," as members refer to him. Having observed and experienced the highly emotional response

Ikeda's presence elicits from members, I indicated that he struck me as being a charismatic individual. In response, the middle-level leader with whom I was speaking bristled and emphatically stated that "Ikeda is not a charismatic individual. President Kennedy and Martin Luther King were charismatic, but President Ikeda is not. He is an extraordinary man, but he is not like other major figures and leaders. You can't compare President Ikeda with them. He's unique."

Sociologically, the suspension of analogical reasoning by converts should come as no surprise. Durkheim ([1915], 1965) has provided a powerful clue for understanding this property of conversion. For Durkheim it is nothing less than the radical distinction between the sacred and profane that defines religion. The sacred is both logically and emotionally antithetical to the profane. The sacred is, in Otto's (1973) words, "the wholly other." It does not admit comparison to the profane; it is ineffable. The sacred is possessed of a uniqueness that defies all efforts at a comparison to the profane. It is literally unknowable and inaccessible in terms of the profane. This helps explain the convert's resistance to analogical comparison between his or her religion and others. For the convert, other meaning systems reside in the realm of the profane. Therefore, "carrying over" the particular from another (profane) meaning system in order to explain the particulars of his or her (sacred) meaning system would be unthinkable. As such, relying on analogy to other religions to explain one's own conversion is more than merely inaccurate and imperfect communication. Rather, it is an affront to the sacred itself. Analogical metaphor is transformed from a linguistic convenience to utter profanation.

Suspending analogical reasoning thus allows converts to assign incomparable value to their world view. By removing other belief systems from the status of eligible competition, a virtually impermeable boundary is established around the convert's world view. The convert's sacred commodity is thereby exempted from the pressures of the free market. Thus the convert is protected from the profaning effects of analogical comparison.

Embracement of a Master Role. The final property of conversion, discernible in both the behavior and the rhetoric of converts, is constituted by the generalization, rather than compartmentalization, of the convert role and its embracement by the convert. Role compartmentalization has long been regarded as part and parcel of modernity (Durkheim [1893], 1964), functional rationality (Mannheim, 1940), and bureaucratization (Weber, 1947). Nevertheless, not all roles are compartmentalized or situation-specific. Hughes's (1945) distinction between master and subordinate statuses suggests that some of our statuses are more central than others both to our behavior and to the way we view ourselves and the way others view us. Banton's (1965) threefold classification of roles based on their differentiation and generality similarly suggests that basic roles determine the allocation and performance of other roles in a wide range of situations. Our observations indicate that the convert role functions in a similar manner but with several crucial distinctions. First, whereas the assumption of a basic role or master status is typically a function of ascription (Banton, 1965), altercasting (Weinstein and Deutschberger, 1963), or labeling (Becker, 1963), the convert role is typically volitional and achieved.

A second and perhaps more significant difference is that the convert role, unlike most master statuses or basic roles, comprises a kind of representative role. While Parsons (1951, p. 100), who coined the term representative role, restricts its usage to leadership roles having to do with affairs external to the collectivity, any group or movement role that leads one to act as a functionary in extragroup activities and relations can be called a representative role. Drawing on this concept in his discussion of ideology and conflict, Coser (1956, pp. 113-114) notes that "in the Marxian labor movement ... any active member, whether or not he had a leadership role in the organization, was expected 'to represent' the movement to the outside world." In a similar vein, all Nichiren Shoshu members are expected to act at all times, in the words of one member, as "representatives of the movement, as ambassadors of President Ikeda." They are constantly instructed by their leaders and the movement's newspaper that in whatever they do, collectively or individually, whether in the context of family, work, school, or leisure, it is to be done with the interests of the movement in mind. As a major leader explained before a gathering of over five thousand members: "The relationship of NSA to the other people in society with whom we work, live, and meet every day is very important. We should keep in mind that how we live our daily life is an exact image of the entire movement. We should become people of whom others will say, 'The members of NSA are really great.' To do that is to advance our cause. Therefore, in every action you make and in every activity you participate, you can be carrying out the movement's mission."

To be sure, not all religions, causes, or movements are as "greedy" (Coser, 1967) as Nichiren Shoshu; nor do all members act in accordance with such demanding expectations and directives. But some movement members appear to consider their group's interests and expectations in the construction of their lines of action in nearly all extragroup activities and domains of life. But unlike many incumbents of traditional representative roles, converts do not view themselves as mere functionaries whose commitment is based primarily on instrumental or extraneous considerations (Becker, 1960). Instead the convert fully embraces the convert role.[6] Not only do converts introject and see themselves in terms of the convert role, but it governs their orientation in all situations. Daily activities and routines that were formerly taken for granted or interpreted from the standpoint of various situationally specific roles are now interpreted from the standpoint of the convert role, which is seen as the embodiment of the movement's interests and mission. Hence the convert does not act merely in terms of self-interest but in the interest of the cause or mission. Daily routines are infused with new meaning and added significance. As a Nichiren Shoshu convert, who aspired to be a nationally ranked tennis player, explained: "Before I started to chant, I had no concrete purpose in playing tennis. I used to think of all the troubles other people had and tennis seemed like a joke. But at those last two tennis tournaments I felt like I was playing for world peace." In a similar vein, a born-again Christian who turned down a $400,000 professional basketball contract in favor of playing for Athletes for Action, the athletic arm of Campus Crusade for Christ, recounts: "As I stand at midcourt during halftime at the AIA games, giving my personal testimony to God's love, my heart swells with the joy of being a Christian ... Most people spend their lives investing for retirement. I spend mine investing for eternity."

A third distinction between the convert role as a master status and traditional master statuses, such as race and gender, is that converts enthusiastically announce their identity in nearly all situations. In fact, the convert seldom lets others forget this role identity during the course of interaction. It is worn like a uniform and is continuously on display (sometimes literally as in the case of Krishna devotees and sometimes figuratively as in the case of converts to Nichiren Shoshu and Christianity). Perhaps this is another reason why conversation with a convert is often a halting and exasperating affair. As the parents of a convert to a Jesus commune lamented when discussing their relationship to their daughter: "It is not so much the fact that she has become what some people call a Jesus freak that bothers us. At least she's not into drugs or come crazy political group. What is bothersome, though, is that when we see each other we can't just sit down and talk without everything being related to Jesus or her communal brothers and sisters." Or as the parents of a Nichiren Shoshu convert similarly noted: "In many ways [our son] is more pleasant to be around since he joined Nichiren Shoshu. He smiles more and is not so argumentative. But he has this irritating habit of relating just about everything we say or do to karma or chanting."

Finally, embracement of the convert role gives rise to what Travisano (1970, p. 605) calls the ubiquitous utilization of the identity associated with the convert role. Metaphorically, it is not merely a mask that is taken off or put on according to the situation. Rather, it is central to nearly all situations. For the convert, such role identities as father, mother, brother, sister, student, and so on pale in comparison to the role identity of the convert. That is because, to paraphrase Hughes (1945), all role identities are subordinate to the identity that flows from the master role of the convert.

SUMMARY AND CONCLUSIONS

At least since the time of Simmel, the identification of social types has been regarded as an important objective of sociological analysis. In keeping with this tradition, we have denoted the convert as a social type. Identifying the convert as a social type helps to refine current conceptualizations of conversion, most of which designate little more than a radical personal change. The precise nature of that change is rarely specified. We argue that the change pertains to the universe of discourse. Furthermore, we have identified and described four properties of conversion observable in the talk and reasoning of converts: biographical reconstruction, adoption of a master attribution scheme, suspension of analogical reasoning, and embracement of a master role. The display of these rhetorical properties indicates the displacement of one universe of discourse by another. The convert is thereby discernible by his or her talk and reasoning.

Several theoretical and methodological implications are suggested by our analysis. First, it suggests that conversion is best conceptualized as the process by which a new or formerly peripheral universe of discourse comes to inform all aspects of a person's life. In short, it involves the ascendance of a universe of discourse to the status of a primary authority. The universe of discourse need not be new but can shift from periphery to center. In the case of religion, for example, conversion need not be restricted to acknowledging only religious migration (the Orthodox Jew becomes a fundamentalist Christian) or the sounding of a religious chord among the previously unreligious (Madelyn Murray O'Hair's son is born again). Moreover, the backslider or prodigal son who reaffirms commitment to a religion from which he strayed can qualify as a convert. Similarly, the citizen of a community of faith may come by a radical redefinition of how God works and apprehend an old and familiar religious belief with a new intensity and clarity of vision. Nominal belief thus becomes True Belief. What was peripheral to consciousness now becomes central.

Second, in arguing that this transformation of consciousness is indicated by the talk and reasoning of those who experience it, our analysis provides the researcher with empirical guidelines for locating the convert. To identify with confidence a transformation of consciousness is an elusive matter indeed. It is in this regard that a focus on language becomes invaluable. Inasmuch as a language is practical consciousness, it stands to reason that transformations of consciousness necessitate transformations of language. Thus, by noting the presence of the four rhetorical features discussed here, we mark the occasion of conversion. It is thereby no longer incumbent on the researcher to guess who has undergone the consciousness transformation that typifies him or her as a convert.

Third, our analysis refines the distinction between converts and other members. While a few scholars such as Nock (1933) have emphasized that adhesion to a religious group is no guarantee of conversion, rarely have such distinctions been noted or pursued. Following Nock, we argue that membership avowal, actual membership status, and participation are inadequate indicators of conversion. Instead, our observations suggest that it is the rhetoric of converts that sets them apart from fellow group members. It is their talk and reasoning that is symptomatic of the consciousness transformation that makes them unique among their peers.

Fourth, our observations raise serious questions about much of the research concerned with the causes of conversion. The bulk of this work has relied largely on converts themselves for data. If conversion is the process through which a universe of discourse comes to function as a primary authority, and if biographical reconstruction is a crucial feature of this process, then converts' accounts of their life and motivation prior to conversion become immediately suspect. Since observations about the past are always refracted by the prism of one's universe of discourse, a change in universe of discourse provides a different vantage point from which to view one's life. thus the medium through which the convert's retrospective vision passes is far from transparent. Rather, it is colored by the spectrum of understandings and meanings that attend conversion. Far from being trusted sources of information about their past, converts are uniquely denied impartial knowledge about the factors that might have precipitated conversion. Hence studies that rely only on converts as sources of background information about conversion are faced with the peculiar paradox of being unable to explain a phenomenon because of a fundamental characteristic of the phenomenon itself.

Finally, we suggest that this portrayal of the convert as a social type is by no means restricted to religion. It is neither institutional context nor ideological content that denotes the convert as a social type. Some of the examples of conversion presented in this essay pertain to politics; others could be found, with equal justification, in the social realms of occupation, psychotherapy, and lifestyle. It is the form, not the content, of claims to truth that betrays the convert as a social type.

NOTES

1.   Nock (1933, pp. 6-7) coined the term adhesion to denote participation in religious group activities and rituals without taking a new way of life. Unlike conversion, adhesion is characterized not by a crossing of religious frontiers but by "having a foot on each side of the fence." Adhesion involves an acceptance of new worships as "useful supplements and not as substitutes."

2.   Demonstration events may function even more importantly as commitment-building activities (Gerlach and Hine, 1970; Kanter, 1972; Shaffir, 1978; Toch, 1965). A public profession of faith, for example, brings into play powerful social forces that help anchor the individual's identities and overall self-conception in the group. As Turner and Killian (1972, p. 33) have noted in this regard: "When the individual goes on record in support of a movement, he becomes committed because persons around him are inclined to treat him as an adherent and to expect continued adherence from him."

3.   Gordon (1974, pp. 165-166) refers to these less radical types of identity change as alteration and consolidation. Thus we have Berger and Luckmann (1967, pp. 157-158) proposing alternation in lieu of conversion; Travisano (1970) contrasting alternation and conversion; and Gordon distinguishing alternation (conversion) from alteration and consolidation. One is left wondering if, as Berger (1967, p. 177) once observed, definitions can amount to more than matters of taste.

4.   Travisano (1970) too employs the concept of a universe of discourse in his thoughtful discussion of conversion. He found that concept to be useful because it "emphasizes that meanings are established and exist in symbolic interaction" (pp. 594-595). Mead's expression appeals to us for a different reason. It is less the symbolic interactionist qualities of the term and more the concern with language that makes it attractive for our purposes. For much the same reason, we prefer the concept of a universe of discourse over similar terms such as meaning system (Berger, 1963, 1967), informing point of view (Burke, 1965), and sacred cosmos (Luckmann, 1967).

5. We do not mean to suggest that some converts never employ analogical metaphors. Close inspection reveals, however, that occasional reliance by converts on analogical metaphor finds them avoiding other meaning systems (particularly if institutionalized) as the points of analogical reference. Rather, naturalistic phenomena such as a birth, panoramic views, and explosions are the points of comparison. Physical sensations such as sudden warmth, a sense of energy, or the perception of sudden illumination are frequently used in analogical comparison. In most instances, naturalistic phenomena and physical sensations are not serious competitors of religious meaning systems.

6. "To embrace a role is to disappear completely into the virtual self available in the situation, to be fully seen in terms of the image, and to confirm expressively one's acceptance of it" (Goffman, 1961, p. 106).

REFERENCES

Aberle, David
    1965   "A Note on Relative Deprivation Theory as Applied to Millenarian and Other Cult Movements." Pp. 537-41 in W.A. Lessa and E.Z. Vogt (eds.), *Reader in Comparative Religion: An Anthropological Approach.* New York: Harper and Row. Second Edition.
    1966   *The Peyote Religion among the Navaho.* Chicago: Aldine.

Agency For Cultural Affairs
    1972   *Japanese Religion.* Tokyo: Kodansha International Limited.

Almond, Gabriel A.
    1954   *The Appeals of Communism.* Princeton, N.J.: Princeton University Press.

Alvarez, Rodolfo
    1968   "Informal Reactions to Deviance in Simulated Work Organizations: A Laboratory Experiment." *American Sociological Review* 33: 895-912.

Anesaki, Masaharu
    1916   *Nichiren: The Buddhist Prophet.* Cambridge: Harvard University Press.
    1963   *History of Japanese Religion.* Rutland, Vermont: Charles Tuttle Co.

Babbie, Earl R.
    1965   "The Third Civilization: An Examination of Sokagakkai." *Review of Religious Research* 7: 101-121.

Balch, Robert W.
    1980   "Looking Behind the Scenes In a Religious Cult: Implications for the Study of Conversion." *Sociological Analysis* 41: 137-143.

Balch, Robert W. and Taylor, David
    1978   "Seekers and Saucers: The Role of the Cultic Millieu in Joining a UFO Cult." Pp. 43-65 in J. Richardson (ed.), *Conversion Careers.* Beverly Hills, Calif.: Sage.

Banton, Michael
    1965   *Roles: An Introduction to the Study of Social Relations.*
            New York: Basic Books.
Becker, Howard S.
    1960   "Notes on the Concept of Commitment." *American
            Journal of Sociology* 77: 32-40.
    1963   *The Outsiders.* New York: The Free Press.
Beckford, James A.
    1978   "Accounting for Conversion." *British Journal of
            Sociology* 29: 249-262.
Bell, Daniel (ed.)
    1964   *The Radical Right.* Garden City, New York: Doubleday-
            Anchor.
Berger, Peter L.
    1963   *Invitation to Sociology: A Humanistic Perspective.*
            Garden City: Doubleday-Anchor.
    1967   *The Sacred Canopy.* Garden City: Doubleday-Anchor.
Berger, Peter L. and Luckmann, Thomas
    1967   *The Social Construction of Reality.*   Garden City:
            Doubleday-Anchor.
Bethel, Dayle M.
    1973   *Makiguchi: The Value Creator.*   New York: John
            Weatherhill.
Bird, Caroline
    1969   *Born Female.* New York: Pocket Books.
Birdwhistell, Ray L.
    1972   *Kinesics and Context.* New York: Ballantine Books.
Black, Mary and Metzger, Duane
    1969   "Ethnographic Description and the Study of Law."
            Pp. 137-165 in S.A. Tyler (ed.), *Cognitive Anthropology.*
            New York: Holt, Rinehart and Winston.
Blum, Alan F. and McHugh, Peter
    1971   "The Social Ascription of Motives." *American
            Sociological Review* 46: 98-109.
Blumer, Herbert
    1969a   "Collective Behavior." Pp. 65-121 in A.M. Lee (ed.),
            Principles of Sociology. New York: Barnes and Noble.
            Third Edition.

1969b *Symbolic Interactionism: Perspective and Method.* Englewood Cliffs, N.J.: Prentice-Hall.

Bolton, Charles D.
1972 "Alienation and Action: A Study of Peace Group Members." *American Journal of Sociology* 78: 537-61.

Boorstin, Daniel J.
1964 *The Image: A Guide to Pseudo-Events in America.* New York: Harper and Row.

Brannen, Noah S.
1964 "Soka Gakkai's Theory of Value." *Contemporary Religions in Japan* 5: 143-54.
1968 *Soka Gakkai: Japan's Militant Buddhists.* Richmond, Va.: John Knox Press.

Bromley, David G. and Shupe, Anson D.
1979a *"Moonies" in America.* Beverly Hills: Sage.
1979b "Just a Few Years Seems Like a Lifetime: A Role Theory Approach to Participation in Religious Movements." Pp. 150-185 in L. Kriesberg (ed.), *Research in Social Movements, Conflict and Change.* Greenwich, Conn.: JAI Press.

Brown, Richard H.
1977 *A Poetic for Sociology.* New York: Cambridge University Press.

Bultena, Louis
1949 "Church Membership and Church Attendance in Madison, Wisconsin." *American Sociological Review* 14: 384-389.

Burke, Kenneth
1965 *Permanence and Change.* Indianapolis: Bobbs-Merrill.
1969a *A Grammar of Motives.* Berkeley: University of California Press.
1969b *A Rhetoric of Motives.* Berkeley: University of California Press.

Cantril, Hadley
1941 *The Psychology of Social Movements.* New York: Wiley.
1965 *The Pattern of Human Concerns.* New Brunswick, N.J.: Rutgers University Press.

Chase, Stuart
1962 *American Credos.* New York: Harper and Row.

Clark, Walter H.
    1958   *The Psychology of Religion.* New York: Macmillan.
Cohn, Norman
    1957   *The Pursuit of the Millennium.* New York: Oxford
            University Press.
Coleman, James S., Katz, Elihu and Menzel, H.
    1966   *Medical Innovation: A Diffusion Study.* Indianapolis:
            Bobbs-Merrill.
Colson, Charles W.
    1976   *Born Again.* New York: Bantam Books.
Conway, Flo and Siegelman, Jim
    1978   *Snapping: America's Epidemic of Sudden Personality
            Change.* New York: Lippincott.
Coser, Lewis A.
    1956   *The Functions of Social Conflict.* New York: Free Press.
    1967   "Greedy Organizations." *Archives Européenes de
            Sociologie* 8: 196-215.
Cox, Harvey
    1978   "Myths Sanctioning Religoius Persecution." Pp. 3-19 in
            M. Darroll Bryant and Herbert W. Richardson (eds.), *A
            Time for Consideration.* New York: Edwin Mellen Press.
Crossman, Richard (ed.)
    1952   *The God That Failed.* New York: Bantam.
Daner, F.J.
    1976   *The American Children of Krishna: A Study of the Hare
            Krishna Movement.* New York: Holt, Rinehart and
            Winston.
Dart, John
    1974   "Growing Buddhist Sect in Southland Thrives on Hopeful
            Image of Man." *Los Angeles Times* (December 8).
Dator, James
    1969   *Soka Gakkai: Builders of the Third Civilization.* Seattle:
            University of Washington Press.
Davies, James C.
    1962   "Toward a Theory of Revolution." *American Sociological
            Review* 27: 5-19.

Deckard, Barbara Sinclair
    1979   *The Women's Movement.* New York: Harper and Row.
Delgado, Richard
    1980   "Limits to Proselytizing." *Society* 17: 25-33.
DeMaria, Richard
    1978   "A Psycho-Social Analysis of Religious Conversion." Pp. 82-130 in M. Darrol Bryant and Herbert W. Richardson (eds.), *A Time for Consideration.* New York: Edwin Mellen Press.
Doughty, William L.
    1955   *John Wesley: Preacher.* London: Epworth Press.
Durkheim, Émile
    1964   *The Division of Labor in Society.* New York: Free Press. (Originally published 1893.)
    1965   *The Elementary Forms of the Religious Life.* New York: Free Press. (Originally published 1915.)
Earhart, H. Byron
    1974   "The Interpretation of the 'New Religions' of Japan as New Religious Movements." Pp. 169-188 in R. J. Miller (ed.), *Religious Ferment in Asia.* Lawrence, Kansas: The University Press of Kansas.
Ebaugh, Helen Rose Fuchs
    1977   *Out of the Cloister.* Austin: University of Texas Press.
Eister, Allan W.
    1950   *Drawing Room Conversion: A Sociological Account of the Oxford Group Movement.* Durham, N.C.: Duke University Press.
Emerson, Robert M. and Messinger, Sheldon L.
    1977   "The Micro-politics of Trouble." *Social Problems* 25: 121-134.
Enroth, Ronald
    1977   *Youth, Brainwashing, and the Extremist Cults.* Grand Rapids: Zondervan.
Epstein, Benjamin R. and Forster, Arnold
    1966   *Report on the John Birch Society 1966.* New York: Random House.

Etzioni, Amitai
    1975   *A Comparative Analysis of Complex Organizations.* New
            York: Free Press.
Feuer, Lewis
    1969   *The Conflict of Generations.* New York: Basic Books.
Fichter, Joseph
    1954   *Social Relaitons in the Urban Parish.* Chicago:
            University of Chicago Press.
Freeman, Jo
    1973   "The Origins of the Women's Liberation Movement."
            American Journal of Sociology 78: 792-811.
Fromm, Erich
    1941   *Escape from Freedom.* New York: Rinehart.
    1950   *Psychoanalysis and Religion.* New haven: Yale
            University Press.
Fujiwara, Hirotatsu
    1970   *I Denounce Soka Gakkai.* Tokyo: Nisshin Hodo Co.
Gallup, George H.
    1978   *The Gallup Poll: Public Opinion 1972-1977.* Wilmington,
            Del.: Scholarly Resources.
Gamson, William A.
    1968   *Power and Discontent.* Homewood, IL: Dorsey Press.
    1975   *The Strategy of Social Protest.* Homewood, IL: Dorsey
            Press.
Geertz, Clifford
    1973   "Religion as a Cultural System." Pp. 87-125 in C.
            Geertz, *The Interpretation of Cultures.* New York: Basic
            Books.
Gerlach, Luther P. and Hine, Virginia H.
    1970   *People, Power, Change: Movements of Social
            Transformation.* Indianapolis: Bobbs-Merrill.
Glaser, Barney G. and Strauss, Anselm L.
    1967   *The Discovery of Grounded Theory.* Chicago: Aldine.
Glock, Charles Y.
    1964   "The Role of Deprivation in the Origin and Evolution of
            Religious Groups." Pp. 24-36 in R. Lee and M. Marty
            (eds.), *Religion and Social Conflict.* New York: Oxford
            University Press.

Glock, Charles Y. and Bellah, Robert N. (eds.)
  1976 *The New Religious Consciousness.* Berkeley: University of California Press.
Goffman, Erving
  1959 *The Presentation of Self in Everyday Life.* New York: Doubleday-Anchor.
  1961 *Encounters.* Indianapolis: Bobbs-Merrill.
  1963 *Behavior in Public Places.* New York: The Free Press.
  1967 *Interaction Ritual.* New York: Doubleday-Anchor.
Goodenough, Ward H.
  1966 "Cultural Anthropology and Linguistics." Pp. 36-39 in Dell Hymes (ed.), *Language in Culture and Society.* New York: Harper and Row.
Gordon, David F.
  1974 "The Jesus People: An Identity Synthesis." *Urban Life and Culture* 3: 159-178.
Greeley, Andrew M.
  1969 "There's a New-Time Religion on Campus." *The New York Times Magazine* (June 1).
Gurin, G., Veroff, J., and Feld, S.
  1960 *Americans View Their Mental Health.* New York: Basic Books.
Gurr, Ted R.
  1970 *Why Men Rebel.* Princeton, N.J.: Princeton University Press.
Gusfield, Joseph R.
  1963 *Symbolic Crusade: Status Politics and the American Temperance Movement.* Urbana, Ill.: University of Illinois Press.
Hall, Edward T.
  1959 *The Silent Language.* New York: Doubleday.
Hargrove, Barbara
  1980 "Evil Eyes and Religious Choices." *Society* 17: 20-24.
Harrison, Michael I.
  1974 "Sources of Recruitment to Catholic Pentecostalism." *Journal for the Scientific Study of Religion* 13: 49-64.

Heider, Fritz
    1958   *The Psychology of Interpersonal Relations.* New York:
            Wiley.
Heirich, Max
    1977   "Change of Heart: A Test of Some Widely Held Theories
            about Religious Conversion." *American Journal of
            Sociology* 83: 653-680.
Hoffer, Eric
    1951   *The True Believer.* New York: Harper and Row.
Hollander, E. P.
    1958   "Conformity,   Status,   and   Idiosyncrasy   Credit."
            Psychological Review 65: 117-27.
    1960   "Competence and Conformity in the Acceptance of
            Influence." *Journal of Abnormal and Social Psychology*
            61: 365-69.
Hughes, Everett C.
    1945   "Dilemmas and Contradictions of Status." *American
            Journal of Sociology* 50: 353-359.
Ikeda, Daisaku
    1966-   *The Human Revolution.* Tokyo: Seikyo Press.
    1967
    1968   *Complete Works of Daisaku Ikeda.* Tokyo: Seikyo Press.
    1974   *Buddhism: The Living Philosophy.*   Tokyo: East
            Publications.
Institute for Social Research
    1979   "Americans Seek Self-development, Suffer Anxiety from
            Changing Roles." *ISR Newsletter,* University of
            Michigan, Winter: 4-5.
James, William
    1896   *The Will to Believe and Other Essays in Popular
            Philosophy.* London: Longmans, Green and Company.
    1958   *The Varieties of Religious Experience.* New York: New
            American Library.
Johnson, Chalmers
    1966   *Revolutionary Change.*   Boston: Little, Brown and
            Company.
Jones, Edward E.
    1964   *Ingratiation.* New York: Appleton, Century, Crofts.

1965   "Conformity as a Tactic of Ingratiation." *Science*: 144-150.

Jones, Edward E. and Davis, Kenneth E.
1965   "From Acts to Dispositions: The Attribution Process in Person Perception." In L. Berkowitz (ed.), *Advances in Experimental Social Psychology.* Vol. 2. New York: Academic Press.

Jones, Edward E. and Nisbett, Richard E.
1971   *The Actor and the Observer: Divergent Perspectives on the Causes of Behavior.* Morristown, N.J.: General Learning Press.

Jones, Edward E. and Others
1972   *Attribution: Perceiving the Causes of Behavior.* Morristown, N.J.: General Learning Press.

Jones, R. Kenneth
1978   "Paradigm Shifts and Identity Theory: Alternation as a Form of Identity Management." Pp. 59-82 in H. Mol (ed.), *Identity and Religion.* Beverly Hills: Sage.

Judah, J. Stillson
1974   *Hare Krishna and the Counterculture.* New York: Wiley.

Kanouse, David E. and Hanson, L.R. Jr.
1972   *Negativity in Evaluations.* Morristown, N.J.: General Learning Press.

Kanter, Rosabeth M.
1972   *Commitment and Community: Communes and Utopias in Sociological Perspective.* Cambridge, Mass.: Harvard University Press.

1973   *Communes: Creating and Managing the Collective Life.* New York: Harper and Row.

Kelley, Harold H.
1967   "Attribution Theory in Social Psychology." In D. Levine (ed.), *Nebraska Symposium on Motivation.* Vol. 15. Lincoln: University of Nebraska Press.

1971   *Attribution in Social Interaction.* Morristown, N.J.: General Learning Press.

1972   *Causal Schemata and the Attribution Process.* Morristown, N.J.: General Learning Press.

Kerckhoff, Alan C. and Back, Kurt W.
    1968   *The June Bug: A Study of Hysterical Contagion.* New
            York: Appleton-Century-Crofts.
Kern, H.
    1963   *Lotus Sutra: Saddharma-Pundarika or The Lotus of the
            True Law.* New York: Dover Publications.
Klapp, Orrin
    1969   *Collective Search for Identity.* New York: Holt, Rinehart
            and Winston.
Kornhauser, William
    1959   *The Politics of Mass Society.* New York: The Free Press.
Kuhn, Thomas
    1962   *The Structure of Scientific Revolutions.*   Chicago:
            University of Chicago Press.
Lande, Nathaniel
    1976   *Mindstyles/Lifestyles.* Los Angeles: Price/Stern/Sloan.
Lang, Kurt and Lang, Gladys Engel
    1961   *Collective Dynamics.* New York: Crowell.
Leahy, Peter J.
    1976   "Mobilization and Recruitment of Leadership to Anti-
            Abortion Movement."   Paper presented at the 1976
            Annual Meeting of the Southwestern Sociological
            Association.
Lee, Robert
    1967   *Stranger in the Land.* London: Lutterworth.
Levine, Donald N.
    1965   "Some Key Problems in Simmel's Work." Pp. 97-115 in
            Lewis Coser (ed.), *Georg Simmel.* Englewood Cliffs,
            N.J.: Prentice-Hall.
Lipset, S. M. and Raab, Earl
    1973   *The Politics of Unreason: Right-Wing Extremism in
            America, 1969-1970.* New York: Harper and Row.
Lofland, John
    1966   *Doomsday Cult.* Englewood Cliffs, N.J.: Prentice-Hall.
    1977   *Doomsday Cult* (new edition with preface). New York:
            Irvington.

1978   "Becoming a World-saver Revisited."   Pp. 10-23 in J. Richardson (ed.), *Conversion Careers*.   Beverly HIlls, Calif.: Sage.

Lofland, John and Stark, Rodney
1965   "Becoming a World-saver: A Theory of Conversion to a Deviant Perspective." *American Sociological Review* 30: 862-874.

Lubrano, Gina
1974   "Buddhist Celebrate Happiness." *San Diego Union* (April 7): B-1.

Luckmann, Thomas
1967   *The Invisible Religion*. New York: Macmillan.

Lyman, Stanford M. and Scott, Marvin B.
1967   "Territoriality: A Neglected Sociological Dimension." *Social Problems* 15: 236-48.

McCall, George J. and Simmons, J.L.
1978   *Identities and Interaction*. New York: Free Press.

McFarland, H. Neill
1967   *The Rush Hour of the Gods: A Study of New Religious Movements in Japan*. New York: Harper and Row.

McCarthy, John and Zald, Mayer
1973   *The Trend of Social Movements in America: Professionalization and Resource Mobilization*. Morristown, NJ: General Learning Press.

McGee, Michael
1976   "Meher Baba - The Sociology of Religious Conversion." *Graduate Journal* 9: 43-71.

McPhail, Clark
1971   "Civil Disorder Participation: A Critical Examination of Recent Research." *American Sociological Review* 36: 1058-73.

Makiguchi, Tsunesaburo
1964   *The Philosophy of Value*. Tokyo: Seikyo Press.

Mannheim, Karl
1940   *Man and Society in an Age of Reconstruction*. New York: Harcourt Brace Jovanovich.

Marx, Gary and Wood, James
    1975   "Strands of Theory and Research in Collective Behavior."
            Annual Review of Sociology 1: 363-428.
Mead, George Herbert
    1932   *The Philosophy of the Present.* (A. Murphy, ed.).
            LaSalle, Ill.: Open Court.
    1936   *Movements of Thought in the Nineteenth Century.* (M.
            Moore, ed.) Chicago: University of Chicago Press.
    1938   *The Philosophy of the Act.* (C. Morris, ed.) Chicago:
            University of Chicago Press.
    1962   *Mind, Self and Society.* (C. Morris, ed.) Chicago:
            University of Chicago Press.
Mehrabian, Albert
    1971   *Silent Messages.* Belmont, Ca.: Wadsworth Publishing
            Company.
Merton, Robert K.
    1968   *Social Theory and Social Structure.* New York: The Free
            Press.
Messinger, Sheldon L.
    1955   "Organizational Transformation: A Case Study of a
            Declining Social Movement." *American Sociological
            Review* 20: 3-10.
Mills, C. Wright
    1940   "Situated Actions and Vocabularies of Motive." *American
            Sociological Review* 5: 904-913.
Morrison, Denton E. and Steeves, Allen D.
    1967   "Deprivation, Discontent, and Social Movement
            Participation: Evidence on a Contemporary Farmer's
            Movement, the N.F.O." *Rural Sociology* 32: 414-434.
Murata, Kokoaki
    1969   *Japan's New Buddhism: An Objective Account of the Soka
            Gakkai.* New York: John Weatherhill.
Newsweek
    1972   "Happy Talk." (June 5): 68.
Nichiren Shoshu of America
    1964-   *World Tribune.* NSA newspaper first published in August
    1975   1964. Santa Monica: World Tribune Press.

1972   *NSA Seminar Report, 1968-71.* Santa Monica: World Tribune Press.

1973-   *NSA Quarterly.* Santa Monica: World Tribune Press.
1975

1973   *The Liturgy of Nichiren Shoshu.* Santa Monica: Nichiren Shoshu Academy.

Niebuhr, H. Richard

1929   *The Social Sources of Denominationalism.* New York: Henry Holt and Co.

Nock, A.D.

1933   *Conversion.* London: Oxford University Press.

Oberschall, Anthony

1973   *Social Conflict and Social Movements.* Englewood Cliffs, N.J.: Prentice-Hall.

Offner, Clark B. and Van Straelen, Henry

1963   *Modern Japanese Religions.* New York: Twayne Publications.

Olson, Mancur

1965   *The Logic of Collective Action: Public Goods and the Theory of Groups.* Cambridge: Harvard University Press.

Otto, Rudolf

1973   *The Idea of the Holy.* New York: Oxford University Press.

Parrucci, D.J.

1968   "Religious Conversions: A Theory of Deviant Behavior." *Sociologial Analysis* 29: 144-154.

Parsons, Talcott

1951   *The Social System.* New York: Free Press.

Patrick, Ted

1976   *Let Our Children Go.* New York: Ballantine.

Pattison, E.M.

1974   "Ideological Support for the Marginal Middle Class. Faith Healing and Glossolalia." Pp. 418-455 in T.I. Zaretsky and M.P. Leone (eds.), *Religious Movements in Contemporary America.* Princeton, N.J.: Princeton University Press.

Peterson, Donald W. and Mauss, Armand L.
    1973   "The Cross and the Commune: An Interpretation of the
            Jesus People." Pp. 261-279 in C. Glock (ed.), *Religion
            in the Sociological Perspective.*   Belmont, Calif.:
            Wadsworth.
Pinard, Maurice
    1971   *The Rise of a Third Party: A Study in Crisis Politics.*
            Englewood Cliffs, N.J.: Prentice-Hall.
Piven, Frances Fox and Cloward Richard A.
    1977   *Poor People's Movements.* New York: Vintage Books.
Pope, Liston
    1942   *Millhands and Preachers.*   New Haven: Yale University
            Press.
Richardson, James T. (ed.)
    1978   *Conversion Careers: In and Out of the New Religions.*
            Beverly Hills, Ca.: Sage Publications.
    1980   "Conversion Careers." *Society* 17: 47-50.
Richardson, James T. and Stewart, Mary W.
    1978   "Conversion Process Models and the Jesus Movement."
            Pp. 24-42 in J. Richardson (ed.), *Conversion Careers.*
            Beverly Hills: Sage.
Richardson, James T., Stewart, Mary W. and Simmonds, Robert B.
    1978   "Conversion to Fundamentalism." *Society* 15: 46-52.
Robbins, Thomas
    1988   *Cults, Converts, and Charisma: The Sociology of New
            Religions.* Beverly Hills, CA: Sage Publications.
Robbins, Thomas and Anthony, Dick
    1979   "The Sociology of Contemporary Religious Movements."
            Annual Review of Sociology 5: 75-89.
Rosen, R.D.
    1978   *Psychobabble.* New York: Atheneum.
Rotter, Julian B.
    1966   "Generalized Expectancies for Internal vs. External
            Control of Reinforcements." *Psychological Monographs*
            80: 1-28.
Schiffer, W.
    1954   "Shinko-Shukyo: A Social and Religious Phenomenon in
            Post War Japan." *Proceedings of the Twenty-third*

International Congress of Orientalists. Cambridge, London: W. Heffer and Sons.

1955 "New Religions in Postwar Japan." *Monumenta Nipponica* 11: 1-14.

Scott, Marvin and Stanford M. Lyman
1968 "Accounts." *American Sociological Review* 33: 46-62.

Seggar, John and Kunz, Philip
1972 "Conversion: Evaluation of a Step-like Process for Problem-solving." *Review of Religious Research* 13: 178-184.

Shaffir, William
1978 "Witnessing as Identity Consolidation: The Case of the Lubavitcher Chassidim." Pp. 39-57 in H. Mol. (ed.), *Identity and Religion.* Beverly Hills: Sage.

Shaver, Kelly G.
1975 *An Introduction to Attribution Processes.* Cambridge, Mass.: Winthrop Publishers.

Shibutani, Tamotsu
1961 *Society and Personality.* Englewood Cliffs, N.J.: Prentice-Hall.

Shupe, Anson D. and Bromley, David G.
1980 *The New Vigilantes: Deprogrammers, Anti-Cultists and the New Religions.* Beverly Hills, Ca.: Sage Publications.

Shupe, Anson D., Spielmann, Roger and Stigall, Sam
1978 "Deprogramming: The New Exorcism." Pp. 145-160 in J. Richardson (ed.), *Conversion Careers.* Beverly Hills, Ca.: Sage Publications.

Simmel, Georg
1964 "The Secret Society." Pp. 345-376 in Kurt H. Wolff (ed.), *The Sociology of Georg Simmel.* New York: The Free Press.

Smelser, Neil
1963 *Theory of Collective Behavior.* New York: The Free Press.

Snow, David A.
1976 "The Nichiren Shoshu Movement in America: A Sociological Examination of Its Value Orientation,

Recruitment Efforts, and Spread." Ph.D. dissertation, University of California, Los Angeles.

1979   "A Dramaturgical Analysis of Movement Accommodation: Building Idiosyncrasy Credit as a Movement Mobilization Strategy." *Symbolic Interaction* 2: 23-44.

Snow, David A. and Phillips, Cynthia L.
1980   "The Lofland-Stark Conversion Model: A Critical Reassessment." *Social Problems* 27: 430-447.

Snyder, David and Charles Tilly
1972   "Hardship and Collective Violence in France, 1830-1960." *American Sociologial Review* 37: 520-532.

Sokagakkai
1966   *The Nichiren Shoshu Sokagakkai.* Tokyo: Seikyo Press.
1971-   *Seikyo Times.* Sokagakkai magazine. Tokyo: Seikyo
1974   Press.
1972   *Nichiren Shoshu and Soka Gakkai: Modern Buddhism in Action.* Tokyo: Seikyo Press.
1973-   *Mainichi Daily News.* A Sokagakkai newspaper published
1974   in Tokyo and Osaka.

Sorokin, Pitirim A.
1937-   *Social and Cultural Dynamics.* New York: American
1941   Book Company.

Spilerman, Seymour
1970   "The Causes of Racial Disturbances: A Comparison of Alternative Explanations." *American Sociological Review* 35: 627-649.

Stouffer, Samuel A.
1955   *Communism, Conformity, and Civil Liberties.* New York: Wiley.

Straus, Roger
1976   "Changing Oneself: Seekers and the Creative Transformation of Life Experience." Pp. 252-272 in J. Lofland (ed.), *Doing Social Life.* New York: Wiley.

Strickland, D.A. and Johnston, R.E.
1970   "Issue Elasticity in Political Systems." *Journal of Political Economy* 78: 1069-1092.

Taylor, Brian
    1976   "Conversion and Cognition: An Area for Empirical Study in the Microsociology of Religious Knowledge." *Social Compass* 23: 5-22.
    1978   "Recollection and Membership: Converts' Talk and the Ratiocination of Commonality." *Sociology* 12: 316-324.

Thomson, Harry
    1963   *The New Religions of Japan.* Rutland, Vermont: Charles E. Tuttle.

Time
    1969   "The Power of Positive Chanting." (January 17): 51.
    1975   "The Super Missionary." (January 13): 26.

Toch, Hans
    1965   *The Social Psychology of Social Movements.* Indianapolis: Bobbs-Merrill.

Travisano, Richard V.
    1970   "Alternation and Conversion as Qualitatively Different Transformations." Pp. 594-606 in G.P. Stone and H.A. Farberman (eds.), *Social Psychology through Symbolic Interaction.* Waltham, Mass.: Ginn-Blaisdell.

Turner, Ralph H.
    1969   "The Theme of Contemporary Social Movements." *British Journal of Sociology* 20: 390-405.
    1973   "Determinants of Social Movement Strategies." Pp. 145-64 in T. Shibutani (ed.), *Human Nature and Collective Behavior.* New Brunswick, N.J.: Transaction Books.
    1976   "The Real Self: From Institution to Impulse." *American Journal of Sociology* 81: 989-1016.

Turner, Ralph H. and Killian, Lewis M.
    1972   *Collective Behavior.* Englewood Cliffs, N.J.: Prentice-Hall.

Tyler, Stephen A.
    1969   "Introduction." Pp. 1-23 in S.A. Tyler (ed.), *Cognitive Anthropology.* New York: Holt, Rinehart and Winston.

U.S. Bureau of the Census
    1971   *Statistical Abstract of the U.S., 1971.* Washington, D.C.: Government Printing Office. 92nd Edition.

Useem, Michael
    1975   *Protest Movements in America.*   Indianapolis: Bobbs-
            Merrill.
Wallace, Anthony F. C.
    1966   *Religion: An Anthropological View.* New York: Random
            House.
Weber, Max
    1947   *The Theory of Social and Economic Organization.*
            (Translated by A.M. Henderson and T. Parsons.) New
            York: Oxford University Press.
Wegner, Daniel M. and Vallacher, Robin R.
    1977   *Implicit Psychology.* New York: Oxford University Press.
Weinstein, Eugene A. and Deutschberger, Paul
    1963   "Some Dimensions of Altercasting." *Sociometry* 26: 454-
            466.
White, James W.
    1970   *The Sokagakkai and Mass Society.* Stanford, Calif.:
            Stanford University Press.
Williams, George M.
    1985   *Freedom and Influence: The Role of Religion in American
            Society.* Santa Monica, Ca.: World Tribune Press.
Wilson, John
    1973   *Introduction to Social Movements.*   New York: Basic
            Books.
    1978   *Religion in American Society.* Englewood Cliffs, N.J.:
            Prentice-Hall.
Wolff, Kurt H. (ed.)
    1950   *The Sociology of Georg Simmel.* New York: Free Press.
Worsley, Peter
    1968   *The Trumpet Shall Sound: A Study of 'Cargo' Cults in
            Melanisia.* New York: Schocken Books. Second Edition.
Wuthnow, Robert
    1976   "The New Religions in Social Context." Pp. 267-293 in
            C. Glock and R. Bellah (eds.), *The New Religious
            Consciousness.* Berkeley: University of California Press.
Zablocki, Benjamin
    1971   *The Joyful Community.* Baltimore, Maryland: Penguin
            Books.

Zald, Mayer N. and Ash, Roberta
  1966   "Social Movement Organizations; Growth, Decay and Change." *Social Forces* 44: 327-41.
Zetterberg, Hans
  1952   "Religious Conversions as a Change of Social Roles." *Sociology and Social Research* 36: 159-166.
Zurcher, Louis A.
  1977   *The Mutable Self.* Beverly Hills, Calif.: Sage.

INDEX